THE HAMPDEN STORY

By the same author

Destiny's Daughter, the Tragedy of RMS Queen Elizabeth
George Square 1919

THE
HAMPDEN
STORY

Russell Galbraith

MAINSTREAM
PUBLISHING
EDINBURGH AND LONDON

First published in Great Britain in 1993 by
MAINSTREAM PUBLISHING COMPANY
(EDINBURGH) LTD
7 Albany Street
Edinburgh EH1 3UG

ISBN 1 85158 445 5

A catalogue record for this book is available from the
British Library

Typeset in Linotype Janson by Servis Filmsetting Ltd,
Manchester

Printed in Great Britain by Butler and Tanner Ltd,
Frome

This book is for Karen and Iain

ACKNOWLEDGEMENTS

Thanks are due to Bob Cowan, for his assistance with research; to staff at the Mitchell Library, Glasgow, for all their help; to Arnold Kemp and Harry Reid for permission to use *The Herald* picture library, and to Robert Tweedie, photo librarian, who knew the whereabouts of the many splendid illustrations used in this book; to architects Thomson, McCrea, of Glasgow, for the use of their artist's impression of what Hampden could look like one day soon, we hope; and to everyone else who helped with interviews or information.

We would also wish to raise a glass to a long succession of marvellous characters, the players and managers, who, whenever they appeared at Scotland's national stadium, brought excitement, hope and joy into the lives of millions.

CHAPTER ONE

Scotland's hopes of qualifying for the finals of the 1994 World Cup in America had been put to the torch in Portugal. Small miracles wouldn't help. Andy Roxburgh, the national coach, considered his words carefully. 'We missed playing our home games at Hampden,' he said.

For the first time in its long and colourful history Hampden Park, Glasgow, had been unable to succour the national side during the early stages of a World Cup qualifying campaign.

'Ibrox is a magnificent stadium and we can't thank Rangers enough for letting us use it when we were homeless,' Roxburgh went on. 'But it would have taken a long, long time, I think, for us to become accustomed to Ibrox as the national stadium.'

There was a time when Hampden Park was, quite simply, the biggest and the best football stadium in the world. For generations, just as the game itself exercised a mesmeric influence over the lives of millions, so the great stadium in Mount Florida, a once-quiet suburb on the south side of Glasgow, could always claim a special place in the nation's heart.

It is no exaggeration, in order to justify its right to a special place in the nation's affections, to suggest that the story of Hampden Park is the story of much of Scottish football, its high points and low points, for almost the whole of the twentieth century.

That it was named after an English patriot might have been judged anathema to most Scots, especially those with a tortured sense of their own history, in the habit of blaming all their misfortunes, real and imagined, on the English.

John Hampden, a country gentleman turned Westminster politician, is rightly remembered as a fearless Parliamentarian who refused to believe in the divine right of kings. Educated at Magdalen College, Oxford, and the Inner Temple, London, and generally admired for his urbanity, veracity and all-round good character, John Hampden was nine years old in 1603, when James, King of Scotland, added England to his realm. Forty years later John Hampden died fighting on the Parliamentary side against King Charles in the English Civil War.

Any additional fame John Hampden might enjoy, more than 300 years after his death, as the man whose name was given to what was once the largest football stadium in the world, is due in part to a certain Mr George Eadie; and members of Queen's Park Football Club.

Eadie, a builder working in the Mount Florida area before the turn of the century, bestowed the name Hampden Terrace, in honour of the great English Parliamentarian, on a row of houses overlooking the site of the first piece of ground ever leased to Queen's Park for the purpose of playing football. This was the original land from which not one but three football grounds, all important to the development of the game in Scotland, emerged; and all named Hampden by order of various Queen's Park committees.

Almost certainly, few of the millions of Scottish fans who packed the famous stadium that took his name had ever heard of John Hampden. But, knowing the facts and given the chance early enough, most of them would have preferred to identify the national stadium with a home-grown hero. To decide otherwise would only confirm the blithe perversity, bordering on wilful bloody-mindedness on the part of the average Scottish football supporter, that quite often distorts an otherwise serious approach to the game.

Except that is exactly the result we are entitled to expect if anyone ever tried to change the name of Hampden to something more appropriate; something quite obviously Scottish, perhaps. If it does survive, who would want to call Hampden anything but Hampden?

Almost 20 years ago, Bob Brown, one of Scotland's most gifted post-war journalists, writing in *We'll Support You Evermore*, an anthology of Scottish football, edited by Ian Archer and Trevor Royle, maintained that 'Hampden stands four square with Bannockburn in the Scottish psyche, despite being indirectly named for the Saxon patriot. Hampden for the Scots is irreplaceable.'

The story of Hampden begins with Queen's Park, the amateur club that totally dominated Scottish football in the early years of its existence. Queen's Park was founded in 1867 when, in the words of a surviving record of the occasion, a number of gentlemen met at 3 Eglinton Terrace, on the south side of Glasgow, sometime during the evening of 9 July, for the purpose of starting a football club.

Interest in the game had been spreading in part from England where the Football Association was founded four years earlier. Kick-about matches were becoming common on Queen's Park Recreation Ground, involving teams numbering as many as 20 a side, who played on a surface 200 yards long and 100 yards wide; and a real club, which could be used to harness this enthusiasm, and organise proper fixtures with other like-minded groups, was a natural progression.

It may be hard to imagine now, considering the attention organised football commands throughout the world, and in the life of Scotland certainly no less than any other place, but these were pioneering days. Games played on the rough ground of Queen's Park Recreation Ground weren't designed for faint hearts. Almost any kind of rough stuff was allowed and most early matches were decided on the basis of strength rather than skill.

Often, in the beginning, although a number of clubs were struggling to emerge, there was no-one for the men of Queen's Park Football Club to play, apart from each other. But people were obviously attracted to the new sport and, within a few years, there was news of several clubs being established in Scotland who were keen to challenge the acknowledged supremacy of Queen's Park.

Word reaching Mount Florida from the south also confirmed the game was taking serious hold in England; and by November 1870, the secretary of the Football Association, Mr C.W. Alcock, was writing to *The Glasgow Herald* to suggest a match between the two countries.

The first full match between Scotland and England was played at Hamilton Crescent, Glasgow, on St Andrew's Day, 30 November 1872, three months before Queen's Park and seven other clubs – Clydesdale, Dumbreck, Eastern, Granville, Vale of Leven, Rovers and Third Lanark – met in Glasgow to form the Scottish Football Association; and almost a full year before a total of 16 clubs contested the first Scottish Cup.

It was a measure of their bold approach to the game, and an indication of their commercial self-confidence, that those in charge of Queen's Park, in the absence of a national association, agreed to accept full financial responsibility for the fixture.

Many people thought England, who had a head start in organised football, and could select their eleven from a hundred clubs, would prove too strong for Scotland with less than ten clubs. National, as well as personal, pride no doubt influenced the home side's refusal to accept the general assumption that England, given the superior size of their available player pool, must win; an example future generations of Scottish players were expected to emulate, no matter the odds.

A no-scoring draw in that first international encounter involving the two countries was a remarkable result for Scotland considering the entire national side was supplied by a single club, Queen's Park.

Hamilton Crescent had been host to the first in a unique series of matches, Scotland against England, home and away, that survived for more than a hundred years. Future matches between the two countries were usually close and drawn matches were not uncommon. But, curiously, it took almost a hundred years for the match to end in another no-scoring draw; in 1970 at Hampden Park.

Matches involving Scotland and England were expected to produce goals. To succeeding generations of Scottish fans, when the fixture meant something, and a game against England, any game against England, always meant something, there was never a more important engagement on a football field, anywhere, any time.

In addition to going some way towards satisfying the on-field ambitions of Queen's Park, the game against England at Hamilton Crescent, more than a century ago, also demonstrated that money could be made from the infant sport.

West of Scotland Cricket Club, who owned Hamilton Crescent, charged £20 for the use of the ground. Other expenses, including guarantees to Mr C.W. Alcock on behalf of the Football Association, totalled £49 11s 6d. Having agreed to pay for the match, Queen's Park could have been left with a serious loss if anything went wrong. But everyone at the club who believed football could become an important spectator sport in the years ahead – and provide profits to those with the foresight to act early – were soon proved right. On the day of the match around 4,000 spectators paid £102 19s 6d to witness an historic event. A surplus of £33 1s 8d exceeded all expectations.

Apart from failing to win outright against the best eleven players the whole of England could muster, Queen's Park were left with a single regret: they didn't own the ground on which the match had been played. As one early historian, Richard Robinson, explained: 'The possession of a private ground would add éclat to the club, in course of time endow its funds, and give it a local habitation, where it would not exist on sufferance, so to speak, as it did on the Queen's Park Recreation Ground.'

With their roots set firmly in the south side of Glasgow there was no question of the club moving to another part of the city. Following the match against England at Hamilton Crescent, it took almost a year for the club to settle on their own ground, rented from the city council, close to Queen's Park Recreation Ground, and within sight of a group of houses with a fateful name: Hampden Terrace.

The majestic turf of the most important football stadium in the world already beckoned.

Queen's Park occupied the first Hampden for ten prosperous years until a new railway line encroached on their territory and they were forced to depart. But not for the first time circumstances proved kind: a search of the neighbourhood established that suitable land was available, on a five-year lease, just 200 yards distant. Known to future generations of football fans as Cathkin Park, home of the doomed Third Lanark, it began service as the second Hampden late in 1884 and continued in this role, as the home of Queen's Park, and one of the most important venues in Scottish football, for almost 20 years.

But in all that time, although they were able to negotiate a series of extensions to the original lease, Queen's Park felt themselves restricted by their circumstances. As described by historian R.A. Crampsey, the problem confronting the club was quite clear-cut. The ground known as second Hampden required to be extended to meet the demands of 'ever-growing numbers of spectators, but with practically no security of tenure it was not wise to sink a great deal of money in the present premises'. The answer was 'simply to buy a piece of ground outright, and on it construct the finest football stadium in the world'.

Work on the new ground began in season 1900–1901, the year Queen's Park finally relented and joined the Scottish Football League.

The Scottish Football League was already ten years old by the time Queen's Park applied for membership. In its early days the new body had been condemned by one prominent critic for pursuing a set of rules which 'stink of finance, money-making and money-grabbing'.

It was hardly surprising that the Hampden side, clinging to their cherished amateur status, wanted to remain outside an organisation which many people believed would soon become a haven for professionals. Clubs in England had been employing professionals since 1885: by the time Queen's Park joined the Scottish Football League five years later a burgeoning market already existed in talented Scottish players moving south; often enticed by the prospect of good employment in addition to whatever terms their football skills were deemed to be worth.

In Scotland, long before the rules were changed to allow professionals, in 1893, hardly anyone bothered to pretend that illegal payments to players didn't exist. But there was also widespread concern that unless Scottish clubs agreed to follow the English example and reward players openly, thus allowing the professional game to flourish, organised football in Scotland would perish; or at best condemn itself to a mediocre existence with all the best players lured to England.

By the turn of the century it was evident that professionally minded clubs had been able to prosper, while the amateur game declined.

Remarkably, in 1890, the first year of the league championship, Rangers and Dumbarton finished equal top of the table. The following year Dumbarton won the title outright. Of the remaining eight championships decided during that first decade Celtic won four, while Hearts and Rangers each won two, Rangers in season 1898–99 achieving the near-impossible, 18 wins in 18 games, earning maximum points.

Twenty years earlier, Queen's Park, hoping to find more demanding competition outside Scotland, had been granted membership of the Football Association. The reward of their fame was a place in the semi-final of the first-ever FA Cup, played at Kennington Oval, on 4 March 1872, without the tedious, and expensive, necessity of having to play in any of the earlier rounds. The result was a no-scoring draw against the much-fancied Wanderers. But, as historian R.A. Crampsey notes in the second official history of the club, 'a draw was tantamount to a defeat, as the finances of the club simply would not stretch to a second visit to London. Queen's were compelled to scratch but they had the partial consolation of knowing that they had forced a draw with the eventual winners of the competition.'

Shortage of funds was the principal cause of the club's continued absence from the FA Cup, in any serious sense, for another ten years. But in 1884, by which time the Mount Florida side was financially secure, thanks largely to profits earned on their Hampden Park investment, it was decided to make a serious assault on England's premier trophy.

In the course of three qualifying rounds Queen's Park scored 32 goals with one against. Drawn to meet Old Westminsters at the semi-final stage, a single goal was enough to decide the outcome in favour of the Glasgow side.

The final was played at Kennington Oval and Blackburn Rovers won 2–1. But two goals disallowed for offside – 'which all who saw the match were emphatic would have counted under the law as applied in Scotland', and a later confession by the referee that 'on one occasion the ball was through the opponents' post by a foot, but nobody in the Scots team had claimed a goal' – left a nasty after-taste, further soured by accusations that the Blackburn side included at least four professionals.

Revenge would have been especially sweet a year later when Queen's Park, appearing in their second successive FA Cup final, faced the same opposition. But on this occasion everyone agreed a 2–0 victory by Blackburn Rovers was a fair result.

However, as R.A. Crampsey also notes in his centenary year account of the club: 'Not many of the crowd which attended the Oval on that day on 22 April 1885, could have known that they were present at the death of an era; from that day to this no amateur side has appeared in the final of the FA Cup and, although soccer is a notoriously chancy game, it is safe to say that no amateur side ever will again.'

Queen's Park had been a founder member of the Scottish Football Association, along with seven other clubs, in 1873, a year after the club, on behalf of Scotland, drew with England at Hamilton Crescent. Ten times winners of the Scottish Cup, and beaten finalists on two occasions, in the Scottish Cup and the FA Cup, their place in the history of the game was assured.

However, just as the growth of professional football as a major sport in Scotland began with the birth of the Scottish Football League, so the decline of Queen's Park as a serious force in the game can be traced to that same year – 1890.

Paradoxically, perhaps, the year the Scottish Football League started, the amateurs from Hampden succeeded in reaching the final of the Scottish Cup for a record ninth time. Unbeaten at this stage of the competition, their victims on this occasion were Vale of Leven who had been seven times finalists, and three times winners, of the Scottish Cup.

Two years later, following a final which included Hearts, a team prominent in the new order, against Dumbarton, who were defeated 1–0, Queen's Park succeeded in reaching yet another final. But this time they were scheduled to meet Celtic, one of the most powerful and influential voices in the new league. The match was played at Ibrox in front of 40,000 spectators. Compared to Queen's Park, the most famous and successful side in the history of organised football, Celtic were viewed as an upstart club by many serious students of the game.

One–nil ahead at the finish, Celtic created a sensation. The celebrations didn't last long, however. Following trouble on the terracing, and a pitch invasion, a replay was ordered for the following week; a decision in favour of the Hampden side that R.A. Crampsey, in his official history, believed 'came perilously near to fraud'.

There was always a chance, in a city polarised by poverty, that this second encounter involving two sides from opposite ends of the social order, could end in serious violence. Little was gained when the SFA, believing it would assist crowd control, doubled the price of admission. Their action was clearly unfair to less affluent fans who wanted to see the game, Celtic supporters, mostly. It also appeared to suggest they had been largely responsible for the earlier trouble; an unsafe verdict perhaps, considering the result.

The gate for the second game almost halved without showing any commensurate drop in income: 22,000 paying double was bound to appeal to treasury-minded SFA officials.

At half-time, Queen's Park were 1–0 ahead and confident the day would end with their name restored to the Scottish Cup for a record tenth time. Unbiased observers could be forgiven thinking events were conspiring, with the Glasgow business establishment, in favour of the Hampden side.

That it was Celtic who scored first following the restart hardly mattered. But another goal at the Queen's Park end was the cause of some real concern; enough, certainly, to encourage a heightened awareness of the flow of play, and with it a growing sense of shock, on the part of the Hampden support. As the whole balance of the match was seen to shift, it was obvious to everyone, including the

Queen's Park, owners of Hampden Park, and Scotland's oldest club, have been ten times winners of the Scottish Cup, starting in 1873 when the first competition was staged

most ardent followers of Queen's Park, that matters were proceeding to an unexpected conclusion.

People who started the day believing the Parkhead side had been unworthy winners of the Scottish Cup were forced to think again. In particular, honest supporters of Queen's Park, mindful of the reputation and best interests of the club, were bound to regret not settling for the original 1–0 result recorded against them. Bad as it looked on the day, it couldn't compare with the 5–1 drubbing Celtic inflicted on their illustrious opponents second time round.

A year later, in 1893, the two sides met again in the final of the same competition. After what happened the previous year, few people gave Queen's Park any chance against the new Cup-holders and reigning league champions. Even when both sides failed to score in the first match and a replay was required, the majority opinion didn't change: Celtic were bound to win in the end.

That they didn't is history – Queen's Park finally winning a bad-tempered game 2–1 against the odds, holders of the Scottish Cup for the tenth time in 30 years.

It was the Hampden side's last recorded victory in the competition. But it wasn't quite their last big hurrah. That came, appropriately enough, in 1900, the year Queen's Park finally decided to seek, and were granted, membership of the Scottish Football League.

By the turn of the century subsequently all-too-familiar names, like Rangers and Celtic, Hearts and Hibs, were beginning to dominate Scottish football.

Rangers' name appeared on the Scottish Cup more often than Celtic's. But in the league, the Parkhead side was marginally ahead in the number of championships won. The two clubs had met twice in the final of the Scottish Cup; with each side winning once. In 1900, the year Queen's Park joined the Scottish Football League, Rangers were reigning champions and Celtic were Cup-holders, as a result of defeating Rangers at Hampden the previous year.

Queen's Park qualifying for the final of the Scottish Cup in the first year of the new century intruded something of their marvellous past on a changing world. Even uncommitted observers would have been forced to admit they were surprised to see the amateurs from Hampden contesting another final. Disputing the game's highest honours was a serious business, best left to professionals, according to the latest wisdom. In the modern game, when professionals played amateurs, people expected only one result.

Fair to say, Celtic never looked like losing. Queen's Park weren't disgraced, however. The match contained seven goals; including three scored by the Hampden amateurs. For supporters of the Mount Florida side especially, each of the Queen's Park goals, against one of the great new powers in the game, was a happy reminder that Scottish football was once dominated by names other than Rangers and Celtic, or Hearts and Hibs, and wasn't always played for money.

When the Scottish Football League at last decided to abandon all pretence that certain players weren't already receiving some kind of financial remuneration for their efforts, an old adversary, the newspaper *Scottish Sport*, endeavoured to convince itself and its readers that there was still a place for amateurism in football. 'Players if they choose can still stand aloof from all mercenary inducements, can still wear the white flower of amateurism, the badge of sport for sport's sake,' a writer insisted. It was the newspaper's earnest desire that professionalism in Scotland would 'not be so professional as to permit our players making football their only living, doing nothing else but train and play'.

But right from the beginning, following a proposal by the Celtic chairman, J.H. McLaughlin, members of the Scottish Football League had been bound by certain considerations which could be judged mercenary – or, at the very least, totally self-serving – including a closed-shop policy which refused to allow a league club to play a non-league club except in competitions sanctioned by the Scottish Football Association.

Apart from making it difficult for Queen's Park to arrange matches against suitable opponents this policy obviously threatened the future development of Hampden Park. There would have been little point in anyone embarking on a scheme to build a great new stadium at enormous cost knowing no-one else would use it.

Faced with the constant threat of eviction, and in some ways, perhaps, bedazzled by their dream of one day building the finest football stadium in the world, Queen's Park decided to think again.

Those who favoured survival were right to argue that, all things considered, membership of the Scottish Football League might eventually prove no bad thing. A place in the league would guarantee regular weekly matches against the best clubs in the country; to which Queen's Park could bring a large and loyal support. The league also agreed to introduce a new rule preventing any of its members poaching players from Queen's Park between the start of the season and the following 30 April.

It would have been difficult for good business sense not to prevail. Fears of extinction, and a healthy regard for the laws of expediency, also helped. Queen's Park joined the league.

That same year work began on a new stadium which Queen's Park officials believed would be without equal anywhere in the world. Their chosen site was on the opposite side of Prospecthill from second Hampden and totalled approximately 12 acres.

The ground on which members of the Queen's Park committee proposed to build their dream stadium had been purchased at a cost of £800 an acre from the previous owner, Mr Henry Erskine Gordon, of Aikenhead House. The asking price had been £850 an acre; starting with £6,000 down and the balance secured at four per cent, due in instalments of £1,000. But once again the canny Glasgow business minds who served Queen's Park so well for so long emerged from the negotiations with an improved deal: the club would pay only £4,000 in cash, and the rest in instalments of £500 at the borrower's convenience.

'It is not every day in the week you can get sufficient ground, large enough for a football enclosure, and in the vicinity of the city,' the club secretary, Mr C.B. Miller, remarked shortly before the official opening three years later. 'We could have done easily with about a couple of acres less ground facing Somerville Drive.' But not wishing to be overlooked by a front of houses, for appearances sake, the club stretched to include the extra ground, Mr Miller explained.

A noted yachtsman, accomplished snooker player, former Queen's Park goalkeeper and lawyer by profession, the Queen's Park secretary could snap a silver threepenny coin between thumb and forefinger, according to an interview in the *Scottish Weekly Record*. 'He does not court notoriety though he moves amid the bustle and hum of a pastime that makes men notorious,' the newspaper claimed, not a little ambiguously.

For the benefit of anyone still upset at the prospect of abandoning second Hampden, where the club had been happy for so many years, Miller was able to explain some of the reasons behind the decision to shift ground. 'At the time we moved into the late Hampden Park in 1884 as a first-class club, it was one of the most up-to-date enclosures,' he told the *Scottish Weekly Record*. 'At the close of our tenancy as a first-class club it was one of the most antiquated city grounds.'

With the growth of football as an important spectator sport, the stand and other accommodation at second Hampden was insufficient for a club of their size, Miller added. There was also the continuing difficulty created by the terms of the club's lease on the ground. 'We had no satisfactory tenancy of the ground,' Miller explained. 'While we had a lease,' the Queen's Park secretary continued, 'the lease simply fixed the rent, because the owner could step in at any moment and resume possession of the ground for building and certain other purposes. That and the fact buildings were coming very close upon us impelled us to shift.'

By the time new Hampden was ready for its official opening on 31 October 1903, the *Evening Times* was able to report with some confidence that Queen's Park probably didn't realise the magnitude of their undertaking. 'It is admittedly a ground for the greatest things, grand in conception and great in area, and only the greatest successes can be deemed adequate reward for the enterprise which rendered such an enclosure possible,' the newspaper warned.

An artist's impression of the great enterprise, published during the week of the official opening, showed a playing surface, surrounded by a cinder athletics track, a twin-towered pavilion, and stands along one side facing comfortably banked terracing. The pitch occupied a basin 33 feet below the level of Somerville Drive where all the main turnstiles had been located. The long sides and wide ends of the ground had been banked with great care.

Crowd safety was the main consideration in the construction of the stadium which surpassed any existing athletics enclosure in size, in originality of design, and the all-important matter of security, the newspaper claimed.

Spectators, accustomed to standing on wooden tiers and steel scaffolding at other grounds, would be accommodated on solid earth at Hampden Park. The new stadium also featured a system of crowd control, described as penning, which had been devised to minimise the dangers of swaying and crushing.

The terracing was divided into sections which, on opening day, were arranged to accommodate 80 people, using barrier posts and wire cable an inch thick. 'The whole oval, with the exception of that portion to be occupied by the stands, will be split up in this fashion, and the beauty and safety of the plan will be realised on sight,' the *Evening Times* reported.

Together with the terracing and other work, which had been shared between Mr Robert Provand of Rutherglen, who had been responsible for excavating the ground, and Messrs McCreath and Stevenson, engineers, the complete cost of the ground alone amounted to around £10,000.

The main stand, which was constructed of steel, had been designed by Mr James Miller and built by Messrs P. and R. Fleming, at a cost of £5,000. It had been designed to accommodate 4,500 spectators seated under cover; with room for an additional 10,000 in the uncovered enclosure. The pavilion, which was expected to cost £3,000, wasn't due to be ready for at least another year.

However, when all of these considerations were added to the original cost of the land, excluding interest charges, the new stadium could be seen to be costing its owners around £30,000.

Queen's Park, with a membership of 800 and a complimentary membership totalling 150, was now a limited company; each of its members committed to a £5 guarantee against misfortune.

On opening day the new stadium was capable of accommodating in excess of 80,000 spectators and no-one anticipated Queen's Park encountering any difficulty achieving a target of 100,000. By extending the system of penning it was thought an additional 40,000 spectators could be accommodated easily and safely.

Sir John Ure Primrose, the Lord Provost of Glasgow, was invited to unfurl a commemorative flag on the occasion of the official opening on 31 October 1903. Celtic, third in the league behind Rangers and Third Lanark, provided the opposition and the Caledonian Railway Company ran special trains from the city

An early view of New Hampden Park, Glasgow, officially opened on 31 October 1903, as the biggest and the best football stadium in the world

Hampden Park, Glasgow, in its heyday. Named after an English patriot, John Hampden,
the huge ground 'stands four square with Bannockburn in the Scottish psyche'

centre to Mount Florida station. One reporter noted there was a large attendance, including many ladies. Someone else thought, 'The glorious spectacle which confronted the spectator at the opening of New Hampden Park was a living testimony to the vitality of Queen's Park. Everybody who was anybody in Scottish football was there to welcome the club to its new home.'

According to another report the turf, always a special feature of a Queen's Park ground, was in magnificent condition for play. Marking a historic occasion, the teams were: *Queen's Park* – I.H. Skene, T.F. Campbell and A. Richmond; Jas.

18

Eadie, W.H. Fullerton and J.F. Templeton; A. Currie, J. Loan, Alex McAllister, D. Wilson jnr and P.F. Jones. *Celtic* – Adams, Watson and Battles; Orr, Loney and Hay; Bennett, McMenemy, Gilligan, Somers and Quinn. *Referee* – Mr Murray, Stenhousemuir.

In its Notes on Sport section *The Glasgow Herald* suggested that, as an exhibition of football, the match provided 'all the features that go to make up an interesting game, the pace being fast, the honours pretty equally divided, and what was of most moment to the bulk of the attendance, the Queen's showing a revival of form which brought them out ahead at the finish'.

The *Scottish Weekly Record* reported it had been present at 'a fast, pleasant struggle, with little or nothing in the strife of unfair play to mar the greatest day in the history of Queen's Park. The character of the game elicited nothing but praise from those who had never previously witnessed a football match.'

Queen's Park, four places from the bottom of the league, with eight points from ten matches, surprised most people by winning 1–0 against the former league champions.

It was never likely, as some of their disappointed fans asserted, that Celtic, with a sentimental eye on the record books perhaps, simply allowed Queen's Park to enjoy the pleasure of victory in their first match at New Hampden. As witnessed by the reporter from the *Weekly Record*, 'Celtic made a bold bid for victory and were quite as determined as their opponents to gain the honours and the points which meant so much for them in the race for the championship'. According to the same observer anyone who thought otherwise was guilty of reckless prating; not a word to be thrown lightly, as an insult or in jest, at the head of a serious Celtic fan, even then.

CHAPTER TWO

When the redoubtable C.B. Miller, and members of the Queen's Park committee, journeyed from their offices in the city centre to Mount Florida and the site of the new dream stadium slowly taking shape on the edge of the city, organised football was already big business in Scotland. A decade earlier a crowd of around 20,000 for the Scottish Cup final was the most anyone could expect. Now it was reasonable to anticipate crowds in excess of five times that number once the largest football stadium in the world was ready for use.

The formation of the Scottish Football League in 1890, and the open use of professional players three years later, had been followed by an explosion of public interest in the game. In 1898 a crowd approaching 45,000 had been present when Celtic met Rangers in a league match at Parkhead. Two years later 63,000 spectators packed the same ground to see Scotland play England. The number of people wishing to attend the fixture had trebled in less than ten years. But most of them probably thought the result – 4–1 in favour of the home side – justified the crush.

Football had become the game of the working classes and, according to social historian Bill Murray, to the worker with magic in his feet it 'offered a way out of the industrial system; to him for whom the magic was only in the mind it offered a few hours of escapist release'.

But even in the dying days of the last century, football in Scotland was settling to a familiar routine: the financial muscle and playing power of the two main Glasgow clubs, Rangers and Celtic, dominated everything.

A presence in every Scottish Cup final except two during the first decade of the new century – when the two clubs also shared a total of eight league titles – suggested, at best, a passing phenomenon, or, at worst, the existence of a new commercial law which many feared might never be repealed.

When the Ibrox side won the Scottish Cup for the first time in their history in 1894 it was Celtic, the league champions, who provided the opposition. Five years later, when the two clubs met for the second time in the final of the same competition, it was Celtic's turn to win; against a Rangers side who were about to set a never-to-be-equalled record in the league championship, winning with maximum points.

In the course of the next ten years, only two Scottish Cup finals actually featured the Old Firm against each other. And of these only one reached a proper conclusion.

Hampden provided a wonderful new stage for the final of the 1904 competition. Rangers, holders and four times winners of the competition, were ahead of Celtic, with only three wins, overall. However, in the all-important tally of finals played and won against each other, the clubs were level.

More important, perhaps, and of genuine concern to anyone who worried about increasing Old Firm domination of the game, for the eighth time in 12 years the Scottish Cup was destined to finish at Ibrox or Parkhead.

Celtic, who were about to embark on one of the most successful periods in their history, claimed the prize; finishing the match 3–2 ahead.

Finals involving both clubs appeared to be settling to a five-year cycle. It was no surprise to anyone, therefore, when the 1909 final of the Scottish Cup again featured the Old Firm.

No-one at Ibrox required the least reminding that, if Celtic won again, the Scottish Cup would be returning to Parkhead for the third year in succession; a record previously established jointly by Queen's Park and Vale of Leven in the early days of the competition.

Since the two clubs last met in the final in 1904, Celtic had twice been winners of the Scottish Cup against other opposition; beating Hearts, the holders, in 1907, and then St Mirren, who were appearing in their first final, a year later. All the Ibrox side could achieve in the same period, in their one appearance in the final, was a no-scoring draw against Third Lanark who went on to win the replay 3–1.

Seeing their old rivals stretch their lead in the record books, in the long-established Scottish Cup, as well as the by now equally important league championship, didn't please anyone associated with Rangers. However, there was considerable public interest in the match and a vintage final was anticipated. As the *Daily Record*, which already boasted the largest sale in Scotland beneath its masthead, reported: 'Nothing draws a Glasgow crowd like a match between Celts and Rangers. The rivalry between the two teams is so pronounced that the football is generally exhilarating. A national final is not usually productive of good football but we shall be disappointed if this 1909 final is otherwise.'

The match itself, which was hard fought, and a splendid tussle by all accounts, ended in a 2–2 draw, thanks to a late goal by Celtic which denied Rangers, led by a new signing from Portsmouth, Willie Reid, a desperately-to-be-desired victory in the competition.

A replay was immediately arranged for the following Saturday. Apart from supporters of the clubs involved, replays in the Scottish Cup were unpopular with the majority of fans because they disrupted league fixtures which provided the main weekend entertainment for a large part of the male population. But drawn matches were common during the early rounds and there was a suspicion, well-nigh impossible to prove and just as difficult to deny, that the prospect of additional income encouraged clubs to play for a draw in the Scottish Cup.

In the interests of achieving a result without the expense of a second game, many people thought extra time should be played before a replay was deemed necessary. Not surprisingly, on the grounds of expense alone, opposition to the idea of a second replay before extra time had been tried was even more widespread.

In fact, although Rangers required two replays to dispose of Hearts at the last stage in 1903, before losing to Third Lanark in a replay two years later, drawn matches, although common enough in the early rounds of the competition, had become something of a rarity in the final of the Scottish Cup.

But whatever the facts of the matter, the men who ruled at No. 6 Carlton Place, Glasgow, headquarters of the Scottish Football Association, were adamant on the subject: in the Scottish Cup, a third match was necessary before teams could be allowed to try and settle a tie in extra time. It was the authorities' stubborn determination to abide by this convention, as much as anything else, that helped produce one of the darkest days in the history of Scottish football: a day when Hampden became a battlefield and the most prestigious trophy in Scottish football was left unwon.

Almost everyone in the crowd of 60,000 who assembled at Hampden Park on 17 April 1909, hoped they would see the Cup won in style; although some people would have settled for winning at any price. In a match featuring the Old Firm, with few neutrals present, there was only one truly good result for either side – victory! Few of those present would have been happy when, for the second time in a week, the two sides finished level; one each.

'I thought the game itself passed off pleasantly enough,' the referee, Mr J.B. Stark, recalled later. 'It's a pity I can't say the same for what happened next.'

According to newspaper reports in advance of the final Rangers and Celtic wanted the match played to a conclusion and players from both sides remained on the park long after the final whistle. In the stand, and on the terracings, as if expecting, or demanding, extra time, thousands of fans waited with growing impatience for the game to continue, unaware that, behind the scenes, a second replay had been ordered for the following Wednesday.

Approached by a number of players, and asked if he would allow the game to continue, the unfortunate referee, who required official approval for such action, was obliged to refuse. Blowing insistently on his whistle, and waving urgently at the players to leave the field, Mr Stark brought the day's official proceedings to a ragged conclusion.

One local dignitary, Sir John Ure Primrose, who had been guest of honour at the official opening of Hampden Park and was now a regular attender at important football occasions, later criticised the SFA for not making their intentions absolutely clear beforehand. 'The fact about half the Rangers team and half the Celtic team remained on the field for about ten or twelve minutes kept the expectations alive that there would be extra time played,' added Sir John, who became chairman of Rangers in 1912 and served in that role for another 11 years.

Given the circumstances, and the explosive nature of the occasion, it would have been impossible for the authorities to establish with any accuracy how the worst of the trouble started. One eye-witness described how 'a few individuals, who invaded the playing pitch more in a spirit of curiosity than mischief, were joined by a crowd numbering several hundreds. Two policemen guarding the narrow passage leading to the players' quarters blocked their path to the pavilion. The policemen refused to stand aside and the crowd tried to overwhelm them with force of numbers.'

As described by one reporter, 'Bottles, stones and ashes were thrown at the officers who pluckily held their ground though unable to prevent about forty venturesome men from making their way to the rear of the covered stand. There the mob were met by mounted constables and driven back on to the playing pitch.'

Meanwhile, other sections of the crowd had invaded the pitch and uprooted the goalposts at both ends. But that appeared to be the worst of it until a number of rioters 'left the field, rushed to the foot of the north terracing, and proceeded to tear down the lining of the barricades', as *The Glasgow Herald* reported bleakly.

'Their object was soon apparent,' the same newspaper continued with ill-concealed horror. 'The timbers were piled on the running track and set on fire. An infuriated crowd surrounded the blazing pile and danced and cheered wildly while willing hands seized more woodwork to feed the flames.'

The bonfire of timbers torn from the barricades grew and spread. A huge crowd cavorted happily and noisily in the vicinity of the flames. Sparks and smoke drifted towards neighbouring tenement homes. Astonished tenants, looking down on the disturbance from three-storey windows, and unaware of any danger to themselves, gaped and cheered.

Hundreds of fans could be seen ducking beneath the penning wires which divided the terracings, and scrambling on to the track, running across the playing field and climbing into the stand.

A small group of mounted policemen guarded the players' entrance to the pavilion. The men wore dark uniforms, with military-style peaked caps. The horses were brown in colour, with large eyes, short manes and long dark tails. Together they represented an élite unit within the Glasgow force. Usually, on match days, the demands made on their time never stretched beyond crowd control and helping to direct traffic in the precincts of the stadium. Everyone took it for granted there was a darker side to their nature and training.

But the average citizen was hardly concerned about what it might be like seeing a policeman seated on a large horse approaching at a gallop, filling the sky with menace, target identified, long baton raised to strike; panic spreading amidst a darkening thunder of hooves, before those who were about to be felled scattered and fled.

Anyone who believed attendance at Hampden Park, on the occasion of the Scottish Cup final, on Saturday, 17 April 1909, entitled them to set the running track alight as a demonstration of anger at the inconclusive nature of the day's main event could be viewed differently, of course.

James Verdier Stevenson would be among those certain to disapprove. An Irishman, born in County Westmeath and educated in Dublin, Stevenson was a tough, uncompromising character, with a strong sense of public order, who had been Chief Constable of Glasgow since 1902. Before coming to Scotland he had been head of the local constabulary in Belfast where he gained a reputation as a hardman. It would have been his considered opinion that any football fan who allowed himself to become part of a mob at Hampden, for whatever reason, inflicted a personal affront on the dignity and reputation of the city.

Following the worst industrial depression in 50 years, those who did so also set a dangerous example which others might follow, on to the streets of Glasgow, in pursuit of some real grievance, such as more jobs and better housing, which were always pertinent.

People expected Stevenson and his officers to use whatever force they deemed necessary to quell a riot. However, as the post-match activities of large sections of the crowd continued at Hampden on 17 April 1909, without strong reinforcements, it was clearly unreasonable for anyone to imagine that six or eight policemen on horseback could make much impression on a riotous mob numbered in hundreds – as *The Glasgow Herald* informed its readers angrily in the aftermath to the day's events.

As the small group of mounted policemen bravely attempted their near impossible task, they were quickly surrounded on all sides, the crowd in huge numbers pushing hard, forcing the horses to stumble, tugging at their harness and the long coats worn by the riders, pulling them out of control, so that, finally, according to one report, 'at least two of the policemen were unhorsed and badly beaten'.

Other reports claimed that, elsewhere in the stadium, policemen who lost touch with their colleagues had been set upon and beaten unmercifully. Ambulancemen who attempted to go to their aid also risked being attacked. Similarly, when the Queen's Park Fire Brigade, with nine engines in attendance, arrived on the scene, hoses were cut, and the firemen forced to defend themselves against the rioters; standing shoulder to shoulder with the police and hurling stones to deter their attackers.

In addition to the bonfire on the cinder-covered running track a burst of flame threatened the roof of the main pavilion at one stage and the entrance to the ground in Somerville Drive was totally destroyed, threatening houses on the opposite side of the narrow street.

At the height of the battle more than 300 policemen on foot and on horseback, who had been rushed to the scene with batons drawn and ready for use, were needed to disperse the crowd, forcing them into retreat, back on to the terracings, where it was found the cables used in penning made an organised charge, and counter-charge, almost impossible.

It appeared to *The Glasgow Herald* that the authorities 'were content to keep the mob on the terracing, hoping that no further mischief would be attempted and that the large covered stands and pavilion would thus escape damage'. To the same source 'the pitch resembled a miniature battlefield, civilians and policemen being carried over the ground in dozens of stretchers or on the shoulders of willing helpers. Inside the pavilion a number of medical men, assisted by four physicians from the Victoria Infirmary, were administering first aid to the injured.'

Queen's Park officials, seeing their splendid stadium threatened with destruction, immediately announced that Hampden would remain closed for the rest of the season. A letter to the SFA complained, with little fear of contradiction, about the behaviour of the crowd at the Scottish Cup final. The club wanted to know who would pay for the extensive damage which had been caused to the pitch, turnstiles and terracing.

Eventually the SFA agreed to meet half the £1,000 involved; with the rest divided between the two finalists and the host club. Queen's Park, not entirely pleased with the outcome, suggested the Corporation of Glasgow should be asked to contribute; which could have meant Glasgow officially accepting a large measure of responsibility for the behaviour of its wilder citizens.

As an idea it was bound to appeal to the austere nature of the men in control at Hampden. Not surprisingly, however, it failed to commend itself to the Corporation who threatened a counter-claim, including compensation for the injured policemen, and damage to city property in the neighbourhood of the stadium.

Following the riot, some people thought the Scottish Cup should be awarded to Rangers and Celtic jointly and both sets of players given commemorative medals. Others wanted to see a third match played outside Glasgow which had shown itself to be unworthy of the event. In fact, there appeared to be some agreement between the two clubs that one of them would scratch from the competition if ordered to play again.

At an emergency meeting, held to discuss the implications of the riot, it was agreed, for the first and last time in the history of the Scottish Cup, to abandon the competition and withhold the trophy and medals. The decision had been taken, SFA president John Liddell was anxious to explain, in order to convey the association's total disapproval of what occurred at Hampden; and to avoid the risk of any repetition of what happened in the previous match.

It was a bad, black time for organised football in Scotland.

Few at the time would disagree with the view, expressed in the *Daily Record*, that football would become 'a thing of the past if a display of brutality like that witnessed in the vicinity of Hampden Park could be traced as an effect of the game. 'No matter under what circumstances the affair occurred public opinion would very soon demand the cessation of a pastime capable of converting a crowd of human beings into an army of savages,' the paper warned.

More than seventy years later, when a different generation of supporters of the same two clubs reprised the riot of 1909, public reaction was much the same. As *The Glasgow Herald* insisted: 'Arguing over which set of supporters was to blame is an irrelevancy – a futile extension of the mindless partisanship that was the real cause of the trouble.'

On this occasion, the final of the Scottish Cup, played at Hampden on 10 May 1980, the crowd was treated to a result. But the score, 1–0 to Celtic in extra time, was never likely to improve the mood of the Rangers faithful. Rangers needed to win to clinch a place in Europe the following year. 'Unless the players have the heart and the guts for the job they can forget it,' a trenchant manager, John Greig, announced before the match.

Celtic were hoping to compensate for the late loss of the Premier league championship to Aberdeen, in a thrilling finale to the season-long struggle, by the margin of a single point. Their manager, Billy McNeill, who had been on the winning side seven times as a player, believed victory in the Scottish Cup final was 'all about players raising their performance and giving that little bit extra. That is what I am looking for from my men at Hampden,' he declared.

A restless, noisy crowd of 70,303 looked on as the teams lined up, in bright, sunny conditions, as follows: *Celtic* – Latchford, Sneddon, McGrain, Aitken, Conroy, MacLeod, Provan, Doyle, McCluskey, Burns, McGarvey. *Rangers* – McCloy, Jardine, Dawson, Forsyth, Jackson, Stevens, Cooper, Russell, Johnstone, Smith, MacDonald. *Referee* – G.B. Smith, Edinburgh.

Afterwards, as people inside and outside football tried to assess the extent of the damage which had been done to the good name of Scotland by the after-match mayhem at Hampden, it was left to the football writers to remind anyone who cared to listen that it had been a match worthy of the final.

As Jim Reynolds argued in *The Glasgow Herald*, the match was one of the most enjoyable Old Firm encounters for a long time: hard and tough, but fair, and laced with good skills from both teams; a view supported by Hugh Taylor in his annual review, *The Scottish Football Book*.

It was hardly surprising the match had been fierce. 'What Old Firm clash isn't fierce?' Taylor demanded. 'But it was fought by true warriors and, even if a few names were taken by a splendid referee, it was a manly and not unsporting affair. For excitement, for goalmouth flurries, for near things and missed chances, the final hadn't been equalled for a long time,' Taylor contended.

Not that any of this mattered to those intent on causing trouble. How many of those responsible for the after-match scenes which disgraced the game in Scotland cared that the winning goal, by George McCluskey after 107 minutes, as witnessed by Alex Cameron of the *Daily Record*, was both cheeky and clever? 'Danny McGrain had shot the ball viciously back as it was headed out,' Cameron wrote. 'McCluskey, back to the goal, flicked the ball with the outside of his left foot, changed direction completely, and sent it well away from McCloy.'

It was only the 11th Scottish Cup final meeting between the two clubs, excluding 1909 when the trophy was withheld. Before the 1980 final neither side could claim any advantage from the record books. Between 1894, when the two clubs first met in the final, and 1928, victory in four finals divided equally. Similarly, following an astonishing gap of 35 years, when Rangers and Celtic never met in the final of the Scottish Cup, six Old Firm finals contested between 1963 and 1977 ended with each side able to claim the same number of wins.

McCluskey's goal put Celtic ahead. It also prevented Rangers enjoying their third hat-trick of wins in the competition since the war. The result also meant that, for the first time in 15 years, Rangers, fifth in the league, failed to qualify for Europe.

The absence of lucrative, and glamorous, European opposition from the Ibrox calendar in the year ahead was a bleak prospect for the always ambitious Glasgow club. And, obviously, a huge disappointment to their army of followers. But whatever the measure of their disappointment, and however great the elation enjoyed by supporters at the opposite end, no-one from either side, and no sensible supporter, could condone the after-match scenes that disfigured the afternoon.

'The trouble started when Celtic fans spilled from the east terracing to acclaim their Cup-winning heroes,' the *Daily Record* reported. 'Then raging Rangers fans swept over the fences at their end and battle was joined.' Showers of bottles, stones and cans rained on to the field. 'Battling fans, armed with iron bars and wooden staves ripped from terracing frames, created the most violent and ugly scenes seen at Hampden in more than 70 years,' the report continued.

There were obvious similarities with events surrounding the Scottish Cup final of 1909, not least the presence of teams representing Rangers and Celtic. But this time, right from the start, instead of turning their immediate attention to the police, the fury of a large number of opposing supporters was directed almost totally against each other.

Gangs of youths, who claimed an undying interest in the fluctuating fortunes of both clubs, pursued rival groups on to the Hampden pitch. And there, in full view of live television cameras which stayed, long after the game was finished, to record the mayhem, they stood and fought; not for the first time, in a city where this was the kind of colour difference that really mattered, blue raging at green.

It was hardly an unusual experience for the majority of Celtic supporters, occupying their traditional place on the east terracing at Hampden, to witness their heroes celebrating victory in the final of the Scottish Cup. On five previous occasions during the past ten years they stood and cheered, roaring their approval, and craning their necks for a better view, as a Celtic captain led his team to the top of the stairs in front of the Hampden stand to take possession of the famous old trophy.

Now it was the turn of Danny McGrain who told reporters the riot left him feeling really sick. 'What should have been a great occasion and a famous victory was completely spoiled,' McGrain complained.

The winners had been given SFA permission to parade the cup in front of their ecstatic followers: in the event of a Rangers victory, the Ibrox side would have been equally entitled, and just as likely, to demonstrate their delight. It was a traditional display enjoyed by everyone attending a Hampden final except, obviously, suppporters of the losing side.

A ten-foot-high perimeter fence had been installed at considerable expense to prevent disgruntled, or excited, fans from either side invading the pitch. Before the final, officials of the SFA, determined to rid the game in Scotland of its persistent hooligan image, appeared inordinately proud of their splendid new fence. Now they watched in horror as hundreds of Celtic fans, intent on joining their heroes' on-field celebrations, clambered across with ease.

'The barriers were completely inadequate,' Chief Constable Patrick Hamill complained later. 'They acted as no deterrent.'

At first, according to an official SFA report which examined the cause of the riot, there was nothing violent in the exchanges between players and fans. Rather, according to the SFA, it was a spontaneous, if misguided, expression of joy, with fans cavorting around and generally celebrating with the Celtic players their exuberance at victory.

But long after the losers' medals had been presented, on the west terracing, at least, disappointment at the result was clearly palpable. Hundreds of Rangers fans, determined to salvage some sort of perverse satisfaction from a disastrous afternoon, remained in their places to hurl abuse at the winners parading the Cup; filling the Hampden air with jeers and taunts. The presence of any number of Celtic fans, chanting and jeering on the Hampden playing pitch, mixing with their idols, triumphant in green and white hoops, happily posing for photographs, waving to their supporters, and passing the Scottish Cup from hand to hand, was unlikely to improve the questionable demeanour of those who watched the celebrations, with angry concentration, from the Rangers end.

And no-one with any real sense of Glasgow was entitled to harbour feelings of surprise, never mind shock, when fans in blue and white scarves, occupying the west terracing, began scaling the inadequate fence that separated them from their tormentors.

Anticipating trouble elsewhere, as jubilant and disconsolate fans clashed on their way home perhaps, or headed for the nearest pub, police numbers at Hampden had been restricted in favour of a large uniformed presence outside the ground and along streets leading to the city centre.

People of a generally pacific nature who remained in the stadium, expecting an orderly end to the match, and millions more watching on television, could only stare in disbelief when, in the words of one eye-witness: 'The thin blue line of police found themselves overwhelmed as fans descended upon them from the terracing, scaling the much-vaunted safety fences with ease.'

Predictably, with not enough police around to restrict them to their own end of the stadium, at least, it wasn't long before the earlier, harmless cavorting at the Celtic end, described in the SFA report, altered course with disastrous effect. No sooner did the first wave of Celtic fans cross the half-way line than a large number of Rangers fans went to meet them – 'ready for war', in the words of one report.

'There was no question of celebration in the minds of the fans who invaded from the west end of the ground,' the SFA reported, ingenuously. 'They had violence in mind and no sooner was it offered than it was returned with enthusiasm.' Before long, 'the pitch had become a battlefield and the police and medical centres outside the south stand looked like a scene from a disaster film'.

Hampden has been the scene of two major riots, the first of which occurred in 1909, the second in 1980. Both disturbances involved Rangers and Celtic fans following a Scottish Cup final

Only the brave intervention of a comparatively small number of police, some of them on horseback, prevented supporters of both sides from killing each other, and anyone else who happened to intrude.

Chief Constable Hamill was later criticised for positioning too few men inside the stadium at the end of the match. However, additional police were assigned to Hampden immediately the extent of the fighting became known. At the height of the trouble, 500 police were on duty inside the stadium, helping to quell the riot. 'Just how many officers does it now take to police such an occasion?' a police spokesman, fielding criticism with ill-concealed anger, inquired later.

The SFA was in no doubt that what happened at Hampden following the match 'brought disgrace upon the two clubs concerned, upon Scottish football generally, and were an affront to Scotland as a nation'.

A fine of £20,000 was imposed on each of the finalists. Celtic felt particularly aggrieved that, in some quarters, they were singled out for special blame. Immediately after the match, the president of the SFA, Willie Harkness, told reporters it was the Celtic players parading the Cup in front of their own fans which helped spark the pitch invasion. Even worse, the Secretary of State for Scotland, George Younger, in a statement to the House of Commons, claimed it was drink, and the actions of the Celtic players, which led to the riot.

Billy McNeill defended his team against all-comers. 'I felt that nothing my players did was anything other than players throughout the world would have done in similar circumstances,' he told reporters. 'For anyone to suggest that they were the culprits for what happened was, in my opinion, irresponsible,' he insisted.

Far from feeling the occasion had been marred by the behaviour of his players, the Celtic manager thought they should be complimented on the way they went about their business. 'Both sets of players can hold their heads high,' McNeill insisted.

His chairman, Desmond White, reacted angrily to a statement issued by Rangers which appeared to support those in authority who criticised Celtic. 'They blame us,' he complained bitterly. 'This annoys me. In fact, it appals me.' According to Mr White, a lawyer, the trouble started when 'a mass of Rangers supporters, who had been hurling cans on to the park, came on and charged the Celtic supporters'.

More than 160 people were arrested inside the ground and another 50 outside. In the words of one report: 'For a time it was mob rule, with hordes of fans, most of whom were drunken teenagers, jostling, swaggering, jeering, swearing and singing along the main routes into the city.'

The Glasgow Herald thought the appalling scenes at Hampden put the whole of Scotland, and especially Glasgow, in a shameful light. 'Years of patient effort to persuade industrialists and others that Glasgow is a desirable place to live are easily negated in a few moments on the national television news,' the newspaper continued sombrely.

Most people acknowledged the religious differences which existed between supporters of the two clubs – 'the root cause of the hatred and bitterness which has existed between the two sets of supporters for decades', the official SFA response noted scathingly.

But more than anything, perhaps, the extent of the riot convinced most people of the need for a ban on drink inside football grounds.

It had been more than two years since a report by a special Government committee, chaired by Gorbals MP Frank McElhone, recommended a ban on drink at all matches. But the full force of the McElhone recommendations couldn't be implemented until the Scottish Criminal Justice Bill became law later the same year. 'The police do not have any power to frisk fans for drink,' a spokesman explained. 'However, in co-operation with the football authorities we make every effort to ensure no drink is taken into a game.'

Anyone at Hampden on the afternoon of Saturday, 10 May 1980, could have been excused thinking the best efforts of the normally efficient Strathclyde Police and the Scottish Football Association, working together to keep the stadium drink-free on the occasion of the Scottish Cup final, had been singularly unsuccessful.

A large measure of public disquiet followed repeated television screenings of the Hampden mayhem. Two days after the riot *The Glasgow Herald* reported: 'In the aftermath of the unprecedented riot alarmed senior police officers asked the Chief Constable, Mr Patrick Hamill, to ban Old Firm matches in the public interest and to save the risk of serious injury to their men.'

In the belief it was unenforceable, many people with a blinkered view of football, and an exaggerated opinion of its importance to the continued well-being of the majority of the population, disregarded the threat. But it was probably just as well for all concerned that clearer heads recognised their responsibility to society as a whole; and were rightly mindful of the likely reaction

Cheers! A familiar sight outside Hampden Park on the morning after a big match before the Scottish Criminal Justice Bill banned fans from entering football grounds carrying alcohol

from uninvolved members of the public to the violent happenings at Hampden.

For example, following the 1980 riot, without rigid enforcement of tough new laws banning drink, future matches between Rangers and Celtic could have been seriously threatened. No-one disputes the likely catastrophic effect of any such ban on the playing standards and financial health of the game in Scotland; or the ramifications of the social and political upheaval it would produce.

The two clubs generate interest, pleasure and heartache for thousands, even millions, of people for most of the year. Matches involving the two sides are national institutions in their own right and Scotland would be a poorer place without them.

But most people with little interest in football are against fighting, in and around grounds, that spreads to the streets, culminating in random violence which endangers anyone who happens to get in the way. They also dislike the idea of wayward football fans spilling their fury and frustrations into their living-rooms by way of television.

Following the 1980 riot, the vast majority of the population, with little interest in organised football, would have been right to remove the threat of a repeat performance. Hampden, 1980, wasn't something anybody with any sense wanted to see repeated ever again.

CHAPTER THREE

At times of political crisis in the governance of Britain there is a tendency to deny the difference that exists from birth between Scots, who proclaim their Scottishness, and the people of England. Anyone who so insists should be present at Hampden on the occasion of a football match between the two countries.

Hard to imagine now perhaps, but for years, before high-profile, full-time managers and various professional assistants appeared to accept the blame, and sometimes the plaudits, for what finally happened on the green bit in the middle of Hampden, a small group of nearly anonymous businessmen were in charge of national team selection.

But anyone who appeared in a Scottish jersey, in a match against England or any other country, represented more than the selectors' frequently flawed choice of the best footballing talent available to their whim from both sides of the same narrow border. Given the opportunity of appearing for his country at Hampden against England, any player, born in Scotland, or of Scottish parents, was never allowed to forget the ancient rivalries whch existed between the two nations; on and off the field.

The fact that most English stars, and their attendant officials, appeared – or pretended! – not to understand the importance of the fixture to almost everyone in Scotland, simply served to make victory, when it came, all the more satisfactory.

Quite often the great tide of national pride and sentiment, always present on the occasion of the bi-annual Hampden gala, threatened to obliterate all good sense. One such recurring lunacy concerned the notion that those who made their footballing careers in England should be banned from the national side at Hampden. Considering the litany of star names who could have been denied a place of honour in winning sides against England, if ever any such nonsense prevailed for all time, then Scotland's chances of securing victory in the great match would have been sorely diminished.

But the theory helped stimulate good pub talk, of a cheery, insane and usually harmless nature. Whenever it worked its way into the papers, which it managed with greater frequency than the idea deserved, it also helped sustain a favourite paper's perilous circulation; thus ensuring a continuing, comfortable billet for several generations of deserving members of the football writers' fraternity.

Remarkably, perhaps, it took England more than 20 years, with a war intervening, to achieve victory at the present Hampden.

Following early matches played at Partick, various grounds had been chosen to house important international fixtures, including Ibrox and Parkhead – there is nothing new in the notion that Scotland doesn't really need a national stadium! But across the best part of eight decades, from 1906, when Sir John Ure Primrose declared new Hampden open, to 1984, when the British international championship lapsed and the fixture was allowed to slip into terminal decline as a serious confrontation worthy of its own great history, the match with England was housed at the Mount Florida ground. During its greatest years Scotland against England at Hampden was certainly the most important, and easily the most emotional, sporting occasion held in Scotland.

That first match, played in 1906, finished with Scotland ahead 2–1. Four other games against England in the international championship, staged at Hampden before the outbreak of the first world war, produced a pair of one-goal draws and two wins for Scotland; 2–0 in 1910 and 3–1 in 1914.

It wasn't until 1927 that an English side succeeded in defeating Scotland in a full international in front of a Hampden crowd.

It was the eighth championship meeting between the two countries since the end of hostilities. Until then various Scottish sides had been enjoying a fine run of success against their oldest opponents. Of the seven matches played, Scotland won four, drew two and lost in only one – an obvious sizzler, played at Sheffield in 1920, which ended with England ahead, 5–4.

The 2–1 Hampden defeat of 1927 was soon avenged, in the most dramatic fashion possible, by the performance of the 1928 Wembley Wizards who destroyed England with their skill; much of it provided by players who earned their living in England.

A total of 35 matches in the British championship played at Hampden between 1906 and 1984 produced 14 victories for Scotland, 13 England wins and eight draws.

Both countries enjoyed periods of sustained superiority. Throughout the 1930s, for example, Scotland lost only once to England in a full international at Hampden.

These were the years of massive crowds at the Mount Florida ground. And there was never one bigger, anywhere in Europe, or, indeed, the world at that time, than the 149,414 who paid to watch the 1937 match against England; with thousands more almost certain to have gained free access by scaling the Hampden wall.

The 1937 match against England was the first all-ticket international ever organised in Scotland. Gate receipts totalled £24,000. Previously, the record Hampden attendance had been set in 1933 when 136,250 spectators paid £13,958 to see Scotland beat England, 2–1. Ground improvements carried out since then included a new north stand, with accommodation for 4,500. This meant the official crowd limit for Hampden had been increased to 150,000.

Alan Morton, nicknamed The Wee Blue Devil during his illustrious career with Rangers, became a Scotland player while still with Queen's Park. His 31 caps included 11 appearances against England

A two-shilling – ten pence now! – ticket was supposed to purchase around one and a half feet of personally-exclusive standing room space on one of the Hampden terracings. Of course, assuming a substantial number of gatecrashers climbing the Hampden walls, even this less-than-generous allocation of body room was almost certainly reduced in 1937.

However, according to *The Glasgow Herald*, which was then devoted, predominantly, to the interests of the Glasgow business class, SFA secretary George Graham delivered a near miracle of organisation when Scotland met England at Hampden on 17 April 1937: 'There was no congestion worth speaking about outside the ground, and the packing of the vast crowd inside, except in the enclosure which fronts the new stand, and in parts of the east terracing, which had been heightened, was remarkably efficient, the number who failed to see the game being practically negligible.'

Others, probably nearer the heart of the matter than the man from *The Glasgow Herald*, claimed nobody could move in the midst of that vast crowd. 'You could hardly move a muscle!' one veteran fan recalled, grinning. 'But what you couldn't see you heard. That was the Hampden Roar!'

On one of the most important days in the history of Scottish sport, the teams were: *Scotland* – Dawson (Rangers), Anderson (Hearts) and Beattie (Preston North End); Massie (Aston Villa), Simpson (Rangers) and Brown (Rangers); Delaney (Celtic), Walker (Hearts), O'Donnell (Preston North End), McPhail (Rangers) and Duncan (Derby County). *England* – Woodley (Chelsea), Male (Arsenal) and Barkas (Manchester City); Britton (Everton), Young (Huddersfield Town), Bray (Manchester City); Matthews (Stoke City), Carter (Sunderland), Steele (Stoke City), Starling (Aston Villa) and Johnson (Stoke City). *Referee* – W. M'Clean, Belfast.

It had been ten years since England last won at Hampden. But from the quality of their first-half performance on this occasion, the massive crowd, predominantly Scottish in character, could be forgiven thinking their heroes were heading for certain defeat. Scotland appeared outclassed for most of the first 45 minutes. But at half-time only a goal, scored shortly before the interval by Freddie Steele, the England centre-forward, separated the two sides.

Two minutes into the second half Frank O'Donnell, of Preston North End, playing in his first international for Scotland, equalised. The roar that erupted from the largest crowd so far assembled anywhere in the world to witness a football match was deafening.

Stanley Matthews, near the start of his brilliant career, and playing in his first match for England against Scotland, later credited the noise of the crowd with the visitors' eventual defeat. If ever a match was won and lost by a roar, this was it, according to the wonder winger.

A more measurable contribution to the outcome was provided by Bob McPhail, of Rangers, who earned 17 full caps for Scotland in the course of a long and distinguished career, five of them against England at Hampden.

McPhail, who was enjoying perhaps his best-ever game in a Scotland jersey, almost scored early in the second half. But an outstanding save by Vic Woodley, earning the first of 19 caps in the England goal, kept the ball out and, as the match developed, robbed McPhail of a hat-trick. Ten minutes before the end, with the crowd roaring itself hoarse, a good through pass from centre-forward Frank O'Donnell found the big Ranger with space to move. And this time, with a shot from 15 yards, he gave Woodley no chance.

Scotland were ahead! The visitors' Hampden jinx wasn't about to be lifted; not yet awhile

England, playing with commendable spirit, looked far from finished. But time was ticking away. Scottish fans, concerned about the narrowness of the score, shuffled anxiously in the small space given to them on the packed slopes of Hampden, barely able to move. But they needn't have worried.

Another goal by McPhail, in the very last minute of the match, put the result beyond doubt. This time a headed pass from Jimmy Delaney, of Celtic, arrived head-high. McPhail elected to finish the move with another header. Woodley shrugged disconsolately as he picked the ball from the back of the net.

Miles from Hampden, the smoke-blackened air around industrial Glasgow filled with a long-sustained and tremendous sound. Unmistakable in its intensity, this was the Hampden Roar at its loudest and happiest.

No-one hearing the noise coming from the direction of the national stadium, needed to be told the result. Only a Scotland victory over England could produce such a triumphant, decibel-laden celebration.

On the terracings and in the stand at Hampden people could judge the size of the crowd with reasonable accuracy. From past experience, most of them guessed right from the start, they were almost certainly part of the biggest football crowd in history. The majority of people, standing shoulder to shoulder on each of the three terracings, and in the enclosure, couldn't move. 'No-one ever saw such a crowd!' people exclaimed, glancing round, and over the heads of their neighbours, in disbelief.

The official attendance figures simply confirmed what everyone present already guessed. But being part of the biggest football crowd in history, in a country which was forever anxious about its own sense of worth and mistaken identity, was also a source of considerable pride.

As the huge stadium emptied slowly, with most of the departing fans barely able to move in the crush, people were thrilled for themselves, and pleased it was Hampden, and not some other place, especially Wembley, which had been host to the largest football crowd in the world.

Some, in jubilant mood, were prepared to believe the day's attendance figures bestowed a rare distinction on the national stadium, everyone present at the match, the entire city of Glasgow, and Scotland as a whole. Victory against England also helped.

Those who celebrated late into the evening of Saturday, 17 April 1937, couldn't possibly imagine how many momentous events, disastrous and calamitous, would engulf the world before they could enjoy another carefree, after-match celebration following a visit by England to Hampden.

The last full international between the two countries, in a British championship match immediately prior to the start of the Second World War, was played at Hampden on 15 April 1939. A draw would have been enough to give Scotland the championship outright for the second time in four years. England winning would result in a three-way share with Wales.

With three minutes left for play the score was 1–1 and another huge Hampden crowd was looking forward to Scotland clinching the international championship title. The teams were: *Scotland* – Dawson (Rangers); Carabine (Third Lanark) and Cummings (Aston Villa); Shankly (Preston North End), Baxter (Middlesbrough) and McNab (West Bromwich Albion); McSpadyen (Partick Thistle), Walker (Hearts), Dougal (Preston North End), Venters (Rangers) and Milne (Middlesbrough). *England* – Woodley (Chelsea); Morris (Wolverhampton Wanderers) and Hapgood (Arsenal); Willingham (Huddersfield

Town), Cullis (Wolverhampton Wanderers) and Mercer (Everton); Matthews (Stoke City), Hall (Tottenham Hotspur), Lawton (Everton), Goulden (West Ham United) and Beasley (Huddersfield Town). *Referee* – W.R. Hamilton, Belfast.

The match had been played in torrential rain and high winds, making the heavy leather ball difficult to control. Scotland, having secured wind advantage on the toss of a coin, employed more calculable methods to score first. Goalkeeper Woodley and right-back Morris combined to leave the England goal at risk. Dougal pounced.

Half-way into the second half an uncharacteristic mis-kick by the Scotland right-back, Jimmy Carabine, let Beasley equalise.

By the closing minutes, with the rain and the wind conspiring to make everyone's life miserable, everyone expected a draw. However, the incomparable Stanley Matthews, with his brilliant footwork and astonishing ball control, disdained the awkward conditions.

A brilliant solo raid on Dawson, as the match neared its end, with even a part share in the championship slipping from England's grasp, earned a corner. The ball was badly cleared. Goulden gave it to Matthews. In front of goal Lawton lurked. Bill Shankly, recognising the danger, ran to intercept. Too late! With perfect timing Matthews delivered the ball straight to the head of Tommy Lawton – who scored.

A part share in the international championship was probably better than no share – although, on the afternoon of Saturday, 15 April 1939, among the thousands of bedraggled, disappointed Scottish fans who trooped home from their latest Hampden encounter with England, not many people really cared. For even then, long before the years of its great decline in the face of soaring competition from World Cup qualifying matches, and interest of a different kind generated by the success of British clubs competing in Europe, only an outright win in the inter-Britain competition attracted much attention.

Invited to choose between winning the championship outright and beating England, the average Scottish fan would almost certainly opt for victory against his nearest neighbours, even if it meant forfeiting the title to Wales or Northern Ireland, with Hampden his preferred venue for the defeat of the Auld Enemy, on the simple grounds more Scots could be there to enjoy it.

It may be difficult for younger fans, weaned on World Cup qualifying matches against the best countries in Europe, to fully appreciate the sense of excitement generated by the presence of England at Hampden. But once every two years it was easy to imagine the great stadium existed for no other purpose than to provide a magnificent stage on which Scotland might inflict some awful, joyful humiliation on their southern neighbours.

That this didn't happen as often as everyone hoped, and the English quite frequently won, or forced an unsatisfactory draw, which didn't please anyone, mattered less in the end than the continuing dream of glory and high expectation which the match always spawned.

Even the concentration of minds and attention demanded by the ultimate horror of the Second World War didn't bring international matches between Scotland and England to an abrupt halt. Far from it! Between 1940 and 1945 the two countries continued to meet on a regular basis, with six-figure crowds not uncommon at Hampden.

There is, of course, a fashionable tendency to dismiss war-time internationals as matches unworthy of serious attention, on the dubious grounds they were simply entertainments, provided, with Government encouragement, to help distract public attention from worries about the war. It is true, of course, that war-time matches only enjoyed the status of friendlies. Players weren't awarded full caps and nobody was supposed to take the outcome too seriously.

As an exercise in psychological warfare, and population manipulation, the theory might be supportable. However, it is hardly sustainable, as a point of view, that any of the star names who took part, and the huge crowds who turned out for many of these matches, considered them non-events.

The nadir of Scotland's war-time torment, in games against England, was a match, played in front of 60,000 spectators, at Maine Road, Manchester, on 16 October 1943. England, leading 5–0 at half-time, added another three goals in the second half without Scotland once finding the net. Lawton scored four, Hagan two, and Carter and Matthews one each.

Despite everyone's preoccupation with the war, it is beyond human understanding, as this frail commodity may be judged in Scotland, to believe someone, somewhere, didn't groan a little on hearing that result.

War-time conditions generally, and the disruption of regular league football, probably put a question mark over the fitness of many of the players. But it would be quite wrong to imagine those selected were somehow second-rate and unlikely to be chosen in normal peacetime conditions, assuming a healthy league and few players of quality absent on war duty.

It was unfortunate for England and, in all truth, the state of the game generally, that so many truly great players who wore the famous white shirt were at the peak of their prowess during the years of the war. Their war-time strength can be judged from just a few of the names who appeared at Hampden – Swift, Hapgood, Cullis, Mercer, Matthews, Carter, Mannion, Lawton.

Not that they were ever allowed to enjoy any feelings of sublime invincibility on their visits to Glasgow, of course. For Scotland could field the likes of Dawson, Carabine, Shankly, Young, Macaulay, Busby, Delaney, Walker, Venters, Gillick, Waddell, Liddell.

In fact, there were few players from either side on active duty who were likely to command a regular place under different circumstances.

Certainly, there couldn't have been many disinterested spectators among the 133,000-strong crowd at Hampden on 14 April 1945, standing in silent tribute before the match to the memory of President Roosevelt, who died the previous day. The teams were: *Scotland* – Brown (Queen's Park), Harley (Liverpool) and Stephen (Bradford); Busby (Liverpool), Harris (Wolves) and Macauley (West Ham); Waddell (Rangers), Bogan (Hibernian), J.R. Harris (Queen's Park), Black

39

(Hearts) and Kelly (Morton). *England* – Swift (Manchester City), Scott (Arsenal) and Hardwick (Middlesbrough); Soo (Stoke), Carter (Sunderland), Lawton (Everton), R.A.J. Brown (Charlton) and L. Smith (Brentford). *Referee* – J.S. Cox, Rutherglen.

The match started wickedly for Scotland. And much too harshly for Tommy Bogan, at inside-right. Forty seconds into the game the little Hibs player collided with the massive frame of England goalkeeper, Frank Swift, and suffered a broken leg.

The snap of breaking bone was unmistakable. The whole of Hampden hushed. Surrounded by players from both sides, Swift lifted the tiny figure of Bogan and carried him to the touchline.

Unfairly, in the view of many observers, Swift, normally a popular man, who enjoyed his reputation as a gentle giant, was accompanied all the way to the line by the boos of the huge Hampden crowd.

Les Johnstone, of Clyde, who was allowed to replace the unfortunate Bogan, soon repaid his unexpected promotion with a goal. But it was the Scots' only goal of the match. A penalty awarded against England, when they were 3–1 ahead, should have been put to better use by Matt Busby.

Busby and Swift were old friends from pre-war days in Manchester. Busby often assisted Swift in training by taking penalty kicks against him. Now, it appeared from the evidence of Hampden, the big goalkeeper was the better learner. At any rate, he rightly guessed Busby's intentions. The penalty, which was Scotland's last real chance to turn the match, was smothered by Swift.

Before the crowd dispersed the names of Lawton twice, R.A.J. Brown, Carter, Matthews and Smith all appeared on the England score-sheet.

Scotland's best performance during the war years was a match played at Hampden on 18 April 1942, when the score was 5–4 in favour of the home side.

Before the match it was thought a crowd of 70,000 could be expected and this figure was fixed as the official limit. On the day, however, a crowd in excess of 90,000 was estimated to have witnessed the match.

The occasion reminded *The Glasgow Herald* of the distant past before 1939. It was the nearest approach to a peace-time Saturday since the war began, the paper added wistfully. But it also noted that: 'Big numbers of servicemen, eagerly seizing this glimpse of old Saturday joys, were in the scrambling crowds seeking to board trams and buses all over the city.'

During the match, according to the same source, the famous Hampden Roar almost reached peace-time strength in response to the quality, high-speed football on view. 'In the ceremonial prior to the match, in quality of play, and in the spirit of players and crowd,' the *Herald* reported proudly, 'the match lived up to the best peace-time standards of Hampden internationals.

'Except for a short time midway through the second half the Scottish attack were superior and held the initiative. It was this superiority, backed by magnificent tackling and service of the Scots wing halves, Shankly and Busby, that finally carried the Scots to victory.'

According to the similarly named, but quite different, *Daily Herald*, Billy Liddell, of Liverpool, was the pride of the crowd. 'After equalising Lawton's opening goal he could do no wrong.'

The teams were: *Scotland* – Dawson (Rangers), Carabine (Third Lanark), and A. Beattie (Preston North End); Shankly (Preston), T. Smith (Preston) and Busby (Liverpool); Waddell (Rangers), Herd (Manchester City), Dodds (Blackpool), G. Bremner (Arsenal) and Liddell (Liverpool). *England* – Marks (Arsenal), Bacuzzi (Fulham) and Hapgood (Arsenal); Willingham (Huddersfield Town), Mason (Coventry) and Mercer (Everton); Matthews (Stoke), Edelston (Reading), Lawton (Everton), Hagan (Sheffield United) and Kirchen (Arsenal). *Referee* – R. Calder, Rutherglen.

In addition to Liddell the scorers for Scotland were Shankly and Dodds who treated himself and the crowd to a hat-trick. Scorers for England were Lawton, who also scored three, and Hagan.

It was the first time in five years that a Scottish side had been able to defeat England in front of a Hampden crowd. Another four years went by before it happened again.

The date was 13 April 1946, and the occasion one of a series of Victory internationals held to celebrate the end of the Second World War.

Although Britain was no longer at war, it had been decided not to give the match full international status. This meant that those who took part in one of the most memorable encounters, in a long history of thrilling matches involving the two countries, were denied proper recognition of their achievement.

Jimmy Delaney, with pre-war appearances against England, Wales and Ireland to his credit, was the only player in the Scotland team who could claim to have been capped before. Similarly judged, only Matthews, who withdrew on this occasion, Mercer and Lawton could claim to be full England internationalists. It didn't matter that many of the players on view had been regular participants in international matches played throughout the war.

A strike by Lanarkshire bus workers failed to prevent a vast army of Scottish supporters descending on Mount Florida. Allegations that the strike had been staged in protest at the small number of tickets allocated to the bus company's social club were denied.

'It was not quite back to the seething crowds of peace-time on international Saturday,' the old Glasgow *Evening News* reported happily, 'but at least the rosette sellers were out in full force, their tartan bonnets and raucous voices loud as ever round every railway and bus station in the city.' In the hours immediately preceding the match, tramcars filled with supporters arrived in the vicinity of Hampden at the rate of one every 20 seconds.

Despite the action of the Lanarkshire bus drivers, an important group then, with thousands employed in the steel industry, mining, and related jobs, requiring transportation to Glasgow for the match, the total number of paying customers was finally put at 139,468. Those chosen to appear were: *Scotland* – R. Brown (Queen's Park), D. Shaw (Hibernian) and J. Shaw (Rangers); Campbell (Morton), Brennan (Airdrie) and Husband (Partick Thistle); Waddell (Rangers), Dougall

(Birmingham City), Delaney (Manchester United), Hamilton (Aberdeen) and Liddell (Liverpool). *England* – Swift (Manchester City), Scott (Arsenal) and Hardwick (Middlesbrough); Wright (Wolves), Franklin (Stoke) and Mercer (Everton); Elliott (West Bromwich Albion), Shackleton (Bradford Park Avenue), Lawton (Chelsea), Hagan (Sheffield United) and D. Compton (Arsenal). *Referee* – P. Craigmyle, Aberdeen.

On the 50th anniversary of the first appearance of Anglo-Scots in international matches, three players who made their living in England had been selected for Scotland – Dougall, Delaney and Liddell. But those in the crowd who disliked the practice, and thought Scotland should be represented at all times by an all-tartan eleven, favouring players who stayed faithful to the game in Scotland, couldn't complain about the performance and commitment of the three Anglos present on this occasion.

Before the match most people thought an England victory was a foregone conclusion and the bookies were laying long odds against Scotland. But, right from the kick-off, the match was all Scotland: fast on the ball, according to *The Glasgow Herald*, quick in shooting, and fierce and relentless in tackling, thrilling the vast crowd which obviously enjoyed England's discomfiture.

Harry Miller, of the Glasgow *Evening News*, one of the few people to forecast a Scottish victory, was clearly elated. 'Never has an English team been so thoroughly outplayed,' he reported gleefully.

The Glasgow Herald, in kindly mood, proffered sympathy to big Frank Swift in the England goal. 'An English defence has not suffered such a pummelling as this for many years, and it required a goalkeeper of Swift's stature to save the side as a whole from complete rout. 'A giant of a man he yet contrived to bring grace and lissomness to his every movement and his rhythmic action, as he leapt high or sideways to punch or clasp the ball in his more than human hands, was too much for patriotic bias and evoked the applause it deserved.'

But for all the superiority shown by Scotland against an English defence that included Billy Wright, making his Hampden debut at the age of 21, and destined to be the first player to win more than 100 caps for England, with less than a minute left for play Scotland hadn't scored.

Not for the first, or the last, time at Hampden it appeared the visitors in white shirts would be allowed to return home with their bruised pride somehow salvaged; the final result an undeserved draw.

The minutes finished ticking away, and the second hand commanded the clock, when Jackie Husband, of Partick Thistle, raised the ball above his head, and steadied himself, for a crucial throw-in. The huge crowd murmured expectantly. Husband was renowned as a long throw specialist.

From Husband the ball soared high into the England penalty area. Swift, seeing the danger, went to meet it. Waddell, the Rangers winger, lying deep in the box, rose too. His leap had been timed to perfection. The ball went right to the toe of Jimmy Delaney.

A flurry of white shirts surrounded the former Celtic player. But they couldn't stop Delaney. His reaction was lightning fast.

There was a moment of silent disbelief on the part of the Hampden crowd. Peter Craigmyle, the flamboyant referee, dressed for the occasion in his well-known striped blazer, didn't hesitate. Adopting a dramatic stance he pointed, with complete authority, in the direction of the centre spot.

Hampden went wild! 'Only an artist could give you that scene half a minute from the end when 140,000 people went stark staring mad and waved, yelled, spluttered and prayed for strength to wave, yell and splutter some more,' the colourful R.E. Kingsley – Rex of the *Sunday Mail* – informed his readers.

Harry Miller believed the match, which gave Scotland the triple crown in the Victory series, would go down in history as one of the great, unforgettable internationals. 'Our players sacrificed individuality to teamwork and it was a triumph of co-operation,' Miller wrote. 'England were fortunate to escape at least a three-goal beating. That Scotland did not effect it was our lack of a marksman.'

Scotland provided three players – Archie Macaulay (Arsenal), Billy Steel (Dundee), and Billy Liddell (Liverpool) – to the Great Britain side which played The Rest of Europe at Hampden on 10 May 1947. Here the Secretary of State for Scotland, Joseph Westwood, greets Steel with Liddell standing alongside. Great Britain proved more than capable of dealing with the invaders, Billy Steel claiming a goal in the 6–1 rout

From the same building in Hope Street, Glasgow, his colleague Rex of the *Sunday Mail* issued a cheerier note: 'When Delaney scored that goal nothing else mattered,' Rex pronounced happily, adding, with cheerful hyperbole: 'This was the greatest game in the world, Hampden the greatest place, and these eleven Scots the greatest players.'

As seen by Kingsley: 'Scottish fans, knee bent by the shackles of demoralising war-time defeats, yanked themselves to the upright and gave vent to the most hysterical joy-crazy manifestation this famous ground has ever known.'

Well, yes, people enjoyed themselves, certainly. But that was probably just as well, considering the dismal years that lay ahead.

CHAPTER FOUR

Few teams arriving in Scotland for a game at Hampden could equal the excitement generated by the appearance, in December 1954, of Ferenc Puskas and his fellow Hungarians.

This was the team that sent shock waves the length and breadth of England the previous November, when they won by 6–3 at Wembley, and then, six months later in Budapest, confirmed their marvellous superiority by winning 7–1.

Scotland were in the middle of a bad patch in their own annual encounters with their nearest neighbour: between 1950 and the end of the decade Scotland won only once against England, and never at Hampden. So, on the principle that few people in Scotland cared who beat England, when or where and by how many, the Hungarians were treated as honoured guests.

Led by the chubby Puskas, reckoned to be the finest inside-forward in the world, they had been beaten in the final of the World Cup the previous year. Against all expectations, West Germany defeated the greatest team in the world, 3–2.

The tournament, held in Switzerland, had been an unmitigated disaster for Scotland. The manager, Andy Beattie, resigned half-way through and the team suffered a 7–0 defeat in their last match against Uruguay, played in sweltering heat. 'As the game went on it got hotter and hotter and the Uruguayans got better and better,' Neil Mochan, of Celtic, who appeared for Scotland, recalled ruefully years later. 'The weather probably suited them more than us. But they gave us no chance. We were just annihilated.'

Six months later the traumatic experience of one hot summer in Switzerland returned to haunt Scotland, shivering now in a cold winter chill. Hadn't the Hungarians, on their way to the final, disposed of Uruguay 4–2? Forget any pain which the Hungarians succeeded in inflicting upon England, humiliation heaped upon humiliation, home and away. It was this single result, against Uruguay in a semi-final of the World Cup which most concerned the average Scottish supporter on learning the wizard Puskas and company were coming to Hampden.

Taken rationally, or less than rationally, in the course of a thousand arguments at work and in the pub, it was hard not to concede there was a gap of sorts between Scotland and the team they were about to confront.

The weather, television and the approach of Christmas all contributed to the attendance falling below an anticipated 123,000. Some of those marked absent also proffered in advance their natural aversion to becoming a witness, far less a participant, in some awful national catastrophe, as their reasons for staying away. But even the enormous differences in ability and achievement that distinguished the two sides wasn't enough to prevent a noisy, hugely nationalistic crowd of 113,000 assembling at Hampden, on a cold, sleet-filled day, hoping for a miracle.

More than anything, including victory, which was probably impossible, anyway, the home fans wanted Scotland to salvage their broken pride, and avoid a similar humiliation to that suffered by England, against the famous Hungarians.

Hampden on a bleak December day, as described by Hugh Taylor in the first of his long series of successful annual reviews, *The Scottish Football Book*, looked stark, stern and grey. Flags fluttered fitfully while the crowd shivered under showers of rain and sleet. 'It was a sombre scene,' Taylor wrote, recalling his feelings months later, 'impressive but melancholy, like a clan lamenting the passing of a chief in a forbidden glen. Hampden, the greatest football stadium in the world, seemed to be brooding, waiting fearfully a football disaster.'

The teams were: *Scotland* – Martin (Aberdeen), Cunningham (Preston North End) and Haddock (Clyde); Docherty (Preston North End), Davidson (Partick Thistle) and Cumming (Hearts); McKenzie (Partick Thistle), Johnstone (Hibernian), Reilly (Hibernian), Wardhaugh (Hearts) and Ring (Clyde). *Hungary* – Farago, Buzanski and Lantos; Bozsik, Lorant and Szojka; Sandor, Koscis, Hidegkuti, Puskas and Fenyvesi. *Referee* – L. Horn, Holland.

It had been hailed as Scotland's game of the century. And the home side surprised and delighted their long-suffering supporters by starting well.

In the opening moments some of the players, perhaps fearful they were about to be overwhelmed by the legendary skills of their famous opponents, showed predictable signs of nervousness. But two in particular, Tommy Docherty and Willie Cunningham, the only Anglos present, were anxious to demonstrate they weren't about to be rubbished on their return home, by strangers: crunching tackles, hard but fair, soon imposed a dour, uncompromising, Scottish presence on the game.

No-one believed for a moment that Scotland could ever begin to match Puskas and the other Hungarians for skill, although Johnny McKenzie tried. Not long into the game the Partick Thistle winger led the Hungarian defence on a merry chase. The huge crowd, huddled in the freezing rain, roared and cheered. An admiring Hugh Taylor enthused: 'His first run couldn't have been bettered by Stanley Matthews himself.'

On this occasion McKenzie outwitted the Hungarian defence and centred accurately. But the chance was squandered. Disappointed, the crowd shivered and sighed. But all those in attendance who supported Scotland – and there would be damn few present who didn't! – were soon cheering again, ignoring the rain, their hearts on fire.

Tommy Ring was performing brilliantly on the Scottish left wing. The ball went from him to Lawrie Reilly who almost scored. Moments later Bobby Johnstone put the ball in the net – but the Dutch referee ruled the little Hibs player off-side. A goal by Scotland looked a real possibility, however.

Then what usually happened to Scotland at such a moment happened: the other side scored. The crowd was stunned but not greatly surprised. For most of them, losing a goal just when it seemed Scotland would score wasn't a new experience. Nor was the maverick nature of the circumstances in which the ball finished in the Scottish net.

From the edge of the penalty area Boszik, the opposing right-half, shot hard and competently at goal. Fred Martin appeared to have the danger covered. But a deflection by an over-anxious Harry Haddock put the ball past him into the net. Hungary were on their way!

'Now Puskas was spraying passes with delightful accuracy. Now the roving Hidegkuti was upsetting the defenders. Now the two wingers were spanking along the touchlines menacingly. This was the brisk football which had put Hungary on top of the world,' an admiring Hugh Taylor recorded, enviously.

It had taken the Hungarians 20 minutes to obtain an unsatisfactory opening goal. Six minutes later they made amends in a manner worthy of their reputation: a perfect pass from Puskas was rewarded with a perfect goal by Hidegkuti.

The defence-splitting pass delivered by Puskas, straight to the feet of his countryman, and Hidegkuti's immaculate response, which allowed Martin in the Scottish goal no chance, was nothing less than a superb demonstration of the level of skill the crowd expected from the Hungarians.

With hearts aching, but knowing its worth, they applauded; an activity which also helped to keep their circulation alive against the bitter cold.

A two-goal advantage to the Hungarians at this stage was probably an improvement on what most people expected before the game. But, clearly, the spirited Scots, who continued to come forward, believed they were far from beaten.

A challenge by McKenzie on Farago appeared to anger the visitors. Puskas looked particularly displeased. But at least Farago then stopped the Partick Thistle winger from scoring. A little later he failed to do the same when faced with Tommy Ring of Clyde. The move which produced the goal was initiated by Cumming, who passed to Johnstone, who found Ring inside the penalty area. With four minutes left to half-time, Ring did the rest.

At 2–1 Scotland looked good. Johnstone and Reilly combined and almost produced an equaliser.

Some in the crowd began to think the unthinkable. Then a shot from Sandor at the other end was blocked by Martin. It was a brilliant save, but the ball returned to Sandor and this time the little winger made no mistake: 3–1.

The match appeared to be going the way most people expected. But no-one could fault the Scots for lack of effort. Early in the second half a marvellous run by Johnny McKenzie ended with him on the ground and the Hungarians facing a dangerous free kick.

Moments later, a beautifully flighted ball, struck perfectly by McKenzie himself, curved over the goal and on to the head of Bobby Johnstone: 3–2.

Scotland were back in the game in earnest. And again quite sensible, rational people, shivering on the terracings and huddled in the stand, together with those occupants of the Press box who would have been happy to see their pre-match forecasts destroyed, found themselves thinking the unthinkable. Never mind winning, a draw would be a marvellous result for Scotland!

'The game grew fiercer as the gloaming crept on,' Hugh Taylor recalled. 'Action never flagged. There were narrow escapes at both ends – a Boszik shot crashing against the Scottish bar, Farago diving at full stretch to stop a McKenzie drive.

'The crowd did its best to inspire Scotland. The players never gave up,' Taylor went on. 'Alas, in the last minute, with darkness closing in, Koscis scored a fine fourth goal for Hungary. Then it was all over. Scotland had lost 4–2.'

But there was pride in defeat. Hugh Taylor, unashamedly sounding for all the world like a fan with a typewriter, spoke for everyone in his end of season review: 'Scotland, the team which wasn't given a hope, had not been disgraced. Their courage was the courage of Bannockburn. They lacked the skill of the Hungarians but football needs more than mere skill – it needs heart and determination as well, and in those qualities the Scots were well endowed.'

Even the great Puskas, famed for his marvellous skill with the ball, and his reading of a game, was forced to concede: 'We of Hungary will have to realise that fighting spirit is still one of the greatest assets in football.'

On the subject of Hampden the great star was even more forthcoming. 'It is the most magnificent stadium I have ever seen, the life and essence of football,' Puskas declared.

Years later, the marvellous Puskas, who won his first cap at the age of 18 in 1945, also figured prominently in another great Hampden occasion, perhaps the finest game of football ever witnessed anywhere in Europe – the 1960 final of the European Cup – Real Madrid versus Eintracht Frankfurt.

There can't be a football fan anywhere who doesn't remember the result; 7–3 in favour of the magnificent men from Madrid, not all of them Spaniards. And this against a team who had been good enough to score 12 times against Rangers, managed by Scot Symon, at the semi-final stage of the same competition: six goals at home in Germany, followed by another six at Ibrox, just for good measure!

Discounting supporters of Eintracht, who travelled from Germany for the match at Ibrox, the majority of those present could scarcely believe the evidence of their own eyes. But it was proving a bad week for Scottish talent pitched against continental opposition generally: the previous evening many of those at Ibrox for the semi-final of the European Cup had been at Hampden to witness a dismal display by the national side against Poland. Although the final scoreline showed that Scotland only lost by the odd goal in five, as seen by the perceptive Hugh McIlvanney, writing in *The Scotsman*, they were 'undeniably inferior in speed, technique and spirit'. McIlvanney especially admired the opposing inside-left,

Pohl, 'a forward whose magnificent artistry demanded that his name be bracketed with those of Puskas, Koscis and the other continental masters who have elevated Hampden with their presence'.

Any ambition Rangers nurtured of providing a home-town presence in the final of the European Cup at Hampden later the same month had been shattered in the away match against Eintracht. The game at Ibrox had been reduced to little more than a formality by the 6–1 score in Germany. Rangers did what little they could in front of their own supporters and scored three times; never a bad effort in a semi-final of the European Cup.

But anyone who witnessed their demolition, and whose football horizons didn't extend beyond Scotland, must have been staggered by the difference in quality between the two sides. Rangers were quite simply outclassed. Eintracht provided a display of football skills totally different from anything normally seen in Scotland. On this evidence, a great new day had arrived in the way football was played around the world – and Scotland, in the guise of their most important clubs, had been left behind.

Already on his way to establishing a reputation as probably the most gifted sportswriter in the whole of Britain during the next three decades, Hugh McIlvanney commented sourly: 'Coming within 24 hours of Scotland's ignominious defeat by Poland the match would cause some among nearly 80,000 spectators to wonder if our sporting future does not lie in shinty after all.'

The greatest club competition in the world, the European Champion Clubs' Cup, otherwise known, quite simply, as the European Cup, was just four years old, and struggling to establish its credentials, when Real Madrid and Eintracht Frankfurt arrived in Glasgow in 1960, each hoping to lay claim to the precious silverware.

There had been various limited attempts to introduce a major competition, involving some of the greatest clubs in Europe, since before the war. But hostilities intervened and the machinery of football always did grind slowly; backwards as well as forwards.

FIFA, the world governing body, was interested chiefly in supervising the World Cup, and keeping control of international matches between the various national associations burgeoning around the world; and preferred to distance itself from a competition designed simply for European club sides. UEFA, the governing body for Europe, also responded coolly. It wasn't until the French daily newspaper *L'Equipe* threatened to go ahead and organise a tournament, with or without their blessing, and a number of major clubs showed an interest, that UEFA was forced to think again.

L'Equipe, unlike other newspapers, confined its daily news and feature coverage to sport. It was also widely respected as co-organiser and sponsor of the Tour de France. The great bike race was easily the most important annual sporting event organised anywhere in Europe. In addition, it was an enormous commercial success which enjoyed the complete support of the French government. If the men behind the *L'Equipe* plan went ahead with their scheme they offered no small threat to organised football.

Any football administrator foolish enough to believe it was beyond the powers of a newspaper to organise a competition of this importance, or that serious commercial interests, with little knowledge of the politics of the game, couldn't intrude on the business of football with any hope of success, would have been on collision course for a rude awakening. Compared to the complexities involved in organising the Tour de France – with its closed roads and mountain stages, its following cavalcade complete with team wagons, motor-cyclists, television vehicles, cars carrying hundreds of journalists and TV and radio crews, food trucks and ambulance vehicles for those who find it all too much, not to mention the small matter of closing the centre of Paris to all other traffic to accommodate the finish (oh, and don't forget accommodating the only people who really matter in the Tour de France, the ones on the bikes) – putting together something as simple as a football tournament would have been easy to the men in charge of *L'Equipe*.

As envisaged by *L'Equipe*, the European Cup would have been organised much as it is today: except, not surprisingly, the newspaper thought the final should be staged in Paris each year! Appropriately enough, considering the stubborn French involvement in seeing the tournament started, the first final was held in Paris in 1956.

It was a new venture and the first final could be excused for attracting a modest turn-out in the French capital: 38,000 at the Parc des Princes for the match between Real Madrid and Reims.

More than three times that number were present in Madrid the following year when a crowd of 124,000 occupied the Bernabeu. But this was hardly surprising considering the defending champions, Real Madrid, were in their second European Cup final: Fiorentina provided the opposition.

A year later about half that number, 67,000, saw Real, the still-defending champions, defeat another Italian side, AC Milan, in extra time.

Stuttgart offered a repeat of the very first final: Real against the French side Reims. And this time a crowd of 80,000 watched as the seemingly invincible Real won again.

Then came Glasgow. And one of the greatest occasions in the history of the game.

A week before the match, when tickets went on sale at Hampden, fans were given less than 24 hours' notice to queue. 'The scenes outside the ground, when I arrived early, were quite unbelievable,' Ernie Walker, who was in charge of ticket sales, recalled. 'The whole of the car park, from Aikenhead Road to Cathcart Road, was black with people. There must have been at least 50,000 people, in orderly queues, no violence, no rushing – everything was correct – and by about four o'clock in the afternoon we had sold 134,000 tickets,' Walker added.

The gods would have been churlish to intrude: long before the appointed day, any mortal with an interest in football knew beyond doubt what to expect. Real – not really Madrid so much as a cosmopolitan compound of football's greatest talents, according to Hugh McIlvanney – would win.

Tempting providence, without exposing himself to any great risk, McIlvanney assured readers of *The Scotsman*: 'History rather than form seems the appropriate word for the achievements of the greatest club team the sport has ever known, but, whatever the term, there is no doubt that their record will leave little room for optimism in the minds of their opponents, Eintracht of Frankfurt.'

Even Ernst Berger, manager of Eintracht, thought Real were the finest team in Europe. 'We will be very happy if we can play as well against Real as we did against Rangers,' he confided cautiously to reporters; unaware perhaps of the nightmares this simple statement encouraged elsewhere. 'So long as we play well and produce a good match, we will be satisfied,' Herr Berger continued philosophically. 'We will play hard and give of our best and may the best team win.'

Emilio Ostricher, the man in charge of Real Madrid, was Hungarian by birth, like Puskas. Both men fled Hungary following the failed revolution of 1956. Hampden was his third European Cup final in a row and life in the west evidently suited Ostricher, who discounted rumours his team of international all-stars would each receive a £1,000 bonus if they won.

The *Scottish Daily Express*, with characteristic initiative then, signed the great Puskas himself to provide Scots fans with an insight into where the game in Scotland was going wrong. 'The one big factor which makes our team such a success is the discipline,' Puskas explained. 'All are highly trained athletes. We know that orders given are for our own good, that they can improve our technique and lengthen our football lives.

'Everyone obeys without question,' the great man continued simply. 'Indeed, we would not be in the team if we did not.'

His team-mate, the marvellous Argentinian, Alfredo Di Stefano Laulhe, confessed to nervousness before the game 'because of the great responsibility we knew we were carrying'.

On the day of the great occasion the teams at Hampden were: *Real Madrid* – Dominguez; Marquitos and Pachin; Vidal, Santamaria and Zarraga; Canario, Del Sol, Di Stefano, Puskas and Gento. *Eintracht* – Loy; Lutz and Hoeffer; Weilbacher, Eigenbrod and Stinka; Kress, Lindner, Stein, Pfaff and Meier. *Referee* – Jack Mowat, Scotland.

Spain and Germany were entitled to enjoy the prestige of providing the two finalists, although the players involved represented several different nations. Santamaria, at the heart of the Real defence, was from Uruguay, and the forward line included only two players of Spanish birth, Del Sol and Gento. In addition to Puskas, from Hungary, and Di Stefano, from Argentina, the right-winger, Canario, was from Brazil.

Scotland provided the stadium and the referee, Mr Jack Mowat, who cited the Royal Burgh of Rutherglen, with its boundaries close to Hampden, as his base. Mowat's extraordinary career as a referee lasted 30 years and included nine Scottish Cup finals, counting replays, between 1950 and 1959.

His memories of the great stadium at Mount Florida went back forty years to the time, as a schoolboy, he attended his first Scottish Cup final in 1920. The protagonists then were Kilmarnock and Albion Rovers who qualified for their one and only final by defeating Rangers, after two replays, at the semi-final stage.

More than seventy years later, Mowat, in sprightly form, recalled a 'very good final. There was a crowd of 95,000 and Kilmarnock won 3–2', he said.

Following his retirement in 1960 Mowat served on the referee supervisors' committee, first as a member, and then as chairman for an unlikely-to-be-equalled three decades. As a consequence, his influence on the game in Scotland was immense.

But for his services at Hampden on the occasion of the first European Cup final ever staged in Scotland, Mowat was paid one shilling and sixpence – about seven and a half new pence – to meet the cost of a rail fare to Hampden from the station nearest his home. The competing clubs contributed mementoes.

Mowat started the most important match of his career in front of 127,621 privileged fans, most of them Scots, who, for a variety of reasons, some of them not unconnected with recent history, favoured Real Madrid.

'Real opened rather like elder statesmen a little weary of great occasions but resolved to find their own tempo in their own good time,' reported *The Times*. 'Eintracht, by contrast, were vigorous, open and resolute in their play and quite unmindful, it seemed, of Real's fearful reputation.'

A swinging shot from Meier, the German left-winger, provided an early test for Dominguez who turned the ball against the bar. Real looked vulnerable as Eintracht attacked in force. Twice the Germans were close to scoring before a pass from Stein, operating along the by-line, found Kreiss six yards out. After 20 minutes Eintracht were ahead.

'Obviously we were a little worried,' Di Stefano, the brilliant Argentinian, who at 33 was the oldest player on the park, admitted later. 'But we knew the game had a long way to go and we were confident we could settle.'

Following the goal Real changed gear. Their pace increased and six minutes later Di Stefano equalised. 'The score was characteristic of the journeyman efficiency of the great Spanish side,' Hugh McIlvanney reported. 'Canario beat Hoeffer simply on the right, and his low cross eluded everyone but Di Stefano, who was perfectly positioned to direct the ball past Loy.'

Three minutes later Di Stefano scored again after Loy failed to hold a shot from Canario. Real were in front! A goal by Puskas, scored from an impossible angle on the by-line a minute from half-time, increased their lead.

Four goals in the first 45 minutes testified to the quality and determination of both sides. No-one dared imagine the quality of play would improve in the second half. Yet it did.

Nine minutes into the second half Lutz, the Eintracht right-back, fouled Gento. Referee Mowat consulted his linesman before awarding a controversial penalty kick. 'Gento had been fouled twice before when he was heading for the penalty area,' said Mowat. 'I waved play on. When he was fouled again the sun was shining straight in my eyes. I went to the linesman and asked, inside or outside? He told me, two yards inside. Penalty kick! The linesman didn't decide it was a penalty kick. I decided it was a penalty kick.'

Alfredo Di Stefano and Ferenc Puskas exchange a victory embrace at the finish of the 1960 European Cup final between Real Madrid and Eintracht Frankfurt which Real won 7–3. At the end of an epic struggle the huge Hampden crowd stayed behind to cheer both teams on a lap of honour

Puskas scored from the spot. Hampden went wild. Six minutes later the great Hungarian scored again, nodding the ball into the net after Gento, eluding Lutz, crossed perfectly; 5–1.

Some in the crowd were having difficulty keeping count. With the German side playing some marvellous football, it didn't seem possible they could be trailing by so crushing a margin. It would have been equally impossible for anyone to guess that, with just 30 minutes left for play in this amazing match, there was still time for another four goals; two from each side. As a scoring rate over the years this would have been enough to secure victory in more than 30 finals of the same competition!

The time available had shrunk to 20 minutes when Puskas picked up a loose ball from Vidal, turned and, from 15 yards, chipped the ball high into the net. Two minutes later Stein scored for Eintracht. His achievement merely stressed that Real were outclassing a good class team, Hugh McIlvanney noted. 'As if to underline the point further, Di Stefano ran through almost immediately, sent several defenders moving in an unprofitable direction, while he steered the ball along the most rewarding route of all – to the net.'

With 15 minutes remaining it was left to Stein, on behalf of Eintracht, to put an end to scoring.

For all who saw it, and those who took part, it had been a marvellous, wonderful occasion; a peerless credit to the game it graced. When referee Mowat finally whistled for time everyone at Hampden, and millions more who watched, second best, on television, knew they had been treated to an unforgettable sporting experience.

'The strange emotionalism that overcame the huge crowd as the triumphant Madrid team circled the field at the end, carrying the trophy they have monopolised since its inception, showed that they had not simply been entertained,' Hugh McIlvanney wrote in *The Scotsman*. 'They had been moved by the experience of seeing a sport played to the ultimate standards. Similarly, their tributes to Eintracht, a team whose quality deserved better than the role of heroic losers, contained a reverence for something Scotland cannot equal.'

The Times thought the match had been a triumph for Puskas, adding that in sustained passages in the second half especially, the quality of the Real Madrid forward play and ball control was of 'such finely drawn skill, of such accuracy, imagination and, indeed, impudence, as to bring thundering down around them vast waves of delighted appreciation from Hampden's mighty crowd'.

Emilio Ostricher, manager of Real Madrid, considered it the finest match in which his team ever participated. 'I don't know if we could ever approach football such as that again, the second half in particular,' he told referee Mowat.

Others thought the match, with all its brilliance, and awesome standards of skill, provided an example – and a warning – to the game in Scotland.

John Mackenzie, writing in the *Scottish Daily Express*, believed, on evidence provided by Real Madrid and Eintracht at Hampden, that it was time Scotland changed its whole approach to the game. Mackenzie wanted football teaching in schools improved, coaches sent to Europe to study the best continental methods, and 500 per cent more effort from players. He also thought managers should be encouraged to discard their results-at-any-price attitude.

The final of the European Cup could be the best thing that ever happened to Scotland, if those in authority accepted the lessons offered; or the worst, if they didn't, because 'the paying public will stop paying for third or fourth best', Mackenzie warned. 'Sentiment must go overboard,' he declared. 'If the small clubs must go under so that the strong can improve and go on to match the best in Europe, then die they must.'

It was a cry, from the man his paper called 'The Voice of Football', that continues to echo down the years.

CHAPTER FIVE

No-one who paid for the privilege ever enjoyed the best view of a match at Hampden. Guests granted access to the comfort of the directors' box, courtesy of the game's current rulers, are also disadvantaged. Perched high above the main stand, the Press box commands an unparalleled view of the action.

On major match days especially the Press box always generates a peculiar kind of excitement among its privileged occupants – the football writers.

'Fans with typewriters,' was how J.L. Manning, a distinguished English scribe with a sense of mischief, once described regular members of the Scottish football writing fraternity.

A famous quip, it was never entirely fair. The same Mr Manning could write glowingly of various sporting heroes, who won gloriously, or lost gallantly, in the service of England.

It would have been impossible for anyone pursuing a successful career on the *Daily Mail* to behave otherwise.

However, as an example of the kind of reporting Manning had in mind, no-one could miss the unrestrained partisanship evident in the following preview of a match against England, written in the *Daily Record*, by Hugh Taylor.

'I am passionately eager for the Scots to win, to take the wind out of the sails of the Champions of the World,' Taylor declared vehemently.

When this duly happened, and Scotland defeated England by three goals to two at Wembley in 1967, the same writer – like his readers and just about everyone else in Scotland who purchased other sheets in which his rivals wrote no less ecstatically – found it impossible not to rejoice.

Perhaps the boys were too arrogant, Taylor admitted with mock remorse. Perhaps they should have concentrated more on getting goals than in humiliating the stricken English. 'But I loved it,' Taylor recalled happily, in the pages of *The Scottish Football Yearbook* which he edited. 'I loved every moment of it. And I can tell you that, even in the Press box, haven of strict neutrality (sometimes), there were cackles of Highland delight as our tartan dream of glory came true.'

On that evidence alone it is hard to imagine a Press box containing Hugh Taylor, who was a popular man, ever qualifying as a haven of strict neutrality, even occasionally, if Scotland were playing England at anything.

However, it is also interesting to note that the *Daily Mail*, describing the outcome of that same Wembley encounter, felt able to reassure its predominantly

English readership: 'The truth is this: in two years Scottish footballers have learned how to beat eight fit men for in 1965 they could only draw against five. Scotland have beaten England, who are World champions, but the win does not give them the crown.'

Perhaps not. However, the length and breadth of the northern part of Britain, the victory provided some welcome consolation for the fact England won the World Cup in a year when Scotland failed to qualify. It also offered all those Scots fans who loved the game, and weren't too fussy who beat England, a brief period of uncorrupted joy; brief because it took another eight matches and seven years before the Scots managed another win against England: 2–0 at Hampden in 1974.

Despite the existence of cross-ownership in commercial television, which dates from the launch of ITV, and a wary respect for the BBC, newspaper journalists tend to be suspicious of television and downright antagonistic to the immediacy of the medium which does nothing to make their own jobs any easier.

For example, given that a crucial World Cup qualifying match involving Scotland is live on television, there is little of real substance for the newspapers to pick at the following morning.

In recent years, encouraged by higher match fees forced on the BBC and ITV by the arrival of highly competitive, and pugnacious, satellite services, there has been a marked increase in the number of matches shown live on television.

To the surprise of many, this has been achieved, in the case of the national side, or crucial league and cup matches featuring the top clubs, with no commensurate collapse in the actual attendance.

Television, with its live cameras, instant replays and direct access to the homes of millions, has been the begetter of previously unimagined wealth; a regular bounty, counted in millions, which the ruling powers in football rushed to accept, with a marked degree of myopic alacrity, and little concern for the consequences.

Unfamiliar kick-off times, arranged to accommodate TV schedules, cup ties moved around the week, even live matches from abroad competing with important home fixtures, are all part of the price football has been obliged to pay in return for the broadcasters' millions.

Many of the consequences which people engaged in football now complain about with less than admirable vigour could have been foreseen before any big money deals were finalised.

Public service broadcasting is a fading concept in Britain. Television is part of the entertainment industry. Like football.

And in the entertainment business, as a number of football administrators have learned to their cost, there is no such thing as a free lunch.

For almost three decades, during which time the broadcasters argued for more live access to important matches, most newspapers could be accused of exercising a blatant double standard.

Clearly, any increase in the number of live matches wasn't in the best interests of newspapers dependent on the quality and extent of their football coverage for much of their circulation.

But knowing there was usually considerable public demand for live coverage, newspapers were forced to be circumspect in their condemnation of the broadcasters' ambitions.

Success in the modern game, with its attendant stardom and enormous financial rewards, is a guarantee of intense media interest. An exaggerated sense of their own importance can afflict many of the star names who climb the narrow stairs to the top of the Hampden stand; or the cluttered TV gantry where the commentators operate beneath the reporters' feet.

Viewed as a whole, and discounting the unwelcome attentions of news reporters representing the more sensational tabloids, Andy Roxburgh, the national team coach, believes football benefits from sustained media attention.

'They promote the game for free,' Roxburgh reasons. 'They advertise the Scottish national team, they advertise football. Just think what it would cost if you had to pay for all that advertising.

'Sometimes what they advertise isn't what I'd choose to promote,' Roxburgh admits. 'But that's part of the price you pay for all the free coverage we enjoy.'

Many senior journalists, particularly those working for the larger newspapers, have been close to the game for decades. Similarly, many prominent officials have been around for years. Usually, it's only the faces of the players that change! As a result some writers, and certain television performers, are often better known than many of the players who command their attention.

Dealing with the occasional awkward star, the men with the notebooks, and their colleagues wielding hand-mikes – including, in recent seasons, the occasional woman who has ventured to join their ranks – are entitled to remind themselves how many others they have known arrive and depart the scene.

As a group the writers and commentators are knowledgeable and, for the most part, fair. Their appraisal of players, managers, directors, owners, and the men who really run football – some elected, some appointed to positions of power within the Scottish Football Association and the Scottish Football League – is often harsh, however.

Not surprisingly, given the degree of pressure surrounding their performance, and the chance nature of many of the happenings which dictate their professional lives, officials, managers and players are often sensitive to criticism.

Following the 5–0 hammering inflicted on Scotland by Portugal in Lisbon on 28 April 1993, the influential, and long-serving, former secretary of the SFA, Ernie Walker, complained: 'I didn't read any sane, commonsense article saying well, that's the end of the run, lads, it was a wonderful run, and great fun while it lasted, thank you football!

'A country of five million people, to be at five consecutive World Cups, the rest of the world are goggle-eyed at what we achieved,' Walker went on. 'But all you hear from the newspapers is what a load of rubbish, sack the lot, they've let us down, they're a disgrace. It's absurd, it's absurd.'

Andy Roxburgh, the man apportioned most of the blame for failing to secure Scotland's accustomed place in the 1994 World Cup finals in America, sounded philosophical. 'It goes with the territory,' he said with a shrug. 'If you don't like it, you can always walk away.

'A kind of immunity builds up,' Roxburgh added, smiling thinly. 'It's a bit like getting injections. You become vaccinated against the criticism to a degree.

'I don't take it personally,' Roxburgh insisted. 'I've developed an ability to read a headline with my name on it as if it was about somebody else. The day you start listening to people in the stands, whether it's a journalist or a spectator, you'll end up sitting beside them.'

Roxburgh recalls the occasion, in Genoa during the 1990 World Cup finals in Italy, when Scotland lost by a single goal to Costa Rica. 'The abuse was unbelievable,' he said. 'It was stop the world we want to get off time!

'The next day there was a scandal with one or two players on the front pages. People were writing that I should be sacked.

'But that, actually, was the best week's work I've ever done. It was a crisis management job.

'And the following Saturday we beat Sweden in what a lot of people said was one of the best nights they ever spent in football. You don't do that by crying, or putting your thumb in your mouth, and sinking into a corner,' Roxburgh declared.

For years football and journalism enjoyed a cosier relationship. The reporters confined their interest to the players' official activities and ignored their social pursuits; although, occasionally, as in Denmark in 1975, when a late night excursion ended the international careers of five Scottish players, there was little anyone could do to prevent the ensuing headlines.

However, both sides need and use each other; an uncomfortable truth which is sometimes denied. The game and those who play it feed on publicity. If the Scottish international team is performing well in Europe or the World Cup there is a voracious public appetite for football and football-related topics. Similarly, if all the big city clubs enjoy a good run in the Scottish Cup, or the League Cup, and there is a tightly contested league championship involving several of the top teams, public interest is guaranteed.

It is this enormous appetite for football, which extends across all sections of the population, that helps sell newspapers in large numbers, boosts television programme ratings and attracts big-money sponsors to the game.

Major companies rarely invest in football for love of the game, or some special interest in any particular team, however successful, alone. It is the repeated exposure, provided by television and newspapers, giving the company name and product access to millions of potential customers, that is the main attraction.

Years ago the late Tom Hart, popular chairman of Hibs, was conducting a rearguard campaign against televised football, in open defiance of an existing contract between the broadcasters and the Scottish Football League. At the height of the row Hart refused to allow television cameras into Easter Road, claiming it was private property to which he could deny access whatever the league agreed. The broadcasters, not wishing to provoke an ugly scene on the streets of the capital, and unwilling, in the interests of their programmes, to commit themselves to a match they might not see, stayed away.

Hart, a stubborn, likeable character, was a successful builder, whose love of Hibs and earthy enthusiasm for the game ensured the Edinburgh club's survival over many years. However, it was his firmly held belief that televised football, whether live or in the form of highlights, encouraged people to stay at home and away from the actual matches. Hart believed, with total sincerity, that this weakened football generally and, ultimately, could destroy the game.

What he was trying to secure, in the midst of the row involving the broadcasters, was a season-long moratorium on all television coverage to test his views.

Asked, at the height of the dispute, to explain why a number of advertising boards had been placed in a prominent position on the opposite side of the ground from the Easter Road stand, where the television cameras were located, Hart didn't hesitate. 'So folk in the stand can see them,' he replied; quite ignoring the regular presence of Scottish Television and BBC Scotland and their audience of millions.

But even then, apart from rights fees, the presence of television cameras generated substantial, and useful, income for clubs operating at the top level. Shirt advertising, now commonplace, was not allowed. But perimeter advertising, covering a wide range of products, including tobacco, since banned, offered important cash-raising possibilities.

For years only a single line of board advertising, itself subject to serious regulation, was allowed. But selling agencies, operating on behalf of the major clubs, were already attempting to double-bank, and even triple-bank.

Now boards which ensure the same company presence at all important matches, and where the presence of television cameras is usually guaranteed, proliferate, to the fury of purists among the broadcasters, who would be happy to see all forms of perimeter advertising banned completely and matches played in so-called clean conditions.

Engaged at the highest performance level, sport has become an important marketing aid for a wide range of products. But it would be wrong to imagine the average marketing director is seriously influenced by sentiment.

What he wants – and expects – is value for money, whatever sport he decides upon as a vehicle for selling his wares.

This means, in simple terms, the sponsor will settle for nothing less than the company name, or product, acknowledged in the newspapers and displayed prominently on television, week in week out, all season long; or as often as possible, and in letters as large as the broadcasters will allow.

Football administrators and broadcasting executives have been arguing for years over what can and cannot be shown, by way of advertising, when television cameras are present at a match.

Noisy squabbles, on the occasion of contract renewals over many years, helped produce a series of ad-hoc rules and regulations about almost everything, ranging from the number, size and positioning of perimeter boards to how a logo will appear on a player's jersey.

Certain conditions are subject to law and not negotiable. Others have been won and lost, haphazardly, in return for concessions by the other side. For years the football authorities argued in favour of match fees commensurate with the size of audience they helped deliver. International matches, the league championship and various cup competitions all provided a popular element in the TV schedules. Some matches guaranteed a large audience, night or day. On a cost-per-hour analysis, football coverage compared well with other types of programming, most of which failed to attract a similar-sized audience.

Objections concerning the unpredictable nature of the product on offer were usually swept aside. Traditionally, however, as each new negotiating round began, the broadcasters fought to contain the cost of rights and win on money. Months of argument invariably produced the perfect stand-off. No television, no sponsorship!

Television controlled access to millions of homes. And football was increasingly dependent on sponsorship money for its survival. Unless domestic competitions, and all the major clubs, featured regularly and prominently on television there would be little sponsorship money forthcoming for football.

People with an important voice in football often argued in favour of banning television from their grounds. Many of them, fearful of its long-term effect on paying fans, believed football could survive without it. Others would have been happy to see the broadcasters part with their money in return for practically no real service, an arrangement the broadcasters were right to resist.

Throughout the whole of the last decade it was evident both sides needed each other. Contrary to some reports, anyone with wide experience of the prolonged negotiating procedures involved expected to achieve agreement in the end.

Caught in an endless spiral of public expectation, and rising costs, football is increasingly dependent on television-generated income to survive. For example:

Umbro will pay the SFA £12 million across six years to supply kit to the national side.

A four-year handle on the Scottish Cup cost Tennent Caledonian, the brewery giants, £2.5 million.

When Scotland played France, in a qualifying match for the 1990 World Cup finals at Hampden in 1989, the SFA levied a £600,000 rights fee on French TV.

A match between Scotland and West Germany, shown live on television throughout Europe, garnered £450,000 from trackside advertising alone.

Bill Wilson, the man responsible for attracting and negotiating big-money contracts on behalf of the Scottish Football Association and the Scottish Football League, argues that Scotland is essentially a one-sport nation. 'No other sport can compete with football when it comes to attracting large crowds,' Wilson insists. 'We have big days in golf, we have big days at racing, we have big days at rugby, maybe once or twice a year. Football has declined but we can still attract tens of thousands of people twice a week,' he declared.

Wilson was a young man, working as a consultant to the SFA in the mid-1970s, when he had 'this wheeze that whoever made our kit could make replica strips'.

'In those days the SFA actually bought their own strips,' Wilson recalled with an air of disbelief.

His first deal netted the SFA £10,000 a year for the rights to produce replica Scotland kit, plus a percentage of all sales. 'Willie Allan, who was then secretary of the SFA, didn't believe me when I told him we might earn as much as £12,000 a year from the arrangement,' Wilson grinned. 'That was a fortune then and I was told to go back to the manufacturers and find out what they really intended.

'It took me four months, and letters from the manufacturer saying they were serious, before he was finally convinced,' Wilson added.

'In the beginning it was strictly strips and tracksuits,' Wilson explained. 'Now, when we introduce a new strip, we also design a range of matching leisure-wear, including sweat shirts, T-shirts, shorts, the lot,' he said.

Market research showed that 92 per cent of people who buy football strips never kick a ball. 'When we started it was strips for football teams to wear that the supporter would buy,' Wilson went on. 'But nowadays you design a strip to go with a pair of jeans that a football team will wear. It's actually gone full circle. We are no longer competing in the football market. We're competing with Marks and Spencers.'

Wilson rejects any suggestion that, in order to serve market forces, the authorities have been cavalier with kit design and the appearance of the Scotland team. 'We never mess about with the home strip,' he said. 'It's always basically dark blue. But we've got to give the manufacturers something for their money. So the away strip, which has no tradition except it must look different from the home strip, is the one we change.'

Challenged to justify the infamous hooped shorts, introduced at Hampden a few seasons ago, Wilson replied: 'That particular design was the biggest shorts seller of all time. The shorts actually sold on their own which is unusual with a football strip.'

Nowadays the SFA kit contract is worth £2 million a year, the largest in Britain, and the association's sponsorship activities alone earn in excess of £5 million a year. In addition to kit, the big money deals involve sponsorship of the Scottish Cup, fees from television, trackside advertising and sponsorship of international matches and the national team.

An appearance in the World Cup finals raises the nation's profile. As former SFA secretary Ernie Walker explained: 'There's a vibrancy about qualifying for the World Cup. You are up there with the big boys, you are a viable entity, the world wants to know you and there are commercial people at your doorstep suggesting all sorts of ideas.'

Wilson believes our record of qualifying late gives him little time to capitalise properly on a place in the finals. 'Last time, in Italy, we only made about £400,000 from commercial activities directly associated with the World Cup. Then, when we qualified for the finals of the European championships, we were in the middle of the recession and made about half that sum as a result of going to Sweden.'

Wilson maintains that, to make a fortune from the World Cup, you've got to be the host or the holder. 'Then you know at least four years in advance you'll be competing next time,' he explained.

'If we fail to qualify, where we lose out is not so much commercially, but in our share of television fees and track advertising,' Wilson added.

Television contracts are usually concluded in advance of the World Cup and last for a period of several years. 'You can't run a business on the off-chance some guy might miss a penalty kick,' Wilson insisted.

But, in practice, this arrangement virtually guarantees one of the principal parties will be dissatisfied with the final outcome. A good run in the World Cup, or the European Nations championship, which ends with Scotland reaching the finals, presents the broadcasters with a bargain and the football authorities wishing they could negotiate fresh terms, an idea they would be quick to refuse on those occasions the national side failed miserably and the broadcasters, faced with a ratings slump, lost interest.

For most of its existence Hampden Park has been home to the Scotland team, the great and the good, and sometimes reckless and feckless, who have been privileged to pull on the famous dark blue jersey.

When they have made 50 appearances in the international side, many of them at Hampden, players are now entitled to a commemorative medal and a place in Scottish football's Hall of Fame. At present this is a modest room concealed behind the imposing white sandstone walls of the SFA headquarters at 6 Park Gardens, Glasgow.

Portraits, mostly commissioned from the young Cumbernauld artist Senga Murray, of the men who have achieved the not inconsiderable target of 50 caps, adorn the walls. Apart from George Young, legendary captain of Rangers and Scotland, who won 53 full caps, including nine appearances against England, in an international career that began in 1947 and lasted 11 seasons, the 17 men with their likenesses already in place in that unimposing little room are players from the modern era.

Look around and you will see some of the best known Scottish players of the last 20 years: Alex McLeish and Willie Miller of Aberdeen; their former club-mate Jim Leighton, who was playing with Manchester United when he assumed the mantle of Scotland's most capped goalkeeper from Alan Rough of Partick Thistle, another with his portrait in the Park Gardens Hall of Fame; Richard Gough, once of Dundee United and Tottenham Hotspur, now with Rangers; Danny McGrain and Paul McStay of Celtic and their old club-mate Roy Aitken who was also capped during his brief spell with Newcastle United; Graeme Souness, who won caps with Middlesbrough, Liverpool and Sampdoria; Gordon Strachan of Aberdeen, Manchester United and Leeds; Billy Bremner who, like Gordon Strachan, in addition to captaining Scotland, led Leeds United to the championship of the English First Division; Joe Jordan, another with a Leeds connection, who also won caps with Manchester United and AC Milan; Asa Hartford of West Bromwich Albion, Manchester City, Everton and Manchester City again; Maurice Malpas of Dundee United; the truly great Denis Law, of Huddersfield, Manchester City, Torino, Manchester United and Manchester City again, who never managed to amass anything like the number of caps his prodigious talent fully deserved; and the only player ever to appear in more than 100 full internationals for Scotland, the remarkable Kenny Dalglish of Celtic and Liverpool.

Unfortunately, members of the public are unable to visit the Hall of Fame, on a whim and as a matter of general interest, to add their own personal tribute to each of their favourites. The headquarters of the SFA is a busy working office, at the centre of a large and important business enterprise. For good and understandable reasons permission to visit the Hall of Fame is not granted readily.

An easily accessible museum of Scottish football, with its own Hall of Fame, which could also chart the growth and development of the game and its importance to the social history of the country as a whole, incorporating modern audio-visual techniques, including video presentations of great matches from across the years, together with a continuing record of all the great players in action, would be a useful and popular addition to the cultural life of Scotland.

The walls at Park Gardens provide an interesting pictorial record of those players who have been deserving and fortunate enough to win 50 full caps for Scotland. Such an achievement is considerable, obviously. Any player with the ability to accumulate 50 caps certainly deserves his own special place and frame in the history of the game.

But it would be foolish to imagine that the players whose likenesses appear on the walls of the SFA headquarters in Glasgow represent the absolute cream of Scottish skill and talent drawn from across more than a hundred years of organised football.

An enhanced World Cup, particularly at the qualifying stages, and the now prestigious European Nations' championship, has made it easier for modern stars to add to their cap count. So, in considering a Hall of Fame for Scottish football, it is clearly a mistake to make caps won the only means of measuring achievement and greatness.

Everyone with an interest in the game will have their own ideas about the names of suitable candidates. No list can be judged exhaustive. But it should be established, right from the start, that any Hall of Fame, covering more than a hundred years of Scottish football, should include major personalities who never shone as players. The men on the park are the heart and soul of the game, certainly. But others, such as managers and administrators, also make their own special mark and their contribution should be recognised.

It would be a poor Hall of Fame of Scottish football that omitted Jock Stein and Willie Waddell, for example. In different ways they have been the twin titans of the modern game.

Stein won the Scottish Cup, as manager of Dunfermline Athletic, before going on to build a Celtic squad that produced the most successful, and possibly the greatest, club side ever seen in Britain. He also managed the national side on its way to the finals of the World Cup in Spain and Mexico, dying, tragically, at Ninian Park, Cardiff, on the very night Scotland qualified for their fourth successive appearance in the World Cup finals.

However, during his own playing career, selection by the Scottish League, for a match against the English League in 1954, was his one and only representative honour. Judged on full international caps alone, Stein wouldn't make the Hall of Fame.

Based on the same narrow criteria, although much more successful as a player than Stein, neither would Rangers' Willie Waddell.

A strong and free-running right-winger, Waddell, who first played for Scotland in war-time internationals, went on to win 17 full caps between 1947 and 1955. As a manager he made Kilmarnock a force in league and Cup, reaching the final of the Scottish Cup, which was lost to Rangers, in 1960 before winning the title in season 1964–65; an achievement that certainly ranks with Stein's Cup-winning efforts with Dunfermline in 1961.

Waddell was also in charge when Rangers triumphed in the European Cup Winners Cup final against Moscow Dynamo in Barcelona in 1972. By general consent, it was his vision that encouraged his fellow directors on the Rangers board to embark on the progressive policy that produced modern-day Ibrox; arguably the finest football stadium in the whole of Britain.

Willie Waddell, like his great rival Jock Stein, should command an automatic right of entry to any Scottish football Hall of Fame.

Similarly, other names, such as Willie Maley, Jimmy McGrory and Sir Robert Kelly, of Celtic; Bill Struth, Scot Symon and Jock Wallace of Rangers; Jim McLean of Dundee United; Bill Shankly of Liverpool; Sir Matt Busby of Manchester United; Tommy Walker of Hearts, who would be entitled to his place as a player as well as a manager; Alex Ferguson of Aberdeen and Manchester United; Tommy Younger, the one-time Hibs and Liverpool goalkeeper who became President of the SFA; together with anyone who was in charge when Scotland qualified, against all the odds, and however unsuccessfully, for the finals of the World Cup, principally managers Willie Ormond, Ally McLeod and Andy Roxburgh; assorted luminaries of the Scottish Football Association, most notably Sir George Graham, Willie Allan, Ernie Walker and David Will; referees, once retired, with the style and lasting power of Tom Dougray, Peter Craigmyle, Charlie Faultless – he of the perfect name! – Jack Mowat, Bobby Davidson and Tom Wharton; not forgetting, perhaps, occasional members of the print and broadcast media whose perception, fragile fame and questionable stamina to survive might command the occasional place, could all be included.

But, obviously, the main thrust of public interest in any such venture would centre on the players selected for inclusion. And rightly so. For it is the players who are the true heart and soul of the game.

From among the giants of the past a more representative Hall of Fame might start with Walter Arnott of Queen's Park. He played 14 times for Scotland, not nearly enough to merit a place on the wall at No. 6 Park Gardens. But ten of his caps were won against England in consecutive years, a rare feat, starting in 1884. He also played in three Scottish Cup-winning sides with Queen's Park as well as in the losing team in the two FA Cup finals which featured the Hampden amateurs.

According to one contemporary, Walter Arnott was a giant among giants. William Pickford, one-time referee and former President of the Football Association turned football writer, said of Arnott: 'Not only was he the best defender, but he was also the most artistic back I have ever seen and no-one ever equalled the ease and elegance of his methods.'

It would be difficult to make a fair assessment of the quality and achievements of many players who were active before any of the people likely to be chosen as custodians of the Hall of Fame were ever born. But football is the people's game. The names of its heroes are passed from generation to generation.

Alan Morton of Rangers, the famous Wee Blue Devil, for example, played his last game for Scotland in 1932 and stopped playing for Rangers the following year. Except as a child, anyone who saw him at his peak would be nearly 70 now. Yet people half that age, and younger, believe the man was a soccer genius.

Morton played 495 times for Rangers and scored 115 goals from the outside-left position. He won nine championship medals and two Scottish Cup medals with the Ibrox side. He also played 11 times for Scotland against England and on 20 other occasions against different opposition.

His first caps were earned while he was still with Queen's Park. But it is with Rangers, both as a player and as a director, that his name is generally associated. To this day a giant portrait of the little man hangs above the marble staircase in the entrance hall at Ibrox. But there is nothing to commemorate his deeds in the Hall of Fame at No. 6 Park Gardens.

The name of Alan Morton is revered because football thrives on legend. The great stars of the Twenties and Thirties, even the fast receding Forties, survive because enough people knew someone who saw them play.

In the event someone ever proceeds to establish a real Hall of Fame, some formal structure would be required for nominating the great and the good, and a few who would be a trifle grey round the edges, for official membership. But until that happens, nominating names for an imaginary Hall of Fame is a game anyone can play.

No-one would seriously argue that Jimmy Johnstone and Jim Baxter, from recent times, neither of whom won anything like 50 caps for Scotland, shouldn't be included. Similarly, from across the years, players with a claim on a place would surely include . . .

Bobby Walker of Hearts, who gathered an astonishing 29 caps between 1900 and 1913, and was thought by some to be the best player in Europe in the early years of the century.

Jimmy McMenemy, of Celtic, who won his first cap in 1905 and his last 15

It would be a poor Hall of Fame of Scottish football that omitted Jock Stein and Willie Waddell – twin titans of the modern game

years later. In all that time McMenemy managed to add only 11 more caps to his total. But he is one of only four players to accumulate seven Scottish Cup medals, the last of them in 1921, when McMenemy was aged 40, and playing with Partick Thistle who, not for the last time, upset all expectations that year by defeating Rangers 1–0 in McMenemy's last final.

Bob McPhail, of Airdrie and Rangers, the first man to equal McMenemy's record tally of seven Scottish Cup medals. McPhail won the first of his medals playing for Airdrie against Hibs at Ibrox in 1924. Twelve years later he scored the goal that brought Rangers victory over Third Lanark at Hampden, and himself a special place in the record books. Between 1927 and 1938 McPhail played 17 times for Scotland.

Hughie Gallacher, who played alongside McPhail at Airdrie, before moving to Newcastle, Sunderland and Chelsea, and various other clubs in the years of his tragic personal decline, was a scoring machine who netted 24 times for Scotland in only 20 international appearances.

Bobby Evans, of Celtic, who finished just two caps short of the present obligatory 50, in an international career that lasted 11 years between 1949 and 1960.

Billy Steel of Morton, Derby County and Dundee, who won 30 caps for Scotland and was one of three Scots who played for Great Britain against the Rest of Europe in May 1947.

Any member of Hibs' Famous Five forward line of the late Forties and early Fifties, which included Willie Ormond, but especially the graceful Gordon Smith, winner of 18 caps for Scotland and league championship medals with three

Hampden regulars, for club and country, for almost a decade, Old Firm favourites Paul McStay and Ally McCoist would be worth a place in any modern Hall of Fame

different clubs, Hibs, Hearts and Dundee.

Eric Caldow, of Rangers, with 40 caps, and many more waiting to be won, when he cruelly broke a leg captaining Scotland against England at Wembley in 1963 and was never as good again.

Billy McNeill, of Celtic, quite simply loaded with honours, including his European Cup-winners medal, seven Scottish Cup medals, to match the record of Jimmy McMenemy and Bob McPhail, as well as six league cup medals; but only 29 caps and another absent face from the wall at No. 6 Park Gardens.

John Greig finished his career just six caps short of a place on that same wall. But the man who captained Rangers to victory in the final of the European Cup Winners Cup in Barcelona in 1972, and was twice winner of the Scottish Football Writers' award as Player of the Year in Scotland, would be sure of a place in any new Hall of Fame.

Of course, McNeill and Greig would be entitled to a separate place on the new wall of honour, together with the rest of the Celtic and Rangers teams that won the European Cup in Lisbon in 1967 and the European Cup Winners Cup in Barcelona in 1972, with the Aberdeen side that won the European Cup Winners Cup in Gothenburg in 1983, followed by the Super Cup, alongside.

The list of players who might qualify for inclusion in an all-embracing Hall of Fame is hardly endless but there can be little argument that caps alone offer an unfair measure of many a career.

Judged across a period of the last 40 or 50 years alone claims for a place in a real Hall of Fame could be made on behalf of everyone already mentioned. But other names also deserve serious consideration.

Bobby Evans, captain of Celtic and Scotland, won 48 caps in a distinguished international career that lasted from 1949 until 1960 – two caps short of a place in the current Hall of Fame

It would be hard to ignore Bill Brown, Martin Buchan, Bobby Collins, Charlie Cooke, Davie Cooper, Jimmy Cowan, Sammy Cox, Pat Crerand, Tommy Docherty, Archie Gemmill, David Hay, Willie Henderson, Sandy Jardine, Derek Johnstone, Billy Liddell, Jimmy Mason, Ally McCoist, Dave Mackay, Johnny Mackenzie, David Narey, Charlie Nicholas, Lawrie Reilly, Bruce Rioch, Ian St John, Ronnie Simpson, Pat Stanton, Paul Sturrock, Willie Thornton, John White and Davie Wilson.

Extend the list to include managers with a strong Scottish connection operating successfully outside Scotland and the claims of Matt Busby, Bill Shankly and George Graham for a place in the Hall of Fame are obvious.

Football is the people's game and it deserves a popular museum, including a Hall of Fame, dedicated to its history. Funds to support the museum could be sought from the Scottish Football Association, the Scottish Football League, the Football Trust, the Scottish Arts Council and other interested parties, including local authorities and sponsors with an established commitment to football; although in time the venture could prove commercially viable in its own right – with its home at Hampden Park!

CHAPTER SIX

Resplendent in green and white ribbons, for the first time in 14 years, the Scottish Cup occupied an honoured place at Parkhead when Jock Stein joined Celtic in December 1951. It had been won, by the narrowest of margins, in a scrappy final with Motherwell, twice defeated by Celtic 20 years earlier in near-consecutive finals of the same competition.

The outcome of the 1931 final had been particularly unfortunate for Motherwell who had been winning 2–0 with only ten minutes of the match remaining. A goal by Jimmy McGrory near the end offered the outclassed Parkhead side something by way of consolation from a match they never looked like winning.

Then, in the final minute, the Celtic outside-right, Bertie Thompson, who admitted later he was hoping to finish the match still in possession of the ball, which he wanted to keep as a memento of the occasion, was forced to part with his intended trophy, and sent a harmless-looking cross into the heart of the penalty area. Alan McClory, the Motherwell goalkeeper, appeared to have the ball covered, with the closing moments of the match ticking away, and Motherwell looking forward to seeing their name on the Scottish Cup for the first time in the history of the competition. But before McClory could take possession of the ball and return it deep into the Celtic half of the field, and safety, Alan Craig, the Motherwell centre-half, rose in front of the goalkeeper and headed the ball into the back of his own net.

Moments later the brightly blazered referee, Peter Craigmyle from Aberdeen, who always enjoyed adding a touch of theatre to his own performance, brought this particular Hampden drama to a close. Celtic couldn't believe they had been given a second chance. But the opportunity wasn't wasted. Motherwell lost the replay 4–2.

Two years later, a single goal, scored by Jimmy McGrory, was enough to separate the two teams a second time.

A final against Celtic was one contest Motherwell fans despaired of winning. As the enigmatic Waverley – W.G. Gallacher – argued in the *Daily Record*, in his preview of the 1951 final: 'Motherwell can be two types of team, and at their best, playing in the fashion which has marked their style of play for many years, they can make themselves the more cohesive eleven of the two. If, however, they desert the smooth soccer of which they have proved themselves capable this season, and go in for the accepted cup brand, they will fall by the way.'

The teams were: *Celtic* – Hunter, Fallon, Rollo; Evans, Boden, Baillie; Weir, Collins, McPhail, Peacock and Tully. *Motherwell* – Johnston, Kilmarnock, Shaw; McLeod, Paton, Redpath; Humphries, Forrest, Kelly, Watson and Aitkenhead. *Referee* – J.A. Mowat, Rutherglen.

The goal which decided the match was scored after 12 minutes by John McPhail, the Celtic captain. 'Believe me, the 78 minutes' play which followed produced nothing to equal it in the way of intelligence skilfully applied and coolness of demeanour,' Waverley, writing in the *Daily Record*, concluded afterwards.

His report, which appeared on the Monday following the match, suggests that Waverley, who had been reasonably optimistic about Motherwell's chances before the match, had been reduced to a mood of despair by what he witnessed at Hampden.

'If a game of classic football could be likened to the alphabet, I would say that the Scottish Cup final on Saturday had everything but the consonants. It was a poor game which I have heard described as producing a lucky triumph for Celtic. Their luck lay in having such mediocre opposition as Motherwell for I have no doubt in my mind that the Parkhead fellows deserved to carry the trophy from the field.'

In the last days of 1951, when Jock Stein presented himself for reserve team duty with Celtic, in addition to the Scottish Cup, a somewhat esoteric object known as the St Mungo Cup was a recent embellishment to the Parkhead trophy room. It had been won in a competition organised by the Scottish Football Association and Glasgow Corporation as a contribution to that year's Festival of Britain celebrations.

Aberdeen, who defeated Rangers, St Mirren and Hibernian on their way to the final, provided the opposition. Celtic, having disposed of Hearts, Clyde and Raith Rovers, enjoyed an easier route to Hampden.

In an age of large attendances, the crowd at Hampden on Wednesday, 1 August 1951, was a barely respectable 80,600, most of whom supported the Glasgow side. The teams were: *Aberdeen* – Martin, Emery, Shaw, Harris, Thomson, Lowrie, Bogan, Yorston, Hamilton, Baird, Hather. *Celtic* – Hunter, Haughney, Rollo; Evans, Mallan, Baillie, Collins, Walsh, Fallon, Peacock, Tully. *Referee* – J.A. Mowat, Rutherglen.

Those in the crowd who expected Celtic to win easily were soon shocked out of their complacency. A goal by Yorston after 20 minutes, followed by a second from former Celt Bogan 12 minutes later, was a harder way than most for any team, least of all the favourites, to set about winning a major trophy.

Nor did it help much when Hunter collided with a post and was forced to go off for treatment. Skipper Bobby Evans donned the goalkeeper's jersey and worked between the posts for fully 12 minutes. It was an unfortunate coincidence, perhaps, and no credit to the man Evans replaced that Hunter, injured when Yorston scored Aberdeen's opener, was back on duty in time to retrieve the ball from the back of the net after Bogan put them further ahead.

There was little doubt, however, that Aberdeen were leading strictly against the run of play. Charlie Tully, especially, was in mesmerising form and treating the northern defence to a very bad time. 'He took corners, right and left, and throw-ins of equal menace,' the *Evening Times* reported approvingly. 'There was class and character in a lot of his work and some of his leading out passes were a delight to behold.'

A joker of note, the controversial Irishman was capable of turning the simplest circumstance to his own cheeky advantage. Handed the ball for a throw-in by the Aberdeen defender Davie Shaw, the Celtic winger, with none of his team-mates immediately available or positioned to his liking, threw the ball against the obliging Shaw's conveniently available back to secure a corner.

Some people thought the action ungentlemanly. Others, less scrupulous, said it was inspired. One thing no-one could dispute – it was certainly productive. For it was from the corner, taken by the ebullient Tully himself, naturally, that his fellow countryman, Sean Fallon, with 40 minutes on the clock, pulled one back for Celtic.

Four minutes into the second half Celtic equalised. A pass from Walsh found Fallon unmarked and, to the great delight of the huge majority of those present, the popular Irishman scored easily.

Twenty minutes later the score finally reflected the true nature of the contest. Typically, with Tully once again at the heart of the action, the winning goal, by Walsh, attracted a storm of protest. Many people thought Tully was over the bye-line before he crossed for Walsh to score. But referee Mowat, who was in a good position to judge, said no.

The St Mungo Cup was on its way to a permanent place of honour at Parkhead. Not a particularly handsome piece of silverware, it soon transpired that the trophy itself had enjoyed an odd history. When captain Bobby Evans accepted the St Mungo Cup from Lady Warren, wife of the Lord Provost of Glasgow, Sir Victor Warren, at a special ceremony held in the Kelvin Hall on the Saturday following the match, few people were aware it served, in a previous incarnation, as the prize in a match featuring Provan Gasworks and Glasgow Police.

It is impossible to know for certain what thoughts motivated the council in their choice of cup for the series of matches launched to mark the Festival of Britain: a sense of history, perhaps; erstwhile frugality, and an unlikely but commendable awareness of the restrictions placed upon them by their higher responsibilities as custodians of the civic coffers; who knows?

It is even possible the Tory council secretly believed there wasn't much point to the Labour-inspired Festival of Britain anyway and an old cup was all the occasion merited. At any rate, as Brian Wilson recounts in his official centenary history of the club, *Celtic, a Century with Honour*, an attempt by Celtic to secure a more appropriate replacement was firmly rebuffed.

However, as Wilson himself ungrudgingly admits: 'In this period, it might be thought, Celtic were not in much of a position to be fussy about the calibre of the trophies they collected.'

But supporters of the Parkhead side who saw Bobby Evans collect the St Mungo Cup from Lady Warren could be excused for believing their team was about to challenge for all the main honours. Winning the Scottish Cup earlier the same year against Motherwell was the first Celtic success, in a major competition, since before the war. A second cup won in the space of a few months – which didn't count a trophy won on a tour of the United States a few weeks earlier – offered additional sweet hope for the future. Keeping possession of the Scottish Cup, and close pursuit of the league championship, would be their main concern during the new season about to begin.

While those who attended the presentation ceremony in the Kelvin Hall waited and watched, and the St Mungo Cup passed from player to player, each one treasuring the occasion, it would have been hard for anyone present to know – and almost as hard to understand – that this was a moment for all Celtic fans to savour; because it was not an occasion easily repeated.

When it arrived at Parkhead the St Mungo trophy – despite its humble football origins – was given a place of honour in the Celtic trophy room beside the Empire Exhibition Cup, won by Celtic in 1938 with war looming and the notion of empire already suffering from terminal decay. Similarly, the St Mungo Cup competition had been staged to help celebrate Britain's lasting greatness in the post-war world. Given the assured absence of empire from any such calculations, even as the Festival of Britain proceeded to a desultory conclusion, it was hard to ignore early signs of the nation's future decline.

So, despite their pleasure at the outcome of the St Mungo Cup competition, seeing both trophies together under the same roof, pessimists with a sense of history – and the best interests of Celtic at heart – could have been forgiven nagging doubts about the future, just as anyone else who happened to believe a vigorous, successful Parkhead side was vital to the general well-being of Scottish football would have been unhappy to learn that a long period of disappointment lay in wait for the club.

It is unlikely, however, that anyone who witnessed the great Celtic recovery against Aberdeen, which ensured a trophy named after the city's patron saint – whatever else its background – remained in Glasgow, realised they would be required to endure another two years of total failure, in all the major competitions, before a different Celtic captain ascended the famous Hampden steps to accept the winning silver at the end of a competition not yet envisaged.

Jock Stein was that man. And in his hands, held proud and high, for all the world to see, was the 1953 Coronation Cup!

Stein had been brought to Parkhead from Wales, where he played for non-league side, Llanelli Town, by manager Jimmy McGrory who was looking for someone to provide short-term cover for the centre-half position.

Stein was already into his 30th year when he signed for Celtic. Before moving to Wales he had been eight seasons with Albion Rovers.

His playing career had been worthy and undistinguished. As a player he was known to be strong, safe and solid, even against quality opposition of the period. 'As a centre-half Stein was a refreshingly pragmatic character,' Tom Campbell notes in *Glasgow Celtic 1945–1970*. 'The things he could do, he did very well: those that were beyond his capabilities, he rarely attempted.'

When he signed for Celtic in December 1951, there was little mention of his arrival in the football-conscious pages of the large number of Scottish newspapers then available. Even in December, with a single star visible above Parkhead, it would have been difficult for even the most perceptive reporter to predict the years of triumph that lay ahead. Celtic were then led by Robert Kelly, as chairman. It may be assumed, however, that no-one at Parkhead was any wiser at predicting the future than their friends and foes writing in the sports pages of the daily papers.

By any standards the fee of £1,200 which changed hands at the end of the transaction was hardly eye-catching. As Bob Crampsey records in *Mr Stein*, a biography: 'The move at the time meant much more to the player than to the club. The supporters, if they had any feelings on the subject at all, saw it as yet another instance of a supposedly major club being content to buy in the bargain basement.'

Tom Campbell, in his history of Celtic between 1945 and 1970, recalls that Stein 'came to Parkhead as a vaguely-remembered nobody. Celtic's team and performances seemed to revolve around their personality players: McPhail, Tully, Weir and Collins, all instantly recognised in the streets, all over-publicised, highly paid stars, all still recalling last season's Scottish Cup triumph – and all members of a side firmly settled in second bottom place in the league table.'

On his first day at Parkhead, Stein was given a peg in the reserve team dressing-room – an indication that Jimmy McGrory, the club's highest-ever goalscorer, and a Celtic legend in his own right, envisaged the big man, who was destined to become probably the most famous Celt of all, providing not much more than a little extra insurance at the heart of the defence.

Stein clearly had other ideas, however. The week he arrived at Parkhead injuries affecting first-team regulars forced McGrory to include him in the team against St Mirren.

Two months later, after a tussle for places which must have delighted the manager, Stein became an established first-team choice, a position he maintained throughout the rest of his playing career which ended, aggravated by injury, four years later.

Born in Burnbank, Lanarkshire, on 5 October 1922, Stein worked as a miner before becoming a professional footballer with Albion Rovers, and the experience showed. There was a rich seam of hard determination in his personality which no-one questioned lightly. Also, his enthusiasm for the game was boundless and with his stop-gap signing it is obvious now that Celtic laid the foundation of their greatest years.

During his years with Albion Rovers there was never much chance of Stein appearing at Hampden, except against Queen's Park in the league, or an early round of some cup competition. However, when he was invited to join Celtic, and quickly became a first-team player, he was entitled to consider his chances of appearing in a major final much improved.

Unfortunately for Stein, and everyone else at Parkhead, he arrived in the midst of lean times for Celtic. When it came to winning the game's highest honours, the Parkhead side rarely figured.

Rangers, managed by Bill Struth and captained by George Young, and Hibernian with their all-star forward line, comprising Gordon Smith, Bobby Johnstone, Lawrie Reilly, Eddie Turnbull and Willie Ormond, and known to supporters throughout Scotland, with affection and fear, as the Famous Five, dominated the league. Six titles contested from 1946, when the championship resumed following the war-time close-down, had been shared by these two clubs.

Similarly, in the years immediately following the war, there had been little requirement for the Celtic team bus to make the short journey across town to Mount Florida and Hampden Park.

Three times winners of the Scottish Cup in the decade before the war, six finals and 14 long years passed before the longest-prized silverware in Scottish football returned to Parkhead in 1951. Celtic didn't even make the final in all that time and Rangers putting their name to the Scottish Cup in three of the first four finals contested after the war was clearly bad news for everyone involved at Parkhead, not least the team's long-suffering supporters.

It is almost impossible for anyone to consider Stein's timely arrival at Parkhead, and his four years as a Celtic player, without indulging in a measure of hindsight.

There was a time, lasting years, when the words Stein and Celtic – Celtic and Stein – were rarely uttered except in the same breath. Considering his achievements, and his subsequent influence on the development of the game throughout Europe, it is tempting to seek evidence that the near heavenly marriage of man and club – for almost as long as it lasted – could be detected from the first wooing; as if it had been 'Robert Kelly himself who dredged up Stein from his own memory and sent for him as another boy David', as Bob Crampsey reflects in his revealing *Mr Stein*. Continuing, a little sardonically, Crampsey observes: 'In his later years the Celtic chairman did nothing to diminish this impression, to Stein's own quiet amusement.'

In fact, it was the reserve team coach, Jimmy Gribben, who first suggested Stein as a possible answer to the club's need for back-up in defence. The ageing recruit's success in achieving a first-team place, and his early elevation to the captaincy, more than confirmed this initial, straightforward, professional assessment.

But to those who rejoiced at the overwhelming success of the Parkhead club in future years, the decision to summon Jock Stein from Wales appeared inspired.

Myth is an essential part of the larger game; and in a city like Glasgow, where people have an acute awareness of time and place, and their own special feeling of identity, a sense of destiny can be willed to order. Given Stein's unbridled determination to make the best of an unexpected career opportunity, more likely Celtic benefited in the long term from unique good fortune rather than spectacular good judgement on the part of anyone at Parkhead, the way it all started.

In time, his immense enthusiasm for the game, coupled with an extraordinary belief in himself and his methods, would combine to produce the most potent group of players ever assembled in Scottish football. But in December 1951, when Jock Stein arrived at Parkhead from Wales, no-one could imagine the great years that lay ahead; not least for the man himself.

Three decades of glittering achievement were waiting to be claimed and enjoyed. For Jock Stein, and the teams he built, the journey to Hampden, the national stadium, became almost commonplace.

When he was still a player with Celtic, the national stadium made few demands on Jock Stein's time. The final of the Coronation Cup at Hampden on 20 May 1953, with a crowd of 108,000 present for the occasion, was a rare highlight in his playing career.

On their way to the final the Parkhead side defeated Arsenal and Manchester United. Their opponents on the last day, Hibernian, likewise proved too strong for no less formidable opposition from the cream of the English First Division, Tottenham Hotspur and Newcastle United.

There was a general feeling, openly expressed, that Celtic had been offered a place in the Coronation Cup because of their guaranteed drawing power, and not as a top team in their own right. A place in the final was the best possible answer to those critics who argued they shouldn't have been invited in the first place. However, complete with their legendary Famous Five forward line, Hibs remained favourites to win.

The teams were: *Celtic* – Bonnar, Haughney, Rollo, Evans, Stein, McPhail, Collins, Walsh, Mochan, Peacock, Fernie. *Hibernian* – Younger, Govan, Paterson, Buchanan, Howie, Combe, Smith, Johnstone, Reilly, Turnbull, Ormond. *Referee* – H. Phillips, Motherwell.

Willie Fernie, on the Celtic left wing, had been chosen to replace the injured Charlie Tully. Early in the match, an unappreciative Hibs support discovered Fernie could be as big a nuisance as the missing Irishman. Twice in the opening minutes Tommy Younger, in the Hibs goal, was forced to launch his massive frame at Fernie's feet to prevent him scoring.

But even Younger's daunting presence could do nothing to stop the opening goal, scored in great style after only 19 minutes, by Neil Mochan, assisted by Fernie. As seen by *The Glasgow Herald*: 'A well directed clearance by Stein was deflected by Fernie onto his centre-forward's tracks. Like McGrory of old he took the shortest way to goal and just as the Hibs defence closed in, he shot with his right foot from 30 yards a ball that Younger, facing the sun, probably never saw.'

Almost on half-time Hibs came close to equalising when Gordon Smith, on the rampage, left the Celtic defence trailing and fed a perfect ball to Lawrie Reilly.

A deadly combination that resulted in a good many goals for the Easter Road side, during the best years of the Famous Five, Smith and Reilly were entitled to believe their efforts on this occasion merited a goal. Reilly's header was well judged and looked destined for the back of the Celtic net. Only a brilliant diving save by Bonnar stopped him scoring.

But that save also set a pattern for the rest of the game. Hibs, it was soon clear, could be judged unlucky: 20 May 1953 was almost certainly the day John Bonnar played the game of his life!

The whole of the second half was dominated by Hibs hammering at the Celtic defence. As one historian, Tom Campbell, recorded for future generations of supporters to ponder: 'On those occasions when the attackers broke through and goals appeared certain, it was Bonnar's daring and anticipation that saved his side.'

A second goal, scored by Walsh three minutes from time, brought welcome relief to the beleaguered Celtic defence. But in some ways it was a formality.

Hibs, judged fairly, were almost certainly the better side. Except they never looked like scoring, not against John Bonnar, not that day anyway; no matter how hard they tried.

A year later Stein led Celtic to a league and Cup double, their first in 40 years.

In the final of the Scottish Cup at Hampden on 24 April 1954, Aberdeen provided the opposition. The teams were: *Aberdeen* – Martin, Mitchell, Caldwell, Allister, Young, Glen, Leggat, Hamilton, Buckley, Clunie, Hather. *Celtic* – Bonnar, Haughney, Meechan, Evans, Stein, Peacock, Higgins, Fernie, Fallon, Tully, Mochan. *Referee* – Mr C.E. Faultless, Giffnock.

To the delight of a large, vociferous majority in the 129,926 crowd, most of the early action was in the vicinity of Martin in the Aberdeen goal. Mochan and Fernie provided the main thrust of the Celtic attack.

Faced with the new league champions, Aberdeen appeared nervous; surprising, in view of the ease with which they despatched Rangers 6–0 at the semi-final stage. At last they settled, however. And the match proceeded at a tremendous pace. Effort, incident and excitement, rather than skill, were the main ingredients

The first half ended with neither side able to score. Inside six minutes of the second half, however, both goalkeepers had been to the back of the net to recover the ball. An own goal by Young, connecting inadvertently with a dangerous, swerving shot from Mochan five minutes into the second half, put Celtic ahead. A minute later Buckley accepted a low pass from Hamilton, waited as Bonnar went to meet him, then calmly scored the equaliser.

The winner, after 63 minutes, was created by the continually resourceful Willie Fernie. Fernie evaded the Aberdeen defence all the way to the goal-line before placing the ball in front of Sean Fallon. The Irishman expressed his admiration for the quality of Fernie's work in the best possible manner. His goal put the name of Celtic on the Scottish Cup for the 18th time, stretching their record in the competition.

Fifteen had been achieved between 1899 and 1937 under the stewardship of Willie Maley, winner of three league and Cup doubles as manager of Celtic. Hardly an unbiased observer at Hampden when Celtic sealed their first double under Jimmy McGrory since his own hey-day as manager, Maley believed Aberdeen deserved a draw. 'But I am happy at the result,' Maley declared. 'Of course I'm happy.'

Speaking for the players, Bertie Peacock, a future captain of Celtic, admitted feeling sorry for Aberdeen. 'They gave us a terrific game,' Peacock acknowledged. 'I shall always remember this final for the terrific spirit they showed in defeat.'

Those few days in April 1954 were the culmination of Stein's success as a player: in addition to his league championship medal, and the satisfaction of raising the Scottish Cup above his head at Hampden, Stein won his only representative honour – a league cap against England on 28 April. Unhappily, it was a match most Scots preferred to forget, the English league winning 4–0 at Stamford Bridge.

Celtic were leading Clyde by a single goal, with less than a minute left for play in the 1955 Scottish Cup final, when an Archie Robertson corner eluded goalkeeper John Bonnar and finished in the net. Clyde, with a goal by Tommy Ring, won the replay 1–0

A year later, with Stein as captain, the Parkhead side finished runners-up to Aberdeen in the league, and were again participants in the Scottish Cup final. The teams on this occasion were: *Clyde* – Hewkins, Murphy, Haddock, Granville, Anderson, Laing, Divers, Robertson, Hill, Brown, Ring. *Celtic* – Bonnar, Haughney, Meechan, Evans, Stein, Peacock, Collins, Fernie, McPhail, Walsh, Tully. *Referee* – Mr C.E. Faultless, Giffnock.

Celtic had been ahead from the first half, with a goal from Walsh, and, with little more than a minute left for play, appeared to be cruising to another Cup final triumph.

There was no reason to believe a corner on the right, taken by Archie Robertson, offered more than the usual danger. With so much at stake, Celtic supporters in the 106,111 crowd were entitled to assume Stein and the rest of the defence could cope.

Give the elegant Robertson credit for a perfect kick, or blame Bonnar, in the Celtic goal, for a moment's inattention. It is also possible Bonnar was a victim of the Hampden swirl. Whatever the reason, Archie Robertson scored from the corner and Clyde were level.

In midweek Clyde gave the men who earned the replay another chance. Celtic, however, elected to drop one of their star performers, Bobby Collins, for no apparent good reason except that he attracted the wrath of the club chairman, Robert Kelly.

Walsh assumed Collins' role on the right wing, John McPhail went to inside-left, and Sean Fallon, who usually performed best in defence, was drafted into the team at centre-forward. 'This was the kind of eccentric selection in which Kelly specialised on big occasions,' Brian Wilson notes drily, in his official history of the club.

Certainly, it didn't help the Parkhead side keep their hold on the Scottish Cup. A single goal by Tommy Ring was enough to take the trophy to Shawfield. It also put an end to the brief period Jock Stein enjoyed in winning medals as a player.

CHAPTER SEVEN

No serious Scotland fan, toasting the latest Hampden triumph over England on the evening of 13 April 1946, would have been prepared to believe a decade and a half would pass before he was entitled to raise a weary, thankful glass in similar celebration again. But it was 1962 before a Hampden crowd – which no doubt included younger fans not yet born when last it happened – saw another Scotland side defeat England in the international championship.

Given that 1937 was the last time England lost to Scotland at Hampden in the same title race, it was just as well Jimmy Delaney was in the right place at the right time in the Victory international at Hampden nine years later.

A decade and a half without victory over England at Hampden sounds bad enough. A quarter of a century without honour would be a good deal worse.

The Fifties didn't provide much in the way of peace and contentment for anyone interested in the good health, success and general well-being of the Scottish international side. A 6–1 win against Northern Ireland at Hampden in the first year of the decade was considered unsurprising then. But it was typical of the deep malaise affecting Scotland throughout the Fifties that three of the next four visits by Northern Ireland to Hampden ended in a low-scoring draw; a 1–0 victory in 1956 the best result various Scotland teams could muster in front of their own unhappy supporters.

Similarly, in matches against Wales, the Scots showed themselves better at achieving a result in Cardiff than at Hampden; starting with a 3–1 victory in 1950, which the Welsh promptly avenged the following year when they won 1–0 in Glasgow. Another four visits by Wales to the Mount Florida ground produced a single victory for Scotland – 2–0 in 1955 – and three drawn matches.

None of it was particularly inspiring. Or of any great interest in the final, crucial analysis. It was how their favourites performed against the might of England that mattered most – too much, by any sensible consideration – to the army of loyal, long-suffering fans, with their high expectations, who never failed to fill the terracings at Hampden.

These were the long wilderness years of the international championship, stretching back to 1937. It was hardly surprising that people who supported Scotland remembered what happened in the Victory international at Hampden so fondly.

During the barren years at Hampden, between 1947 and 1961, Scotland fared little better at Wembley.

Eight appearances at the famous London ground actually produced two victories and a couple of draws. But such statistics conceal the nightmare of two of the worst defeats ever inflicted on a team in Scottish colours, including the World Cup.

Two men took most of the blame and praise for the measure of a 7–2 defeat in 1955: Fred Martin, in the Scottish goal, and Stanley Matthews, still playing for England at the advanced age of 40, and still destroying Scotland, despite his years.

Six years later England won 9–3. Before the match Stanley Matthews, the great destroyer himself, actually tipped Scotland to win. But once again it was the Scottish goalkeeper, Frank Haffey of Celtic on this occasion, who shouldered most of the on-field blame.

However, a number of privileged and well-dressed spectators, occupying some of the best seats at Wembley, also took a drubbing; almost as bad as the one inflicted by the England players on the unfortunate Scotland team. Seated, embarrassed and uncomfortable, amidst the VIPs attending the match, were the men who decided the names of those who appeared for Scotland – the SFA selection committee.

Not for the first time a large body of fans, including a few who travelled with typewriters, and could claim access to hundreds of damning, excoriating column inches in the following weeks' newspapers, wanted their heads. 'It's time to put professionals in charge,' was the unsurprising, and oft-heard cry.

On 14 April 1956, a crowd totalling 132,817 thought the painful years of failure against England at Hampden were about to end.

The referee, Mr Leo Callaghan, of Merthyr Tydfil, had been seen to glance at his watch. An unofficial reckoning put the time left for play at less than 30 seconds – with Scotland, a forgotten treat at this stage of a game at Hampden, a goal in front!

The teams were: *Scotland* – Younger (Hibernian), Parker (Falkirk) and Glen (Aberdeen); Leggat (Aberdeen), Johnstone (Manchester City), Reilly (Hibernian), McMillan (Airdrie) and Smith (Hibernian). *England* – Matthews (Coventry City), Hall (Birmingham) and Byrne (Manchester United); Dickinson (Portsmouth), Wright (Wolverhampton Wanderers) and Edwards (Manchester United); Finney (Preston North End), Taylor (Manchester United), Lofthouse (Bolton Wanderers), Haynes (Fulham) and Perry (Blackpool). *Referee* – L. Callaghan, Wales.

No-one, especially the star writers filling the back pages of the so-called national newspapers based in London, thought much of Scotland's chances before the match. A complex mixture of national pride, prudence and a sensible eye on their circulation figures, encouraged their Scottish counterparts, operating out of Glasgow, Edinburgh and Aberdeen, to sound at least a little more encouraging. There wasn't one among them who didn't pray Scotland would win. The last time a Scottish team beat England in a full international at Hampden, many of the reporters present hadn't yet started on their own careers.

Looking out across the tenement roofs of Glasgow, reliving the match, at work on their copy, finding the right word to describe that marvellous, unfamiliar moment, when everyone could see beyond all possible doubt that Scotland had beaten the Auld Enemy at Hampden at last, would be a new and exciting, and altogether pleasant experience.

So it seemed, as the seconds ticked away on a dull-looking day in 1956.

Scotland had been ahead for half an hour after Graham Leggat, running through the middle, took possession of a cross from John Hewie. Matthews, in the England goal, had been off his line. Leggat, playing in his first international, saw a chance. A high, deliberate lob left the goalkeeper stranded.

Not surprisingly, the visitors, urged on by their skipper, Billy Wright, responded strongly. Johnny Haynes, always dangerous, hit a post. George Young, at the heart of the Scottish defence, was injured.

The last time Scotland won at Hampden, in 1937, the illustrious Stanley Matthews thought the crowd played a key role. It was larger then, of course – and indulging its roar at a time when the home side was used to winning against England.

Who knows, in different circumstances, with the entire Scottish support hungry for victory, if a crowd of 132,817 mostly desperate people could really expect to out-roar 149,415 quite complacent souls? At Hampden, in 1956, they certainly tried! As the dying seconds of the match ticked away, the noise from the crowd, in support of Scotland, was deafening.

But if the great roar was actually intended to frighten the English, in all fairness, the men in white shirts under the command of Billy Wright showed no sign of feeling intimidated. They tried, right to the end. And none harder than tragic Roger Byrne of Manchester United, the England left-back. With probably just enough time left for one last attacking run in support of his forwards Byrne crossed to the head of his club-mate, Tommy Taylor, like Duncan Edwards who was also playing, would become a victim of the Munich air disaster two years later.

Now Taylor nodded the ball to the alert and waiting Haynes. Before the awful truth of what was happening really dawned on the huge Scottish support, Haynes equalised. There was barely time to restart before the referee brought the match to a cruel and disappointing close for Scotland.

Some, including the Scottish captain, George Young, thought Haynes handled before he scored. It didn't matter: the goal stood.

Two years later, on 9 April 1958, England won 4–0. Many people who witnessed this latest Hampden rout found it difficult to forgive the Scotland team.

It was Hampden's saddest day, according to Hugh Taylor, a good judge, who saw more than most in the course of a long career. Despairingly, he wrote: 'What worried the Scottish supporters was the lack of fight by their team in the second half when they were in with a chance. The native fight and the native genius were missing and, in the end, England hesitated to prod a prostrate foe.'

The teams were: *Scotland* – Younger (Liverpool); Parker (Falkirk) and

Haddock (Clyde); McColl (Rangers), Evans (Celtic) and Docherty (Preston North End); Herd (Clyde), Murray (Hearts), Mudie (Blackpool), Forrest (Motherwell) and Ewing (Partick Thistle). *England* – Hopkinson (Bolton Wanderers); Howe (West Bromwich Albion) and Langley (Fulham); Clayton (Blackburn Rovers), Wright (Wolverhampton Wanderers) and Slater (Wolverhampton Wanderers); Douglas (Blackburn Rovers), Charlton (Manchester United), Kevan (West Bromwich Albion), Haynes (Fulham) and Finney (Preston North End). *Referee* – A. Dusch, Germany.

Billy Wright won the toss from Tommy Docherty and elected to make the Scots play against the wind. By half-time, following goals by Douglas and Kevan, Scotland were already two down.

England always looked the better side. But most people agreed the fierce wind probably helped. Scotland, with wind advantage in the second half, were bound to improve. They didn't. Instead it was England who increased their lead with goals by Charlton and Kevan.

A crowd approaching 130,000 saw the match kick-off. But long before Herr Dusch signalled the end Hampden gaped with space. Some of those who left early, summoned by the attractions of home and pub, could have been born on the day Scotland last beat England in a full international at Hampden.

Any who were would be just eight days short of celebrating their own majority. It was a sobering thought, whichever direction they were headed.

Two years later, on 9 April 1960, another England side came and went, again unbeaten. As were the Scots on this occasion. But a 1–1 draw was about the last thing anyone wanted to see in a match between Scotland and England at Hampden

Some blamed the Hungarian referee, one Jeno Sranko, for being over-zealous in his interpretation of the rules. But the Hungarian official refused to accept any suggestion that the frequency with which he brought the game to a halt spoiled the match. It was only by dealing firmly with every infringement as it happened that he was able to ensure a sporting game, Mr Sranko insisted.

Certainly it would have been difficult for anyone to accuse the referee of courting favour with the vast majority in the near-130,000-strong crowd when he awarded England a dubious second-half penalty for a McKay foul on Charlton.

Scotland were already a goal ahead from the first half, when Graham Leggat beat Springett, in the England goal, with a shot from 16 yards. But nobody could reasonably accuse the referee of favouring the visitors. For example, what appeared an acceptable equaliser, netted by Joe Baker soon after Leggat scored, had been disallowed in favour of a free-kick to Scotland.

Now, as Bobby Charlton prepared for the penalty, an equaliser was just a moment away: Haffey, predictably, going the wrong way, as Charlton intended.

It wasn't a result the Scots fans relished. But it could have been worse. Who, in that huge Hampden crowd, would have bet on Bobby Charlton, given another penalty, and two chances from the spot, to miss each time?

His first shot went straight to the goalkeeper. Haffey couldn't believe his unexpected good fortune. But all self-congratulation on his part ended almost as

*A penalty kick, taken by England great Bobby Charlton during the 1960 home
international at Hampden, is saved by Frank Haffey in the Scotland goal. Ordered to take
the kick a second time Charlton, uncharacteristically, shot wide. The match ended 1–1*

soon as it started. Charlton was allowed another kick, Mr Sranko explained later,
because a Scottish player ventured into the penalty area just as the first spot-kick
was about to be taken. Perhaps it was the shock of it all – but, unbelievably,
Charlton missed again, his second attempt going wide.

It was an uncharacteristic lapse which even the most fervent Scottish
supporter, short on praise for visiting England stars, never expected to see. The
teams on that unhappy occasion were: *Scotland* – Haffey (Celtic); McKay (Celtic)
and Caldow (Rangers); Cumming (Hearts), Evans (Celtic) and McCann
(Motherwell); Leggat (Fulham), Young (Hearts), St John (Motherwell), Law
(Manchester City), and Weir (Motherwell). *England* – Springett (Sheffield
Wednesday); Armfield (Blackpool) and Wilson (Huddersfield); Clayton (Blackburn Rovers), Slater (Wolverhampton Wanderers) and Flowers (Wolverhamp-
ton); Connolly (Burnley), Broadbent (Wolverhampton), Baker (Hibernian), Parry
(Bolton Wanderers) and Charlton (Manchester United). *Referee* – J. Sranko,
Hungary.

Twenty-five years is a long time for people to be deprived of something they believe is important: it can sour the mind and harden the soul. And in football there was nothing more important, or depressing, to the average Scottish supporter, than the continued absence of a home victory against England at Hampden.

Resilience is a common characteristic among followers of Scotland's national team. It is a necessary part of their match-day armour. But two and a half decades of Hampden failure against England, in the international championship, was too great a burden for most of them to bear with any kind of equanimity; not least the men who chronicled the fortunes of the national side, the Scottish football writers.

It would have been Sunday, 15 April 1962, when the normally calm Cyril Horne, football correspondent of *The Glasgow Herald*, confessed to his typewriter, for the benefit of his regular Monday morning readers: 'Scotland's succcess at Hampden has made some of us more than a little hysterical.'

Evidently, it was an excitement that stayed with many people a long time. Months later, at least one senior Scottish scribe felt able to suggest that Saturday, 14 April 1962, was the greatest day for a quarter of a century. 'Great, great, great, everything was just great,' *The Scottish Football Book* exulted. It was a day when, 'Tears filled your eyes. You were so hoarse you could hardly croak.'

What was great, great, great, of course, and the cause of so much sustained, and barely contained, national excitement, was the result of the international championship match between Scotland and England, which had been played at Hampden on Saturday, 14 April 1962: Scotland 2 England 0.

It was the most stirring victory ever seen at Hampden, the first win over England anywhere for 11 years, *The Scottish Football Book* recorded; adding, improbably, but for good measure, that the heroes who comprised the winning team could go down in history as Scotland's greatest of all time. On a bright spring day in Mount Florida the teams were: *Scotland* – Brown (Tottenham Hotspur); Hamilton (Dundee), Caldow (Rangers); Crerand (Celtic), McNeill (Celtic), Baxter (Rangers); Scott (Rangers), White (Tottenham), St John (Liverpool), Law (Turin), Wilson (Rangers). *England* – Springett (Sheffield Wednesday); Armfield (Blackpool), Wilson (Huddersfield); Anderson (Sunderland), Swan (Sheffield Wednesday), Flowers (Wolverhampton Wanderers); Douglas (Blackburn Rovers), Greaves (Tottenham), Smith (Tottenham), Haynes (Fulham), Charlton (Manchester United). *Referee* – L. Horn, Holland.

It didn't take long before everyone at Hampden, outside the England team, knew, just knew, that this was going to be Scotland's year – at last!

Right from the start, the match was dominated by the blue shirts of Scotland. Cyril Horne reported: 'Crerand, set the task of containing Haynes, the England captain and principal tactician, was not in the slightest perturbed. McNeill, a centre-half of great authority, gave Smith hardly a look at the ball. Baxter, whose ability in defence has often been suspect, gave all of us a pleasant surprise by playing England's scoring hope, Greaves, right out of the match.'

It was Davie Wilson who scored first. Springett, together with three of his colleagues in the England defence – Flowers, Anderson and Swan – were all

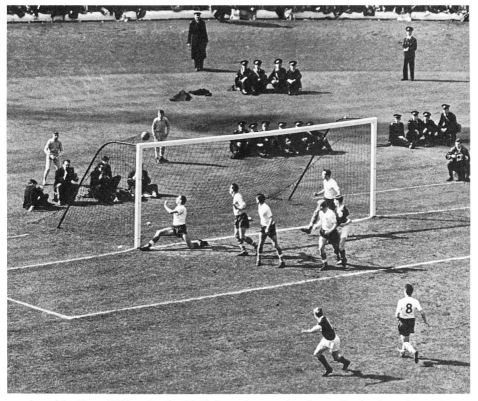

A goal by Davy Wilson in the 1962 home international puts Scotland on the road to victory against England at Hampden for the first time in 25 years. As one reporter admitted: 'Scotland's success has made some of us more than a little hysterical'

between Wilson and the England goal when the little Ranger fastened on to a ball from Denis Law and whacked it into the net.

Wilson scored the opening goal after only 13 mintues. But it wasn't until two minutes from the end that a penalty, taken by Caldow after Swan handled, made the prospect of a home victory absolutely certain.

As chance after chance was squandered, hardened troops in the crowd were entitled to share the occasional nervous glance as the minutes ticked away. It would have been a travesty if Scotland lost. But Scotland had been known to lose, or draw, in similar circumstances often enough before. And, no doubt, it would happen again.

Springett, in the England goal, was outstanding. At times he appeared virtually unbeatable. Cyril Horne, in his summing up, noted: 'The goalkeeper had superb saves from Law, St John, White and Wilson and was lucky more than once, notably when St John headed against the crossbar.'

However, the visitors almost scored when a superb shot from Charlton came off the goalkeeper to the feet of Haynes. But with Bill Brown beaten, Haynes' shot was cleared off the line by an alert Caldow. Later, all glory went to Brown when he stopped a lightning fast free-kick, taken by Haynes, with only one destination in mind.

That England didn't score was largely due to good fortune and a highly controversial decision by the referee. Half-way through the second half Greaves, on the right, crossed to Haynes. An explosive shot hit the underside of the bar. The ball appeared to drop inside the line for a goal. Fortunately for Scotland, the referee, Mr Leo Horn, of Holland, decided otherwise.

But the match, as most people saw it, was all Scotland. 'England, outplayed for long spells, should have lost by half a dozen goals,' Cyril Horne noted.

That they didn't was typical of Scotland, of course. Untypical, after 25 years, was any kind of victory over England in the international championship. An outright win in the championship, with six points from three matches for the first time in more than ten years, was nice too. Those involved were entitled to enjoy their lap of honour.

People waited 25 years for this moment! The Scotland team who defeated England 2–0 at Hampden on 15 April 1962 enjoy their lap of honour

88

In the international championship, at least, these were good years for Scotland.

On 6 April 1963, playing with ten men for most of the match, after skipper Eric Caldow broke his leg in the eighth minute, Scotland won for the first time in a dozen years at Wembley; 2–1. For the second year running, additional victories against Wales and Northern Ireland brought the title to Scotland with maximum points.

In the entire history of the international championship a run of three consecutive wins was rare in matches between the two countries. Thus, in the minds of many fans, the match against England at Hampden on 11 April 1964, soon assumed a special, potentially heroic, status.

Scotland hadn't won three-in-a-row against England since before the turn of the century. In the present century, only England managed to achieve this feat, before 1964, registering three wins between 1957 and 1959, two of them at Wembley.

Now, on a rainy, wind-swept day at Hampden, Scotland, managed by Ian McColl, could match them in the record books; if only they could score. The teams were: *Scotland* – Forsyth (Kilmarnock); Hamilton (Dundee), Kennedy (Celtic); Greig (Rangers), McNeill (Celtic), Baxter (Rangers); Henderson (Rangers), White (Tottenham Hotspur), Gilzean (Dundee), Law (Manchester United), Wilson (Rangers). *England* – Banks (Leicester City); Armfield (Blackpool), Wilson (Huddersfield Town); Milne (Liverpool), Norman (Tottenham Hotspur), Moore (West Ham United); Paine (Southampton), Hunt (Liverpool), Byrne (West Ham United), Eastham (Arsenal), Charlton (Manchester United). *Referee* – Leo Horn, Holland.

For the best part of an hour there wasn't much excitement from either side, although England looked dangerous in the early stages. Twice it took quick thinking by new cap Campbell Forsyth in the Scotland goal, to put an end to flashing raids by Roger Hunt. 'Gloom mounted as England, playing a fluid 4–2–4 game, mounted nonchalant attack after nonchalant attack and they seemed to be piercing the Scottish defence as they pleased,' Hugh Taylor recalled later. 'Would Scotland never come to life?'

Raymond Jacobs, at Hampden for *The Glasgow Herald*, found the match disappointing. 'Neither side gave an exhilarating performance and the match left little feeling of elation,' he complained. Much of the play was untidy, mistakes were frequent, and excitement around the goalmouth was spasmodic, Jacobs added.

Twice in the second half Scotland might have been awarded penalties. But referee Leo Horn, the Dutchman who had been so kind to Scotland on the occasion of England's last visit to Mount Florida, refused all appeals. Some observers believed it was his denial of Law, whom many people thought had been held by Bobby Moore when he was about to score, that galvanised the Scots into serious action.

Willie Henderson caused havoc whenever the ball arrived at his feet, *The Glasgow Herald* reported, adding: 'Time and again Henderson's unparalleled sense of balance and timing took him past Moore and Wilson deep into the penalty area, and desperate, even ruthless, measures were employed to stop him and the other forwards.'

Baxter, Law, Wilson and Gilzean also contributed greatly to the visitors' sense of discomfiture in the face of superior forces. There was nothing England could do to stop Baxter taking complete control of the game. Nor were they capable of deciding where Law would turn up next. The men in the white shirts were clearly rattled. Finally, the goal most of Hampden wanted, arrived.

Eighteen minutes from the end, Davie Wilson took a corner on the left. Gordon Banks went out to meet it. Alan Gilzean reached the ball first. A nod of his head, and Scotland, deservedly, went in front.

Of course, it wouldn't have been Scotland, playing in front of a home crowd, with so much at stake, each of the players burdened with the dreams and hopes of thousands, if there wasn't a moment before the end when the match, already won, appeared lost. This time, with less than a minute left for play, Norman emerged from the heart of the England defence to connect with a corner from Paine. Forsyth and the rest of the Scottish defence looked beaten. The crowd gasped and groaned as the big centre-half's header went inches wide. Rarely was the sound of a final whistle more welcome.

Nobody grudged the Scottish players their lap of honour. They were all participants in a small moment of football history; even if the match itself offered little to encourage superlatives.

A win against England was always nice. Two wins in succession was nicer still, of course. But three in a row against their oldest opponents, for the one and only time this century, was almost certainly the nicest football experience just about everyone in the Hampden crowd could remember.

Four-in-a-row against a country already on its way to winning the World Cup, under the strict guidance of Alf Ramsey, was always too much to expect, probably. But in advance of the next Wembley encounter few such sensible considerations, and proper regard for the abilities of their neighbours to the south, did much to discourage the vast majority of Scottish supporters from rubbishing England. 'Easy! Easy!' was the standard approach to a match that was rarely anything but difficult, and often downright impossible, for Scotland.

A 2–2 draw in the England capital appears, at first glance, not a bad result. But for a large part of the game the home side played with only nine men!

A year later, with England grudgingly assured a place in the World Cup finals, as hosts, and Scotland once again failing to qualify, thanks largely to a disastrous performance against Poland at Hampden the previous year, the most important bi-annual event in Scottish sport offered an opportunity for some kind of desperate, frustrated revenge.

Only two of the England side – Newton and Connelly – who appeared at Hampden on 2 April 1966, weren't included in the team that won the World Cup a few weeks later. Yet, somehow, Scotland were expected to dismiss them with ease.

Scotland hadn't lost at Hampden since 1958; England hadn't won at

The supreme stylist, Jim Baxter, questioned
England's reliance on blackboard tactics

Wembley since 1961. Raymond Jacobs, writing in *The Glasgow Herald* on the morning of the match, believed 'the record of past years, and the evidence of more recent years, suggests that Scotland will beat England this afternoon at Hampden Park'. In support, Jacobs cited 'individual ability, flair and initiative, and, not least, the compelling urge felt by Scottish teams in any sport to beat English opposition'.

Forty-eight hours, and one football match later, the same writer confessed: 'The predominant sound was not the Hampden roar but the eating of words.'

Even the bookmakers thought Scotland would win. As *The Scottish Football Book* recalled later: 'For once, in a country where caution is legendary, there was hardly a voice raised to point to the folly of taking anything for granted in international football.'

England, masters of method, were often accused, in their greatest year, of lacking flair. Scotland, with Jim Baxter, Denis Law and Jimmy Johnstone all at their peak, enjoyed an abundance of flair. Some other ingredient essential to success – application, perhaps, discipline, sometimes, and even, on occasion, good fortune – was often missing from their performance.

However, in the Sixties at least, Scotland were rarely short of flair if that is taken to mean a spontaneous, joyous, unorthodox approach to the game. 'When

91

you watch the rigid tactics of England you wonder if all the blackboard planning is worthwhile,' no less a judge than Jim Baxter once mused.

Of course, prior to the kick-off at Hampden on 2 April 1966, there was also a strong element of pique in the Scottish attitude. England hosting the World Cup rankled. To most Scots it seemed an underhand way of reaching the finals – but typical of their neighbours!

A crowd of 130,000 saw the teams line up as follows: *Scotland* – Ferguson (Kilmarnock), Greig (Rangers), Gemmell (Celtic), Murdoch (Celtic), McKinnon (Rangers), Baxter (Sunderland), Johnstone (Celtic), Law (Manchester United), Wallace (Hearts), Bremner (Leeds United), Johnston (Rangers). *England* – Banks (Leicester City), Cohen (Fulham), Newton (Blackburn Rovers), Stiles (Manchester United), J. Charlton (Leeds United), Moore (West Ham), Ball (Blackpool), Hunt (Liverpool), R. Charlton (Manchester United), Hurst (West Ham), Connelly (Manchester United). *Referee* – M. Faucheux, France.

For most of the first 45 minutes the unfancied visitors, soon to be world champions, dominated the match. In little more than half an hour they were comfortably, and deservedly, ahead, with goals from Geoff Hurst and Roger Hunt. Having started the day expecting too much, the despondent Hampden crowd was now beginning to fear the worst. However, a goal by Denis Law shortly before half-time kept Scotland in the match.

Those who considered Scotland fortunate to be no more than a goal down at the interval nodded knowingly barely three minutes into the second half, when England went further ahead, with Roger Hunt again the scorer.

However, before Hunt scored, the crowd could see a distinct improvement in the Scottish performance. Baxter was beginning to take command of the midfield, while Law and Johnstone, in particular, were the cause of considerable upset to the England defence.

Twelve minutes into the second half it was a pass from Law to Johnstone that brought Scotland's second goal: 3–2! With more than half an hour left for play, everyone sensed this was a match either side could win.

A goal by Bobby Charlton, almost half an hour into the second half, shortened the odds on England. Scotland, however, were far from finished. Seven minutes after Charlton scored, Jimmy Johnstone nabbed his second. Baxter delivered a free kick straight to Johnstone's feet. The happy beneficiary then despatched an unstoppable ball past Gordon Banks in the England goal: 4–3!

People consulted their watches, anxiously. With ten minutes of the match remaining, anything could happen.

A draw would have been a fair result. Scotland dominated the last few minutes of the match. In its dying seconds, Stiles was a hero for England, heading off the line, with Gordon Banks beaten.

With an uncertain, but exciting, summer ahead, England were entitled to feel satisfied with their performance. Few people in the huge crowd thought the visitors were potential world-beaters. But, mostly, the dissidents were Scots with a poor opinion of England generally. Something they might have found hard to deny, if they were honest: although Scotland finished on the wrong side of the result, seven goals, in a match against England at Hampden, wasn't a bad afternoon's entertainment.

Wishing the victors well at Wembley in June would have been more difficult to concede. The fact Scotland could lose, by four goals to three on their home ground, Hampden, to the would-be world champions, a year before they totally dominated the actual world champions on their home ground, Wembley, should have been the cause of no great surprise, given the most rudimentary understanding of the Scottish character.

Defeating England was always fun. Losing, occasionally, was a consequence imposed by the law of averages, with little regard to talent, or just reward, at the end of a difficult match.

With characters like Denis Law and Jim Baxter around to remind them, there was never any likelihood of a young player, with a chance of appearing for Scotland against England, being allowed to forget the importance of the occasion. And there wasn't a Scots fan anywhere worth the price of his half and half-pint who didn't know Scotland were ahead in matches won since the annual fixture started with a goalless draw at Partick in 1872. His counterpart from England, invited to dispute this remarkable record, was unlikely to respond with anything like the same certainty; or fervour.

Denis Law scores against soon-to-be world champions England at Hampden on 2 April 1966. Another six goals distinguished the afternoon. Unfortunately for Scotland, the result favoured England, 4–3

CHAPTER EIGHT

In Scotland, at the start of any season, four major trophies – domestic and European – are waiting to be won by the previous year's league champions. In no great order of priority they are the league championship, the league cup, the Scottish Cup and the European Cup. In less complex times, if the club concerned happened to come from Glasgow, for good measure they could also seek to add the now moribund Glasgow Cup to their list of honours.

For reasons other than the obvious – it just hadn't been done before – few people believed, prior to season 1966–67, that a single club could win each and every one of them in the course of a single season.

It just didn't seem possible, in the face of so much competition both at home and abroad, that one man could organise a campaign of such cunning, intensity and sheer management brilliance that each and every one of them would be won by the same club. Or, given the manager, that he could assemble a group of players with the strength and skill, the season-long discipline, and enough ambition and belief in themselves to make such an impossible dream a reality.

But that was the measure of Celtic's achievement, captained by Billy McNeill and managed by Jock Stein, in season 1966–67.

It would be difficult to invent the odd series of coincidences surrounding Jock Stein's departure from Parkhead in March 1960, and his return in March 1965, after more than four years with Dunfermline and almost another year in charge of Hibs.

Stein had been put in charge of the Celtic reserves after an ankle injury forced his retirement as a player in 1956. Four years later most people were sorry to see him go to try his luck as a manager at Dunfermline. But if there was a pang of regret then, at the departure, perhaps for good, of a hard-working club servant, everyone at Parkhead was entitled to feel a good deal sorrier a year later when Stein steered his new club to the final of the Scottish Cup for the first time in their 75–year history.

Celtic, who hadn't won the Scottish Cup since 1954, when Stein was captain, provided the opposition!

With the exception of Willie Fernie, who played in the same league and Cup-winning teams as Stein, the whole of the Celtic side had been coached by him when he was in charge of the reserves at Parkhead. But this didn't stop him

The 1961 Scottish Cup final brought glory to Dunfermline for the first time in their 75-year history. Two games against his old club Celtic ended in triumph for manager Jock Stein – thanks, largely, to an amazing performance by Eddie Connachan in the Dunfermline goal

insisting, straight-faced, for the benefit of reporters, that his knowledge of Celtic was out of date and wouldn't help Dunfermline.

Considering the Fifers were forced to play without right-winger Tommy McDonald, ill with appendicitis on the eve of the match, and then lost centre-half Jackie Williamson for the last ten minutes because of injury, a no-scoring draw in front of 113,618 spectators at Hampden on 22 April 1961, was a remarkable achievement.

Hugh McIlvanney, writing in *The Scotsman*, considered Dunfermline's performance 'a triumph for the little club from the country who held their own against a team acknowledged to be the slickest of city slickers when it comes to knock-out competitions'.

R.E. Kingsley, of the *Sunday Mail*, writing in praise of Stein, emphasised: 'In nearly every move you could trace the touch of the man who is teaching Dunfermline to be big.'

Stein himself thought, 'Every lad played magnificently to plan.'

On the eve of the replay at Hampden on 26 April 1961, Celtic released Bertie Peacock to play for Northern Ireland in a friendly match against Italy in Bologna; a similar request to Dunfermline, for the services of Willie Cunningham, was refused. Twenty-four hours before the final, when Celtic were forced to improvise their team selection, due to the loss of Jim Kennedy through illness, many observers believed the experienced Irishman could have been put to good use in the Celtic defence.

By an odd quirk, Kennedy, the Celtic left-back, had been hospitalised suffering from appendicitis; the same ailment that robbed Tommy McDonald, the Dunfermline right-winger, of his place in the final.

The teams for the replay, with a crowd of 87,866 substantially reduced from the first match, were: *Dunfermline Athletic* – Connachan, Fraser, Cunningham, Mailer, Miller, Sweeney, Peebles, Smith, Thomson, Dickson, Melrose. *Celtic* – Haffey, McKay, O'Neill, Crerand, McNeill, Clark, Gallacher, Fernie, Hughes, Chalmers, Byrne. *Referee* – H. Phillips, Wishaw.

Two goals – the first after 67 minutes by Davie Thomson, the second from Charlie Dickson two minutes from the end – decided the match in favour of Dunfermline, and concluded an historic day for the ancient town. But the real credit for winning went elsewhere: to the manager, Jock Stein, for his meticulous preparation, and the goalkeeper, Eddie Connachan, for the sheer brilliance of his performance across two games.

Hugh McIlvanney, assessing Connachan's contribution to a day of triumph for Dunfermline, assured readers of *The Scotsman*: 'Seldom can one player have so influenced the destiny of an important game.' As an example McIlvanney described what happened after Davie Thomson opened the scoring for Dunfermline. 'Almost immediately,' he recorded, 'Connachan had the most memorable moment of a gloriously memorable game when he leapt at a fierce 20–yard shot from Crerand, hung in the air for a second as if supported by its power, and then dropped on to the ground and into football history.'

Accompanied by his wife, who assisted with the presentation of the Cup and medals, Mr Robert Kelly, President of the Scottish Football Association and chairman of Celtic, could have been forgiven reflecting on the irony of the moment: much of what the big man in charge of Dunfermline knew about football at this level had been gathered while he was an employee of Celtic.

Stein had been near the end of an honest, but undistinguished career as a player when Celtic offered him his first taste of the big-time. Kelly's own policy of taking his players to see the best teams in the world perform widened his horizons. And, finally, his work coaching the Parkhead youngsters let Stein develop many of the ideas which helped Dunfermline defeat Celtic in the final of the Scottish Cup.

It would have been little wonder if Robert Kelly didn't ask himself – 'Were we right to let him go?'

There was a curious symmetry about some of the events which attended Jock Stein's return to Parkhead in March 1965. One of his last acts as manager of Hibs was to mastermind the elimination of Rangers, winners for the past three years, from the Scottish Cup.

The first Old Firm final in 35 years had been contested two years earlier, on 4 May 1963. The last time the two clubs met in the Scottish Cup final Rangers were struggling to recover from an abysmal 25–year slump in the game's oldest competition.

A world record crowd for a club match filled Hampden on 14 April 1928, with thousands more locked outside. There was good reason for all this excitement: Celtic, the holders, were due to defend the Scottish Cup against their oldest rivals, Rangers.

Those with long memories in the 118,115 crowd hadn't forgotten the most recent Scottish Cup final involving the Old Firm: the infamous occasion in 1909 when the trophy was withheld due to rioting.

Rangers, winners of the league championship 11 times during the same period, hadn't won the Scottish Cup since 1903. On those occasions when Rangers succeeded in reaching the final, the Scottish Cup always left Hampden in the possession of others; namely Celtic, Third Lanark, Partick Thistle and Morton.

The teams at Hampden on 14 April 1928, were: *Rangers* – T. Hamilton, Gray, R. Hamilton, Buchanan, Meiklejohn, Craig, Archibald, Cunningham, Fleming, McPhail, Morton. *Celtic* – J. Thomson, W. McStay, Donoghue, Wilson, J. McStay, Macfarlane, Connolly, A. Thomson, McGrory, McInally, McLean. *Referee* – W. Bell, Motherwell.

Their first-half form suggested Celtic were about to extend their tally of cups won. For much of the time only a courageous performance by Tom Hamilton, in the Rangers' goal, prevented the Cup-holders taking the lead. In particular, a tremendous save from the Celtic right-winger, Pat Connolly, half-way through the first half, probably saved the game for Rangers.

Less than ten minutes into the second half the match finally turned when

Rangers were awarded a penalty after Willie McStay punched the ball clear, with Thomson beaten. 'It must still rank as the most important penalty kick ever taken by a Rangers player,' Bob McPhail informed his biographer, Allan Herron.

Meiklejohn appeared calm, although he admitted later, in the whole of his life he never felt more nervous! 'If our skipper had missed then Celtic would have won that final,' was the matter-of-fact judgement offered by Bob McPhail many years later.

Meiklejohn didn't. And ten minutes later McPhail himself put Rangers further ahead, to be followed, almost immediately, by Sandy Archibald, scoring the first of two goals from a distance of 25 yards.

Celtic, demoralised by the sudden loss of their authority, failed to score.

For fans of the Ibrox club, it was a great way to end the wilderness years at Hampden: 4–0 in their favour against Celtic in the final of the Scottish Cup.

Thirty-five years later when the two most powerful clubs in Scottish football next met in the final of the Scottish Cup, for only the sixth time in their history, a performance by the often-maligned Frank Haffey, in the Celtic goal, stopped Rangers, the favourites, winning comfortably. 'It was goalkeeping perfection,' according to *The Scottish Football Book* for 1963. 'Not only did Haffey make saves that broke the hearts of the Rangers' forwards, his composure, confidence and brilliant positioning encouraged his colleagues.'

There was a lot at stake for both clubs. Rangers, in addition to their eighth league and Cup double – itself a record – were hoping to equal their great rivals' record of 17 wins in the Scottish Cup, or see Celtic go further ahead.

As league champions Rangers were guaranteed one of the top places in Europe. And even if they were to finish as losing finalists Celtic knew they would be competing in the following season's European Cup Winners Cup competition. However, it would be a lot more satisfying for everyone at Parkhead if they were able to qualify in their own right.

In front of 129,527 fans at Hampden on 4 May 1963, the two sides were forced to settle for a 1–1 draw, with Brand and Murdoch the scorers.

Eleven days later a midweek crowd which totalled 120,263 brought the combined attendance for the two matches tantalisingly close to quarter of a million. The teams for the replay were: *Rangers* – Ritchie, Shearer, Provan, Greig, McKinnon, Baxter, Henderson, McMillan, Millar, Brand, Wilson. *Celtic* – Haffey, McKay, Kennedy, McNamee, McNeill, Price, Craig, Murdoch, Divers, Chalmers, Hughes. *Referee* – T. Wharton, Glasgow.

Without the inspired performance of Frank Haffey in the first match there would have been no need for a replay. But no-one ever accused Haffey, the man who lost nine goals against England in the course of a single afternoon at Wembley, of being a model of consistency.

In the 1963 Scottish Cup final, second time around, Rangers were no doubt wondering if this was to be one of Haffey's good nights, or another of those eccentric displays for which he was perhaps unjustly famous, and people remembered for years.

It was clearly in Rangers' interests to attack right from the start, in the hope of unsettling Haffey. Given time, the unpredictable Celtic goalkeeper might decide there was a lot to be said for the role of hero and switch to his inspired mode once again.

Six minutes into the match, those who believed Rangers would be right to continue with their policy of sustained attack, pursued in the previous match, nodded knowingly when a copybook goal put them ahead.

Kennedy was left standing as Henderson fastened on a neat pass from Millar. The pugnacious little winger's cross found Brand. At close range Brand was generally lethal. Haffey, who defied Rangers for more than 40 minutes in the first match, and thereafter right to the end, did what he could to stop him scoring. But it wasn't enough.

Just on half-time Brand figured again. A ball from Millar provided the chance of a shot which Haffey stopped but couldn't hold. The ball fell to Davy Wilson who scored.

Two goals down at half-time, Celtic would have been struggling to recover even at their best. But the team who played at Hampden on 15 May 1963 bore little resemblance to great Celtic sides of past and future years.

Rangers, with the sauntering, swaggering, audacious Jim Baxter playing at the top of his form, controlled everything. 'Only the persevering Billy Price, the resolute Billy McNeill and the sturdy Duncan Mackay were making any gestures of protest against this Rangers domination,' *The Scottish Football Book* noted in a tone of some despair.

Most people expected the Ibrox side to increase their lead, perhaps by a considerable, humiliating margin at the finish, not least several thousand crestfallen Celtic supporters who left Hampden early.

In fact there was only one more goal, a strange, bouncing effort, despatched from 20 yards 17 minutes from the end by Ralph Brand, which somehow eluded Haffey, adding considerably to the debit side of his reputation.

At the final whistle, his own reputation as a master craftsman intact, Jim Baxter could afford to indulge the mischievous side of his complex nature, cheerfully purloining the match ball, which he tucked inside his jersey, as a gift for Ian McMillan. McMillan, a great Ibrox favourite nearing the end of his career, had been recalled from the reserves to replace George McLean, missing because of an ankle injury, and played superbly. When referee Tom Wharton failed to recover the ball the men who ruled Scottish football were not amused. The Cup final ball was the property of the Association and they wanted it returned. The secretary of the association, Mr W.P. Allan, pursued the matter in his usual vigorous and punctilious manner. There was no question of the SFA taking a lenient view of such a serious lapse of discipline. Baxter – and Rangers – were in trouble.

In the end a ball was despatched from Ibrox to the headquarters of the SFA and an uneasy peace was restored between the game's ruling body and its leading club. Those who thought the episode funny continued to find it funny. Those who didn't – didn't!

Hibs dismissing Rangers at the quarter-final stage of the 1965 Scottish Cup competition, two days before Jock Stein left Easter Road to return to Parkhead, was a bonus for Celtic, delivered courtesy of the new manager.

Hibs and Celtic were both through to the semi-finals of the Scottish Cup. The draw, which kept them apart, raised the prospect of an intriguing final. For the last club to benefit from Stein's style of management had been drawn against the first, Dunfermline.

There was little Stein didn't know about either side. Barely a year ago, before the move to Hibs, he had been in charge at Dunfermline. Now he was directing his unique talents, and considerable energy, in the service of Celtic.

It showed how easily loyalties can change in a notoriously transient profession. If his new charges could overcome Motherwell in the other semi-final, Stein would be plotting an end to one of his old club's dreams of glory.

Celtic needed two matches to dispose of Motherwell and reach the final at Hampden on 24 April 1965, when their opponents were the club where Stein served his apprenticeship as a manager, Dunfermline.

Scottish football's oldest trophy hadn't been seen at Parkhead since 1954 when Stein was captain. There had been seven unsuccessful trips to Hampden, including replays, in pursuit of the Scottish Cup. But on every occasion it was their opponents – Clyde, Hearts, Dunfermline and Rangers – who won in the end.

It would have been difficult to forget the driving force provided by their former captain on the occasion of the 1961 final against Dunfermline when the Scottish Cup finished in Fife for only the second time in its history, East Fife registering a solitary victory, following a replay, against Kilmarnock in 1938.

That was Stein's first Scottish Cup campaign in charge of his own team. Everyone at Parkhead hoped he could concoct the same magic and achieve a similar result, in even quicker time, with Celtic.

Credit for taking Celtic through the early rounds belonged to manager Jimmy McGrory and chairman Robert Kelly, the ruling duopoly at Parkhead before Stein, with the chairman, in and out of the boardroom, the dominant figure. However, with the return of Stein, team selection became the prerogative of the manager at Parkhead.

Aside from how the players performed, people with a close interest in the outcome of the 1965 Scottish Cup final anticipated a battle of wits and tactics involving the managers.

Willie Cunningham, the Northern Ireland player who sacrificed a cap against Italy to help Dunfermline beat Celtic on the occasion of their last Hampden confrontation, had been appointed manager of the Fife side in succession to Stein.

It had been Stein, on his arrival at East End Park, who persuaded the highly experienced Cunningham to continue playing after it appeared he was about to retire early following a dispute with his last club, Leicester City. Cunningham, who played 27 times for Northern Ireland, first with St Mirren and then with Leicester, before his talk with Stein, won another three caps at Dunfermline where Stein made him captain. Similarly, it was Stein, when he was still at Dunfermline, who encouraged Cunningham to become a coach.

If the day ended with the Scottish Cup trailing black and white ribbons Stein would have been entitled to reflect, with a wry shrug, on the ironies of fate – and football!

John Rafferty expected Dunfermline to play with the slickness of good organisation and the efficiency of well-trained craftsmen. 'But efficiency and craftsmanship are cold qualities, and the Hampden field today could well be for the emotional, for roused men fighting for a cause,' he reflected, a shade mysteriously, for the benefit of readers of *The Scotsman*. Celtic would be 'stimulated by the occasion, by the new manager, by the feeling that great days are just ahead, and that a surge of spirit will add devastation to their play', Rafferty added.

The teams at Hampden on 24 April 1965 were: *Celtic* – Fallon, Young, Gemmell, Murdoch, McNeill, Clark, Chalmers, Gallagher, Hughes, Lennox, Auld. *Dunfermline Athletic* – Herriot, W. Callaghan, Lunn, Thomson, McLean, T. Callaghan, Edwards, Smith, McLaughlin, Melrose, Sinclair. *Referee* – H. Phillips, Wishaw.

Twice in the first half the men from Fife went ahead. The opening goal was scored after only 16 minutes. Fallon pushed frantically at a dangerous cross from Willie Callaghan, marauding down the right. With the Celtic goalkeeper out of position, it would have been difficult for anyone in front of goal to miss the empty net. Melrose, when the ball arrived enticingly at his feet, despatched by the alert Sinclair, didn't.

Another 16 minutes of the match was played at a hectic pace before Celtic managed to equalise. A 25–yard drive from Charlie Gallagher hit the bar and rose high in the air, with Herriot beaten. Auld, running in, rose to meet the ball as it fell. With the goalkeeper on the ground, and Auld following his header into the back of the net, the teams were level.

But two minutes from half-time Celtic were again behind. Melrose, who had been fouled, didn't wait for the Celtic defence to assume their preferred positions. Reacting quickly, he pushed the ball in front of McLaughlin who hit it perfectly to score a glorious goal beyond the reach of an unhappy John Fallon. As *The Scottish Football Book* for the year recalled: 'This was a goal – we thought then – fit to win any final, a dreadful blow to Celtic, coming as it did so near the interval, and great encouragement to Dunfermline, who would have the wind behind them in the second half.'

Celtic, enthused and cajoled during the break, no doubt, by their new manager, began the second half in a brisk and determined mood, moving the ball about with confidence, pace and skill.

The match was far from finished. Anyone in the 108,800-strong crowd who thought otherwise would have been wise to pay close attention to the inspirational form of the Celtic captain, Billy McNeill, and the combined talent for destruction presented by Lennox and Auld on the Celtic left flank.

Six minutes into the second half it was a pass from Auld to Lennox, then back again to Auld, which produced the equaliser, Auld adding to his tally from inside the six-yard box with Herriot well beaten.

It was already looking like a repeat of 1961 when a single game wasn't enough to separate the two sides. Then the first match finished with neither side able to score; this time it appeared two goals apiece wouldn't be enough.

The crowd, knowing they were present at one of the great finals, loved every minute of the surging, end-to-end action that continued throughout the afternoon. 'It was a super advertisement for Scottish football, a dramatic, blood-tingling battle,' *The Scottish Football Book* enthused. 'So fast was the play, so furious was the excitement, that the on-field tension could be felt even on the highest stretches of the vast terracings.'

The winner, nine minutes from the end, was a goal to match the afternoon. It started with a corner on the left, taken by Charlie Gallagher. Gallagher rarely wasted the opportunities offered by a corner. His kick was perfectly judged.

The ball began to drop around the middle of the six-yard line. Herriot, in the Dunfermline goal, might have been expected to reach it first. But as he rose to clutch the ball, and put an end to the danger, the flying figure of Billy McNeill, the Celtic captain, appeared between him and the ball. Just as the corner kick taken by Gallagher put the ball in absolutely the right place at precisely the right moment, McNeill's run and header couldn't have been bettered: with the unfortunate Herriot left grabbing at air, and the rest of the Dunfermline defence transfixed, Celtic went into the lead.

And there they stayed to the finish. It was the club's eighth visit to Hampden for a Scottish Cup final match in 11 years. However, given all these chances, it was the first time a Celtic captain collected the prize.

Writing with the benefit of hindsight, Brian Wilson, author of the club's centenary history, could claim with complete justification that 'Celtic's victory clearly heralded the birth of a new era in Scottish football. The supporters' faith in the manager's potential for greatness was reinforced,' Wilson went on. 'So too was the players' faltering belief in themselves.'

According to Wilson even Jock Stein believed Celtic might have been less successful during the great years of the late 1960s and early 1970s if the 1965 Scottish Cup final had been won by Dunfermline.

At the time John Rafferty suggested Dunfermline had been rushed out of the Cup in a hard and exciting final in which it seemed they had the better all-round quality. 'This was very much a manager's victory,' Rafferty added.

However, the same good judge discounted talk that turned Jock Stein into a football magician. 'In fact,' Rafferty declared, 'he has no more than common sense, a knowledge of modern football, the ability to talk to players, and enough independence in his bulky frame to be able to make up his own mind.'

On 29 October 1966, with Rangers providing the opposition, a goal by Bobby Lennox kept the League Cup at Parkhead for the second year in succession.

Unusually, it was the third meeting in consecutive months between the two teams since the season started and the Parkhead side were already two up in matches won. In August their old rivals had been humiliated on their own ground in the first round of the Glasgow Cup when Celtic won 4–0, Bobby Lennox scoring three and Billy McNeill adding his captain's share. A month later it was Rangers' turn to travel. In a league match at Parkhead in September goals by Auld and Murdoch brought another Celtic victory and more misery to Rangers, who failed to score.

Now the two sides were scheduled to meet again. But this time a major trophy was the prize. The teams were: *Celtic* – Simpson, Gemmell, O'Neill; Murdoch, McNeill, Clark; Johnstone, Lennox, McBride, Auld and Hughes. *Rangers* – Martin, Johansen, Provan; Greig, McKinnon, D. Smith; Henderson, Watson, McLean, A. Smith and Johnston. *Referee* – T. Wharton, Glasgow.

As the teams emerged for the start, the men who fixed the odds had no doubts about the eventual outcome: Celtic were quoted at 7 to 4 on and it was hardly surprising that the Parkhead side appeared to enjoy a psychological advantage long before the first ball was kicked.

But those who joined a crowd of 94,532 at Hampden believing a surprise result was possible were right to live in hope. The big, dark-suited figure occupying the Celtic dug-out always said there was nothing in football quite like an Old Firm game. As Jock Stein explained later: 'Matches involving Rangers and Celtic are different from any other. The tension, atmosphere and the high stakes tend to produce a physical game.'

The wisdom of Stein's judgement became clear right from the start. Rangers, skippered by John Greig, refused to accept the role of underdog. They were fast, courageous, determined to score. However, Celtic, led by Billy McNeill, were superb in defence.

There were appeals for penalties at both ends, first, at the Celtic end, when Alex Smith was blocked in the goal area by McNeill and Clark; then, moments later, when a crushing tackle by John Greig put an end to a Bobby Lennox initiative.

In the end, a goal scored by Lennox ten minutes later, was all that separated the two sides. Except this was a goal taken at breathtaking pace, a goal that combined artistry and accuracy, according to one report, a goal fit to win a cup final. 'Although Rangers had played football that was attractive, entertaining and modern,' *The Scottish Football Book* for the year concluded, 'Celtic had the edge in finishing – and in today's football, with its accent on method, defence and tight marking, the team with the forwards who strike like lightning and thunder the ball at goal must be supreme, and always more likely to win.'

Yet, despite the bookmakers' gloomy predictions, and the worst fears of the Rangers fans, this was a game to remember. There was something in it for everyone at Hampden. Celtic kept the League Cup, of course, and were entitled to believe they deserved it – just!

Rangers, on the other hand, having fought splendidly for the whole of the 90 minutes, succeeded in salvaging a little of their bruised pride. It might take time but most certainly they would win that particular cup again, with Celtic their preferred opponents – always.

Celtic, in the eyes of their manager, played below their best in the league cup final against Rangers. But even Jock Stein, scanning the far horizons of possibility, patiently building, experimenting, searching, and forever looking into the depths of himself to find the perfect team from a combination of remarkable individual talents, didn't dare believe what no-one else could even begin to contemplate: that, for Jock Stein and Celtic, victory against Rangers in the final of the League Cup, on a sunny afternoon at Hampden Park, Glasgow, was the first step on the road to a unique record – and a special kind of glory.

CHAPTER NINE

Ordinarily, it is doubtful if anyone, apart from statisticians and the clubs immediately involved, would remember who won the Glasgow Cup in any given year. It is mentioned now only because, on 7 November 1966, a week after Celtic disposed of Rangers in the league cup final at Hampden, luckless Partick Thistle found themselves crushed 4–0 – Lennox scoring three, Chalmers one – leaving Celtic to collect their second domestic prize of that unforgettable season.

By the time the old year ended Celtic were also into the third round of the European Cup, qualifying comfortably on aggregate against Zurich and Nantes. Their next European date was set for 1 March 1967. But before then they were faced with the likelihood of playing two rounds in the Scottish Cup.

Beginning in January 1967, a good opening draw, and a 4–0 margin in front of a boisterous Parkhead crowd, soon settled Arbroath's ambitions. Then came February and further good fortune which brought Elgin City to Parkhead. The result was unsurprising: Lennox three, Wallace two, Chalmers and Auld one goal each – 7–0.

In any other circumstances, three goals by Queen's Park, on the occasion of their third-round visit to Parkhead, might have been enough to dispel the general impression that Celtic were cantering to the final of the Scottish Cup.

The previous ten days had been spent securing a place in the semi-finals of the European Cup at the expense of Vojvodina of Yugoslavia. And few people believed Queen's Park could prevent Celtic reaching the same late stage in the domestic competition.

But memories of strenuous encounters involving the two clubs in three different finals of the Scottish Cup – stretching to five games – echoed down the years.

Queen's Park, once the most famous club in Scotland, were celebrating their centenary year. Celtic were into the semi-finals of the European Cup. Their progress on all fronts appeared unstoppable. In the style of all great champions who believed totally in their own superiority as a fact of life, victory was usually achieved with an air of confidence and certainty; arrogant, and almost infallible, in its appearance and execution.

Dukla Prague, home and away, could put an end to all their dreams and all such notions, of course. But at Parkhead the players, at least, were confident their place in football history, as the first British side to reach the final of Europe's premier club competition, was assured. Stein, as usual, took nothing for granted. So far, in addition to their exploits at home and abroad in pursuit of various pieces of much-coveted silverware, the Parkhead club had been defeated only once in 25 league matches, losing by the odd goal in five to Dundee United at Tannadice.

Queen's Park, from the second division, drawn against Celtic in the fifth round of the Scottish Cup, on 11 March 1967, weren't expected to cause the aspiring champions of Europe any trouble. Despite their distinguished pedigree, and exclusive mailing address, it went against logic for anyone to imagine a group of amateurs could go to Parkhead and, in the space of a single afternoon, outwit a normally splendid Celtic defence on no fewer than three occasions.

Under different circumstances, Jock Stein would have been right to worry: losing goals, even against inferior opposition, was never part of his preferred way of working. However, the final result offered no real cause for alarm. With effort to spare, Celtic won 5–3 and now faced the prospect of three semi-final matches, in two different competitions, in the space of as many weeks.

When they lined up against old rivals Clyde in the semi-final of the Scottish Cup at Hampden on 1 April a first-leg encounter with Dukla Prague, at the same stage of the European Cup, was less than two weeks away. Clyde, who had been defeated 3–0 at Shawfield in the opening league game of the season, and then 5–1 on their return visit to Parkhead in January, made the short journey to Hampden with little hope of achieving a surprise result.

Three times winners of the Scottish Cup, their record included a 1–0 defeat of Celtic, captained by Stein, following a drawn first match in 1955. On this latest occasion some observers believed a certain preoccupation with Europe on the part of the Celtic players might present the Shawfield side with an outside chance of victory.

In the Scottish Cup the worst possible result for Celtic, short of defeat, was a replay within a week of facing Dukla Prague at Parkhead. But a no-scoring draw on 1 April brought Clyde to the brink of their first Scottish Cup final in almost ten years.

A replay was scheduled for 6 April. Celtic were due to play the first of their semi-final matches in the European Cup against Dukla Prague six days later.

Jock Stein, faced with a unique challenge, refused to compromise. Stein was convinced Celtic could win both trophies. Clyde were a moderately talented side from Scotland; Dukla Prague, the Czech army side, represented a great footballing tradition, a nation with appearances in the final of two World Cups – in 1934 against Italy, when the match went to extra time, and in 1962 against Brazil – to their credit.

However, regardless of such considerations, to Stein, both sets of opponents provided an uncomfortable mirror image of the same problem: Scot or Czech, both teams stood between his treasured Celtic and a place in two important cup finals. Both required to be defeated before Stein and his men could demonstrate the true value of their unique talent to the world.

Stein believed in careful planning. He preferred to dispose of one problem before moving to the next. At any level of competition, he believed in the principle of giving the bulk of his attention to one game at a time; taking nothing for granted, least of all the quality of the opposition.

Given this philosophy, and Stein's total belief in the ability of his players to defeat all-comers, there was never any chance Celtic would apply anything less than the whole of their attention to the match against Clyde at Hampden.

Goals by Lennox and Auld duly produced the result Stein expected. For the 32nd time in their 80-year history, Celtic were into the final of the Scottish Cup.

Their opponents at Hampden on 29 April would be Aberdeen, appearing in their fourth final in 15 years. It had been 20 years since the northern club achieved their only success in the final of the Scottish Cup, a 2–1 victory against Hibs in 1947. But following back-to-back defeats by Rangers and Celtic in 1953 and 1954, and a further loss at the last stage of the competition to St Mirren in 1959, given the opportunity, Stein knew Aberdeen would be in a mood to reverse this discouraging trend.

Before he could give the matter his full attention Stein and his men were required to overcome the champions of Czechoslovakia in the semi-final of the European Cup.

Goals by Jimmy Johnstone, in the course of a dazzling individual performance which left his opponents baffled for most of the game, and Willie Wallace, twice, in front of 75,000 fans, should have been enough to settle the tie at Parkhead on 12 April. But a goal by Strunc kept Czech hopes alive.

Writing in *The Glasgow Herald*, Glyn Edwards warned: 'It will not be easy in Prague for, as Dukla showed last night, they can move the ball about with astonishing speed and skill and, in Strunc and Masopust, they have two players who have the ability to create havoc in opposing defences.'

Fortunately for Celtic, in the European Cup, away goals didn't count double in the event of a draw on aggregate across two games. Dukla Prague needed to win by three clear goals to qualify for the final. A two-goal margin in favour of the home side, resulting in a draw on aggregate, would have meant a play-off in a neutral country.

People who expected Celtic to provide a constant diet of non-stop, joyous, attacking football were disappointed by their return performance against Dukla Prague at the semi-final stage of the European Cup. For almost the entire 90 minutes, before a 22,000 maximum crowd packing the government-owned Juliesky Stadium, the Scots concentrated on defence, determined to protect their hard-won advantage from the first leg.

It could have proved a dangerous way to proceed: two goals by the marauding Czechs would have been enough to turn the match and leave Billy McNeill and his men scrambling to survive. But although Dukla attacked with determination throughout, they never seriously threatened Simpson in the Celtic goal. The final result was a goalless draw. Celtic were into the final of the European Cup, a new experience for any British club.

Stein didn't waste time arguing with anyone critical of the spoiling, negative tactics employed against Dukla Prague. 'Our job was to get through to the final – and we did.'

To reporters covering the match, Billy McNeill added: 'At the start of the season we had a dream. It's coming true. We're only a step away.'

Players, officials and guests on the two-hour flight to Glasgow were happy to endorse the McNeill dream. They talked about little else than the successful European campaign for most of the journey, boisterously recalling great moments from the previous seven months, and looking ahead, with uncontained excitement, to the great finale in Lisbon barely a month away.

At 40,000 feet, with the whole of Europe laid out below, cheerful self-justifying optimism was the prevailing mood; although Jock Stein, relaxed and smiling now, refused to let the euphoria of the occasion sweep him away. Better than anyone, probably, he could imagine the peaks of character and strength, determination and skill, which were waiting to be scaled in pursuit of their European dream, by everyone involved at Parkhead, not least the 11 players selected to contest the final.

Stein studied the faces of the men who would carry the burden of Lisbon. It was a matter of understandable pride on his part that, under his influence, a mixed group of players, in attitude, application and skill, from small towns and villages around central industrial Scotland, within 30 miles of the Glasgow heartland, had been assembled at little cost to the club and become a team, a formidable cohesive unit able to tackle the best in Europe, and win.

If victory in the final of the European Cup was the eventual outcome for Celtic, their place in football history was assured. If they lost . . .

For the moment Stein, who hated to contemplate the possibility of defeat, kept his thoughts on that bleak prospect to himself. In his heart he knew if that was how the great adventure ended, with victory for the other side, what he wanted most of all was for people everywhere to remember Celtic 'because of the football we played. We want to make neutrals everywhere glad that we qualified.'

Stein still didn't know who Celtic would meet in the final of the European Cup in the National Stadium, Lisbon, on 25 May. The other semi-finalists, CSK Sofia and Inter Milan, were due to meet in their second-leg match the following day. A 1–1 draw in Milan at the end of the first game appeared to favour the Bulgarians, although Stein would have been the last person anywhere to underestimate the Italian side's powers of recovery. Not that it mattered greatly to him who won: Celtic would be ready.

There was also no point in wasting time worrying about events and matches he couldn't control, never mind influence. Least of all, he might have thought, as the aircraft bringing them from Prague began its descent towards Glasgow, with one of the most important games of the year, the result of which he was expected to influence directly, due to be played in just four days time – the final of the Scottish Cup, against Aberdeen, at Hampden.

Just as Celtic had been revitalised by one man, Jock Stein, and much of their current success could be traced to his relationship with the club chairman, Bob Kelly, so those who welcomed the return of Aberdeen to Hampden after a lapse of eight years believed their current success was due to the influence of one man, Eddie Turnbull, and the support offered by his chairman, the much-respected Dick Donald.

A successful player with Hibs, one of the Famous Five forward line that brought so much glory to the Edinburgh club in the late Forties and early Fifties, Turnbull had been a member of the Hibs side defeated by Aberdeen in the 1947 final of the Scottish Cup.

Now, under his no-nonsense style of management, this latest Aberdeen side were considered capable of preventing Jock Stein's all-conquering Celtic side from routinely claiming yet another trophy on their way to achieving an unprecedented grand slam. And that in advance of their eagerly awaited appearance in Lisbon the following month, thus allowing Aberdeen to return home with the Scottish Cup for only the second time in their history.

Turnbull, who could be a tough and taciturn man, liked to declare, 'The greatest thing a footballer can have is heart.' He didn't bother to deny his own perceived truth that the Aberdeen players under his command were all heart. By way of excusing the hard-team reputation that followed them around, he was also prepared to concede they could be over-enthusiastic at times.

There had been two previous Scottish Cup final meetings at Hampden involving the two clubs, both won by Celtic.

In 1954 the team from the north, appearing in their second consecutive final, lost 2–1; the same narrow margin Rangers enjoyed a year earlier when they disposed of the Pittodrie side by a single goal, in a replay, following a 1–1 draw.

All three matches attracted large crowds. In the first game against Rangers, on 25 April 1953, Hampden responded comfortably to a crowd totalling a mere 129,861. For the midweek replay the attendance dropped to 112,619. A year later, however, it again nudged the 130,000 mark, with 129,926 passing through the Hampden turnstiles.

These are respectable figures for any match, stunning, in fact, by modern standards. But for sheer size they don't even begin to approach the crowd who watched Celtic defeat Aberdeen, by the odd goal in three in the first of their Hampden encounters 17 years earlier. At the Scottish Cup final played on 24 April 1937, the official attendance was put at a staggering 147,365; with another 20,000 estimated to have been turned away when alarmed officials ordered the turnstiles closed 15 minutes before the kick-off. The official attendance numbered little more than 2,000 fewer fans than the world record crowd who watched Scotland defeat England at Hampden the previous Saturday.

Remarkably, if the gates had been left open until Hampden was considered full, or those arriving had been more evenly spread around different parts of the ground, the 149,415 world record figure for the international would have been surpassed within a week. But then, for the first time ever as a means of crowd control, the match was all-ticket in anticipation of a huge turn-out. A similar level of interest in their own Cup final evidently surprised those responsible for organising the match.

For the Scottish Cup final between Celtic and Aberdeen, a crowd of around 120,000 was expected at Hampden. It was thought no more than 15,000 fans would travel from Aberdeen for the match. In the end it was estimated at least twice that number made the long and inconvenient journey south. SFA secretary George Graham announced afterwards that future Cup finals would be all-ticket, like the England match.

Of course, if several thousand additional spectators had been allowed to gain admission to Hampden on the day of the Cup final, safety considerations apart, not many would have been privileged to view much of the action. Even then a maximum crowd of around 135,000 would have been a more considerate limit for the men in the best seats to impose.

But it was a historic occasion, nonetheless, and certain never to be repeated anywhere in Britain. Those who appeared in front of the largest crowd ever assembled for a match between two club sides were: *Celtic* – Kennaway; Hogg and Morrison; Geatons, Lyon and Patterson; Delaney, Buchan, McGrory, Crum and Murphy. *Aberdeen* – Johnstone; Cooper and Temple; Dunlop, Falloon and Thomson; Benyon, McKenzie, Armstrong, Mills and Lang. *Referee* – M.C. Hutton, Glasgow.

Aberdeen were appearing in the final of the Scottish Cup for the first time; Celtic could now claim a total of 23 appearances at the last stage of the competition.

Aberdeen, according to the colourful wordsmith Scrutator, writing in the Glasgow *Evening News*, were 'the neophytes from the north, making their first palpitating plunge into unknown waters'. By comparison, Scrutator believed, the Parkhead side appearing at Hampden represented 'inspiring history'.

The columns of *The Glasgow Herald* also reflected concern about Aberdeen's ability to deal with the strains and upheavals of the great occasion. Both sides were lying joint second in the league behind Rangers, who were assured of the title. 'As their positions indicate there is little between the teams so far as playing strength is concerned,' *The Herald* conceded.

However, in his pre-match appraisal, the paper's football correspondent also felt Hampden was a most disconcerting place for players. Temperament would play a large part in the outcome. Readers were reminded: 'Against Stenhousemuir and Motherwell, in earlier rounds, Celtic seemed to be doomed to defeat. But they rallied, forced draws and won the replays.' These were the qualities that made Celtic great cup fighters, *The Herald* enthused. 'Aberdeen have football strength but they have yet to demonstrate their ability as fighters – the power to take a blow and then retaliate and give more than they have taken,' their reporter argued.

The first blow to Aberdeen came after only 12 minutes, with Celtic attacking right from the start. A shot by McGrory was pushed out by Johnstone in the Aberdeen goal. The ball fell to Crum who netted.

The man from *The Glasgow Herald* who questioned the resilience of Aberdeen didn't have long to ponder their powers of retaliation, however. A minute after Crum put Celtic ahead, Armstrong equalised for Aberdeen.

The goal was almost a repeat of what happened earlier. Kennaway in the Celtic goal parried a shot from Mills. Armstrong, like Crum before him, reacted quickly. Now it was Kennaway's turn to retrieve the ball from the back of the net.

One-all at half-time, the goal that decided the match was scored 20 minutes from the end. Protesting furiously that McGrory handled before ridding himself of the ball, Aberdeen made the elementary mistake of not waiting for the referee to confirm their suspicions. No-one bothered to intercept Buchan when he accepted a pass from McGrory and headed determinedly in the direction of the Aberdeen goal.

That the Celtic inside-right didn't stop to discuss the niceties of the moment with anyone from the other side was hardly surprising. Nor was the outcome of his unopposed raid on the Aberdeen goal. With no-one around to offer support and assistance, the unfortunate Johnstone found himself beaten at the near post.

It was generally agreed Celtic deserved to win. In the words of one report: 'They struck with a swiftness, and passed with a precision, that Aberdeen never equalled.'

Now, on 29 April 1967, almost 30 years to the day since Celtic and Aberdeen established the European record for a match between club sides, another huge crowd packed Hampden, expecting to witness an enthralling clash. The teams were: *Celtic* – Simpson, Craig, Gemmell; Murdoch, McNeill, Clark; Johnstone, Wallace, Chalmers, Auld and Lennox. *Aberdeen* – Clark, Whyte, Shewan; Munro, McMillan, Peterson; Wilson, Smith, Storrie, Melrose and Johnston. *Referee* – W. Syme, Glasgow.

Celtic skipper Billy McNeill won the toss and elected to play against the wind. A crowd of 126,102 testified to the importance of the occasion.

Those who pinned their hopes on the men in the red shirts were entitled to bemoan the absence from Hampden of one man – Eddie Turnbull, ill and unable to attend. His presence was obviously missed. As Glyn Edwards, writing in *The Glasgow Herald*, reported: 'Had he been at the match he would doubtless have advised Aberdeen to change their tactics by the end of the first half hour, by which time Celtic, despite having the wind in their faces, had established a clear superiority in midfield and were practically encamped in their opponents' half of the field.'

According to Edwards the team from the north displayed an unrealistic dedication to caution. As a result 'play rarely reached the level of entertainment and skill which the crowd of 126,102 had every reason to expect'.

Two goals by Willie Wallace settled the match. *The Glasgow Herald* believed a third goal would have been superfluous. Their man at the match was also of the opinion that Aberdeen had been completely mastered by a Celtic team which never fully extended itself.

Hugh Taylor, in his review of the year, recalled that Aberdeen, who had been

111

crude and destructive early on in the match, performed with spirit, speed and skill towards the end. But what impressed him most was the sheer professionalism of Celtic which had been breathtaking throughout. 'Confidence,' recorded Taylor, 'belief in themselves and their colleagues, and faith in the tactics of manager Jock Stein, enveloped Celtic like a suit of impregnable, shining armour. They reminded one of a champion boxer at the peak of his prowess, carefully conserving energy, breaking out only when there's a glimpse of a chance – but always taking care to be well on top of an opponent.'

In such circumstances a blow on the chin from Dundee United – who earned full points from a league match at Parkhead in midweek – could be absorbed without forcing the defending champions to falter seriously on their relentless march to another title; which was duly confirmed with a 2–2 draw against Rangers at Ibrox on 6 May.

Celtic – with four cups won – were on the verge of realising their impossible dream. Only one team stood between them and glory – the champions of Italy, and twice winners of the European Cup, Internazionale of Milan, who, as Stein suspected might happen, had been successful in their semi-final against CSK Sofia.

Stein didn't doubt that Inter, who would be contesting their third European Cup final in four years, provided the greatest challenge yet to everything Celtic had been working to achieve. A marked contrast in style between the two teams was bound to produce an intriguing contest of method and will. Celtic usually opted for an attacking style of play, whatever the state of the game, while Inter Milan always sought to score first and thereafter defend their slim lead: *catenaccio*, the Italians called it, with ill-concealed pride. The system, which everyone else hated, had been developed over many years by Helenio Herrera, coach of Inter Milan, and an acknowledged master tactician.

When it was known Inter Milan would be going to Lisbon to face Celtic in the final of the European Cup, everyone recalled how Jock Stein, in his early days as a manager at Dunfermline, had been to Italy to study Herrera's methods. Now that Celtic, managed by Stein, had qualified to meet Inter Milan, bossed by his old tutor, in the final of the European Cup, admirers of Stein were quick to claim that Lisbon would demonstrate, for the whole of the football world to see, how the master-pupil relationship which once existed between the two men had been reversed, and the Italians' reviled system of *catenaccio* discredited forever.

When Celtic lined up against Internazionale of Milan to contest the 12th annual final of the European Champions' Cup, on 25 May 1967, only four names adorned the huge trophy waiting to be won – Real Madrid of Spain, Benfica from Portugal, and from the same northern Italian city, AC Milan and Internazionale. On five consecutive occasions, between 1956 and 1960, the engravers employed by UEFA became well-practised in the art of spelling out the name of Real Madrid. Amazingly, for all these years, starting with the first competition, the men in white were masters of the entire continent.

Then came their neighbours on the Iberian peninsula, Benfica, in consecutive seasons; followed by the Italians, AC Milan and Internazionale, who also won twice, in 1964 and 1965; before Real Madrid commandeered the competition for an incredible sixth time in 11 years, by defeating Partizan Belgrade 2–1 in Brussels in 1966.

Generally, these were high-scoring days. Real Madrid, on their way to victory in the first five finals of the European Cup, scored 18 times. Their losing opponents, Reims twice, Fiorentina, AC Milan and Eintracht, between them scored eight.

The records show that, in the 1967 final against Internazionale, the Scottish champions, with goals by Gemmell and Chalmers, beat the Italians by the odd goal in three. What the records cannot possibly convey was the glorious manner of that marvellous achievement – 'the exhilarating speed and the bewildering variety of skills that destroyed Inter', as witnessed by Hugh McIlvanney of *The Observer*.

In the Portuguese capital, as the day and hour of the match approached, Stein confided a little about his methods, and what he thought of the players under his control, to Albert Barham, the man from *The Guardian*. 'Success has not altered them. I have boys I have to bark at, others I must encourage,' Stein told him. 'Each I treat differently. Their success is my success.

'You could not buy the prestige this season has brought us,' Stein went on. 'Nor gain a greater height to which the club's stature has been raised.'

For the benefit of his predominantly English readership – nobody in Scotland who studied the sports pages, however casually, needed to be told! – Barham noted that Celtic were poised to accomplish something no other European side had ever achieved – League, National Cup and European Cup – in the same season.

Celtic had been brilliantly prepared, physically and mentally, the always thoughtful John Rafferty assured readers of *The Scotsman* – 'and today', Rafferty continued happily, on the day preceding the match, 'the green and white hordes have been pouring into Lisbon to give them encouragement'.

Rafferty was in no doubt it would be a great night for Scottish football, and British football generally, if Celtic could break the continental monopoly of victories in the European Cup; adding, for the benefit of anyone who might have missed the high-level nature of his own expectations, that this was the result, in all honesty, he anticipated.

By the time his familiar by-line next appeared no-one enjoyed saying I told you so more than John Rafferty!

It didn't matter that Inter scored first, after only seven minutes, from a penalty, conceded by Jim Craig, the Celtic right-back, and scored by Mazzola. Or that the Italians spent the next 55 minutes defending desperately, their hearts set on proving *catenaccio* worked, before Gemmell, the other Celtic full-back, took a pass from the previously unfortunate Craig, appropriately enough, somewhere outside the Inter Milan penalty area, and blasted an unstoppable shot past the helpless Italian goalkeeper, Sarti, leaving Chalmers to score the seemingly inevitable winner five minutes from time.

Playing in front of 56,000 spectators – many of them sporting the green and white colours of the first British side ever to reach the final of the European Cup, plus millions more watching on television – the teams were: *Celtic* – Simpson, Craig, Gemmell, Murdoch, McNeill, Clark, Johnstone, Wallace, Chalmers, Auld, Lennox. *Inter Milan* – Sarti, Burgnich, Facchetti, Bedin, Gaurneri, Picchi, Domenghini, Bicicli, Mazzola, Capellini, Corso. *Referee* – K. Tschenscher, West Germany.

There was only ever one team in it – and no-one could grudge Celtic their latest, and greatest, title: Champions of Europe!

It should have been the cause of some complaint against a higher authority that the official scoreline showed only a single goal separating the two teams. This was a churlish and truly misleading statistic, as most observers later agreed, including millions of television viewers world-wide who had seen Inter outclassed – no, not outclassed, but annihilated, as John Rafferty reported. 'If annihilated needs explaining, it should be said that Celtic – after losing a goal to a penalty kick and being pestered and frustrated by an unsatisfactory referee – destroyed the theorising of the alleged magician, Herrera, with refreshing, attacking football. Had they won by four goals it would have been a fair reflection of the play,' Rafferty insisted.

Hugh McIlvanney, writing in *The Observer*, thought Celtic 'a team without a serious weakness and with tremendous strengths in vital positions. But when one has eulogised the exhilarating speed and the bewildering variety of skills that destroyed Inter – the unshakable assurance of Clark, the murderously swift overlapping of the full-backs, the creative energy of Auld in midfield, the endlessly astonishing virtuosity of Johnstone, the intelligent and ceaseless running of Chalmers – even with all this, ultimately the element that impressed most profoundly was the massive heart of this Celtic side.'

On the subject of Stein himself, he added: 'Despite the extreme tension he must have felt, he never lost the bantering humour that keeps the morale of his expeditions unfailingly high.'

There was also praise for Celtic from Helenio Herrera who, gracious in defeat, conceded the better side won. The manager of England, Sir Alf Ramsey, who watched the game on television with the England side in Vienna, said he thought Inter had been completely outclassed. Speaking for the entire England party, Ramsay added: 'Everyone here is delighted with the result.'

An old friend, Bill Shankly, manager of Liverpool, and a man with a peculiar sense of the importance of football to the world at large – according to Shankly the game was more important than life itself – expressed the view that Stein, having steered his side to victory in the European Cup, was now immortal.

When the triumphant Celtic party flew into Glasgow, to a heroes' welcome from thousands of fans, the chairman of Rangers, John Lawrence, was waiting at the airport with a generous handshake and a personal message of goodwill for his Old Firm counterpart, the chairman of Celtic, Bob Kelly.

Regardless of their usual differences, people throughout Scotland recognised a unique triumph, a great victory which they were more than happy to share and acknowledge without rancour.

A telegram despatched by the Right Reverend Dr W. Roy Sanderson, Moderator of the General Assembly of the Church of Scotland, meeting in Edinburgh, crossed the official religious divide by extending 'congratulations to the Celtic Football Club on a splendid achievement that has added so greatly to our country's prestige in sport'.

In nine games in the European Cup the Glasgow side scored 18 goals and conceded five. Seven players – Simpson, Gemmell, Murdoch, McNeill, Clark, Johnstone and Chalmers – played in every one.

Up to, and including, the European Cup final, their high success rate meant Celtic were obliged to field teams on 62 different competitive occasions that season. It was a record, some commentators observed, which did little to support the widely held view that British clubs played too many games to win anything worthwhile.

The idea that the European Cup had been won by Celtic, not just for themselves and their own supporters, but for the benefit of everyone in Scotland, soon took hold.

Stein himself was always the first to admit his men could be as hard and professional as anybody; and, with characters like Gemmell and Auld around, Celtic knew how to look after themselves whatever the circumstances. But that day in Lisbon, in the tree-fringed amphitheatre of the National Stadium, the men from Glasgow put their name on the European Cup with a dazzling display of the game's highest skills and a demonstration of courage and determination that left the Italians gasping.

'What a performance!' Stein said, talking to reporters afterwards. 'What a performance!' Stein could have added, just as sincerely, and without risk of anyone suggesting otherwise, 'What a season! What a season!'

It is hard to imagine the achievements of that special Celtic team, during season 1966–67, being repeated. Although, for the unimaginable good of Scottish football, those who follow the game are entitled to hope that others, most notably Rangers – even Celtic again – will try.

CHAPTER TEN

Following the exhilaration of Wembley in 1967, despite the English critics' reservations about the measure of Scotland's achievement, there was little in the way of good news for followers of the national side, either home or away. For most of the seven bleak years that followed it was hardly surprising the English kept saying they had been right to question the lasting value of their neighbour's performance against the world champions.

At Hampden a 1–1 draw in 1968, and a no-scoring draw in 1970, sandwiched a 4–1 drubbing at Wembley. The four defeats in a row which followed would have been enough to induce a state of near catatonic shock in many otherwise healthy followers of the dark blue side.

The pain of a 3–1 defeat at Wembley in 1971 was made worse by the contemptuous manner with which it was inflicted. Even the most enthusiastic Scottish supporter, flinching before the arrogance of the men in white shirts, was forced to admit England won easily.

Hampden, a year later, provided on-field pain of a different kind.

The crushing burden of carrying Scottish aspirations had been removed from the quiet, gentlemanly figure of Bobby Brown. Tommy Docherty was now in charge of the national side.

Captain of Scotland in his days as a player, Docherty was a robust and cheerful character whose curriculum vitae also included periods as manager of Chelsea, Rotherham, Queen's Park Rangers, Aston Villa and Oporto in Portugal. 'Every time a Scot takes on the world and wins I feel proud,' Docherty once asserted.

With his appointment it wasn't surprising that Hampden attitudes were soon restored to their customary condition: a potent mixture, on the part of the vast majority of supporters, of sublime hope, blind faith and not much charity when it came to affording any England team due credit for its achievements.

Fortunately, it was a sublime view of the world not shared by the manager. 'The players know the score about England,' he insisted prior to the 1972 Hampden match which England were expected to lose. 'They know they are not as poor as they are being made out to be. They know there is likely to be a backlash and are prepared for it,' Docherty added.

However, with his mind no doubt on the World Cup qualifiers ahead,

Docherty also believed the old conception of Hampden as a show match was changing. 'We have always got to be looking ahead to something bigger,' he told a saddened John Rafferty before the match.

Scotland required only one point from the match, played at Hampden on 27 May 1972, to secure the British championship. John Rafferty, writing in *The Scotsman*, forecast that England would try and smother play in midfield. 'There is, into the bargain,' he continued angrily, 'the real fear that this team will kick the good football out of the opposition.'

In front of a crowd totalling 119,325, the teams were: *Scotland* – Clark (Aberdeen), Brownlie (Hibernian), Donachie (Manchester United), Bremner (Leeds United), McNeill (Celtic), Moncur (Newcastle United), Lorimer (Leeds), Gemmill (Derby County), Macari (Celtic), Law (Manchester United), Hartford (West Bromwich Albion). *England* – Banks (Stoke City), Madeley (Leeds), Hughes (Liverpool), Storey (Arsenal), McFarland (Derby County), Moore (West Ham), Ball (Arsenal), Bell (Manchester City), Chivers (Tottenham Hotspur), Marsh (Manchester City), Hunter (Leeds). *Referee* – S. Gonella, Italy.

It wasn't a match made memorable by the quality of its play or the excitement generated by a solitary, mesmerising, wonderful goal. The goal that settled the match was a scrappy affair, scored by Alan Ball midway through the first half.

The main talking point among the spectators was the high level of crunching violence that began, with carefully applied ferocity, in the first few minutes of the game, most of it coming from the England side. As usual, however, provoked or not, there were few on the Scottish side prepared to allow the toughest methods to go unchallenged.

Just as England led by the narrowest of margins at the finish so they were just ahead in the number of physical fouls awarded against them by the Italian referee: 24, to 22 incurred by Scotland. Apparently, the referee thought the game had been hard but correct.

Sir Alf Ramsey, the England manager, appeared to disagree. 'The physical aspect of the match I disliked intensely,' he admitted later to reporters. Sir Alf thought the violence, which was largely confined to the first 20 minutes, could be blamed on the fact both teams were intent on winning, the atmosphere in the ground, the wind, rivalry between players, including rivalry between players of the same club playing on opposite sides.

Tommy Docherty pronounced himself disappointed but not discouraged by the result. 'The physical aspect was partly due to the occasion,' he shrugged.

However, during this period, the 5–0 destruction inflicted on Scotland by England on an ice-bound pitch at Hampden in February 1973, lives in the memory as probably the worst experience of these dispiriting years.

To be thrashed 5–0 by England at Hampden would have been bad enough at any time, of course. The fact that this particular match had been arranged as part of the SFA centenary celebrations simply made it all the more painful and humiliating to endure. If anyone believed the visitors should show their hosts a little respect and kindness on their hundredth birthday the final scoreline suggests no-one bothered to inform them of this fact.

Right from the start something about the evening didn't sit right. The choice of date missed the actual anniversary by several weeks and, given the weather, there was little joy in the Hampden atmosphere.

A meagre crowd, which only just exceeded 48,000, risible considering the importance of the occasion in the history of organised football in Scotland, could have been forgiven thinking the birthday celebrations had been hi-jacked by Bobby Moore, the England captain.

A splendid player and a first-class England skipper, Moore could never be described as a great favourite with the Hampden crowd. But this was hardly surprising. The sight of the England captain at Wembley, holding the World Cup aloft, was an enduring, but less than happy, memory to the vast majority of Scottish fans. His tenancy of the England leadership also coincided with a dismal period in Scottish football history, particularly when the national side was forced to confront an England team with Bobby Moore at its head.

That the elegant, fair-haired, smiling Moore quite clearly enjoyed his role, and always appeared happy to do whatever he could on a football field to add to Scottish discomfiture, was another, quite understandable, reason, he was never likely to win a popularity contest at Hampden.

Few, on a bitterly cold night, at snow-covered Hampden on 14 February 1973, would have been prepared to elect, as a celebration of 100 years of Scottish football, a match in which Bobby Moore won his 100th cap for England. An on-field ceremony before the kick-off, during which Moore was presented with a silver salver to mark his 100 caps, only added to the aggravation of the crowd.

But that was nothing to the speed with which Scotland's birthday celebrations, already in part eclipsed by the presentation to the England captain, collapsed. It was soon evident that those few Scots who braved the icy conditions, in the hope of participating in a memorable Hampden occasion, would be bitterly disappointed; their hearts were as cold as their feet at the finish.

It was Willie Ormond's first appearance as manager of the national side, following the resignation of Tommy Docherty to take charge of Manchester United. Ormond was the man responsible for team selection. But most of the players who lined up at the start had been favoured by Docherty during his period in charge.

The teams appeared as follows: *Scotland* – Clark (Aberdeen), Forsyth (Manchester United), Donachie (Manchester City), Bremner (Leeds United), Colquhoun (Sheffield United), Buchan (Manchester United), Lorimer (Leeds United), Dalglish (Celtic), Macari, Graham, Morgan (all Manchester United). *England* – Shilton (Leicester), Storey (Arsenal), Hughes (Liverpool), Bell (Manchester City), Madeley (Leeds United), Moore (West Ham), Ball (Arsenal), Channon (Southampton), Chivers (Tottenham), Clarke (Leeds), Peters (Tottenham). *Referee* – R. Wurtz (France).

In his preview of the match for *The Glasgow Herald* Ian Archer thought the Scotland manager had chosen the best available side. 'Scotland tonight celebrates 100 years of football history, seeking once more the only kind of victory that has ever mattered to the ordinary people of this country,' Archer enthused.

One of Ormond's keenest admirers during his period as manager of Scotland, and also no lover of the England football team and what he considered its sterile ways, Archer believed Scotland could win 'if they decide to tease and torture their opponents and not charge into a hand to hand combat'.

'That is not always our natural style,' Archer admitted, 'but at Hampden Park victory will go to the cool ones. We must for once not be our own worst enemies.'

The game actually started well for Scotland with Lorimer and Macari both active in the England goal area. But long before any sense of hopeful anticipation developed on the snow-covered terracing, England went ahead.

The unhappy nature of the goal should have been a warning, to the meagre Scotland support present, that they were about to endure an evening of horror unmatched at the Mount Florida ground in the present century, and, therefore, an experience previously confined to the realms of nightmare. For England went into the lead without the serious involvement of a single player dressed in a white shirt.

Five minutes into the game Peter Lorimer connected with a harmless-looking cross; and watched stunned as the ball finished behind Clark in his own goal.

Nine minutes later England went further ahead. A long ball from Hughes found Chivers who passed to Clarke. The Leeds man didn't stop to wonder about the coincidence and chances, of an Englishman called Clarke confronting a Scotsman called Clark in such dramatic and historic circumstances at so famous a ground. He scored.

A minute later Clark of the Scottish name was probably wishing he was somewhere else, in warmer, gentler company perhaps, celebrating St Valentine's Day, rather than at the national stadium, on a freezing cold night, playing in goal for his country, on the occasion of the unhappy 100th birthday celebrations of the Scottish Football Association.

This time it was a long throw-in by Martin Chivers which confused the men operating immediately in front of Clark. At odds with the treacherous conditions, Bremner and company were unable to stop Mike Channon adding a dispiriting third goal to the England total.

It would have been out of character for the Scots, led by the pugnacious Billy Bremner, to do anything other than try. But their opponents, with a three-goal lead, were already too far in front, and too strong in defence, all the way back to Peter Shilton in goal, to be caught. The game was over as a contest, friendly or not, whatever that might be, considering the teams involved, when Channon scored.

Scotland came close to reducing the England lead only once when the seemingly invincible Shilton failed to hold a thunderous free-kick from Peter Lorimer. The ball slipped from his grasp and Colin Stein, who replaced the injured Willie Morgan early in the first half, put the ball in the England net, only to be judged off-side by Monsieur Wurtz.

The goals that followed, by Chivers and Clarke, simply added to the humiliation of an ill-starred night which ended with what remained of the crowd booing the dejected Scotland players into the Hampden tunnel. 'The customers were entitled to be angry,' fumed an aggrieved Alex Cameron, writing in the *Daily Record*. 'It was a diabolical performance.'

Ian Archer was also prominent among the mourners. He told readers of *The Glasgow Herald*: 'It is hard to avoid the conclusion that this match marked the end of a time in which we could claim even rough equality with the English.' It had been a sad end to 100 years of history, Archer wailed. 'Increasingly, we will have to tell our youngsters of our prowess through the history books and not by living example.'

Before the match, Willie Ormond, the new Scotland team manager, had been saying he thought his side could win the centenary match comfortably. Afterwards he was forced to admit: 'This was a terrible blow.'

It was a measure of the spirit and tenacity of the man that, following another 1–0 defeat at Wembley the same year, he was able to recover in time to qualify for the World Cup finals in Germany the following year – and inflict a 2–0 defeat on non-qualifiers England at Hampden. This was a side that owed everything to

Jimmy Johnstone, following an incident on the Firth of Clyde in an open boat, was in superb form against England at Hampden on 18 May 1974. Scotland – heading for West Germany and the World Cup finals, while non-qualifiers England stayed at home – won 2–0

120

Ormond's own preferences and vision, and little to the departed Tommy Docherty.

In its assessment of a season most people remember with pride, *The Scottish Football Book* listed a miserable afternoon in May 1974 as the day of national recovery. That was the day the lions roared back!

'Suddenly it all came back – all the old Scottish arrogance, artistry and shooting power,' *The Scottish Football Book*, exuding its own rampant enthusiasm, recalled colourfully. 'And once again Hampden, dripping rain, was a Scottish fortress, grim, grey but triumphant, with the tartan-favoured thousands drunk with emotion and ecstasy, cheering wildly and transforming the bleak day into a festival of colour with flags waving like a field of lilies in the breeze.'

This was the year of the 'Jimmy Johnstone nearly lost at sea' carfuffle. While the Scottish squad prepared at Largs, it will be remembered, the little Celtic winger took advantage of an evening excused the rigours of normal team discipline to celebrate his release perhaps a mite unwisely.

It all ended with Johnstone alone in an open boat, minus an oar, the Firth of Clyde drifting past and the Irish Sea beckoning.

Rescue, when it came, was accompanied by banner headlines, questions concerning the manager's methods and much hilarity at Johnstone's expense – all of it disguising great and genuine relief that the little Celtic star, with his own enduring place in the hearts of the majority of Scottish supporters, regardless of their usual loyalties, was safe.

Appearing in the match against England, dripping wet from nothing more serious than the heavy downpour which characterised an otherwise happy day, Johnstone was in superb form. With a crowd of 93,271 resolutely defying the conditions, the teams at Hampden on 18 May 1974 were: *Scotland* – Harvey (Leeds United), Jardine (Rangers), McGrain (Celtic), Bremner (Leeds), Holton (Manchester United), Blackley (Hibernian), Lorimer (Leeds) Johnstone (Celtic), Jordan (Leeds), Dalglish (Celtic), Hay (Celtic). *England* – Shilton (Leicester City), Nish (Derby County), Pejic (Stoke City), Hughes (Liverpool), Hunter (Leeds), Todd (Derby), Channon (Southampton), Bell (Manchester City), Worthington (Leicester), Weller (Leicester), Peters (Tottenham Hotspur). *Referee* – Van der Kroff, Holland.

The score at the finish was 2–0 in favour of the home side. The fact that both Scotland goals were converted by Englishmen wasn't the result of any great carelessness on the part of Shilton or anyone else in the England defence. From the visitors' point of view it was unfortunate they succeeded in scoring not once but twice against themselves in the course of a single Hampden afternoon.

It wasn't an experience any side crowded with famous names would wish upon itself at any time. But an England side sporting a new manager, Joe Mercer, who had been appointed to a caretaker role following the departure of Sir Alf Ramsey, being made to suffer so cruelly in front of a Scottish crowd was a rare sort of humiliation best avoided.

It would have been better all round if Jordan and Dalglish, the players who saw their final shots turned past Shilton by Pejic and Todd, had been able to claim sole credit for the goals. On both occasions, however, Scotland went ahead as a result of intense pressure on the England defence.

The opening goal was inspired by Bremner who split the England defence with a beautifully judged ball which was heading straight to his club-mate Lorimer. The towering Shilton, knowing the likely outcome if the Leeds player, with his instant reflexes and devastating shot, was given the slightest chance in front of goal, dived at his feet. The ball skidded towards Jordan, another player accustomed to wearing the white outfit of Leeds who could show an unfriendly streak in front of goal.

When the ball left Jordan most of Hampden believed it was on its way to the back of the empty England net. Pejic did what he could to stop it. The unfortunate Stoke City player was unlikely to consider assisting the ball into his own net the best way to mark his first Hampden appearance.

When the Scots went further ahead after 31 minutes, Todd was probably more culpable in putting the ball into his own net than Pejic before him. But once again England were in all kinds of trouble when Shilton was beaten for the second and last time that afternoon.

The incident that brought the goal started with Jimmy Johnstone, in brilliant form, back-heeling to Lorimer who immediately despatched a powerful cross towards Dalglish. When the Celtic star connected with the ball, there was always a chance the generally reliable Shilton was in a good position to put an end to that particular Scotland attack. It was his misfortune, and that of Todd, that the desperately lunging Derby County defender reached the ball first. With the England goalkeeper lying helpless on the ground, Scotland were two up.

And back in the business of convincingly beating England, on their own home ground at least.

After acknowledging the plaudits of the large Hampden crowd, many of whom stayed behind to cheer themselves hoarse long after the match ended, Willie Ormond was rewarded with praise from all sides.

The reaction of his beaten rival, the hugely experienced and thoroughly likeable, Joe Mercer, was particularly welcome. 'Scotland always impressed me as a fine World Cup side,' Mercer revealed without rancour.

Ormond acknowledged it had been a good victory. However, he also thought Scotland should have scored more goals. 'We can do better yet,' he promised.

It was typical of Scotland, and not at all surprising to anyone who followed the country's football fortunes with close attention, that a more than creditable performance in the World Cup in Germany was immediately followed by another heavy defeat at Wembley in 1975.

On this occasion the match ended with England 5–1 ahead, a score which did much to avenge the horrors, for England, of the previous year's Hampden experience.

Those who continued to resent England's absence from the World Cup finals in Germany, from which Scotland emerged, almost miraculously, unbeaten, were also entitled to assume an air of satisfaction at the humbling of Ormond's impudent warriors. But honest folk among the huge army of travelling Scottish supporters would have been forced to admit it wasn't much different from the way they behaved in 1967.

Before the 1975 Wembley match Don Revie, the England manager, had been predicting victory for Scotland. 'They have settled well, played well and must be favourites,' Revie contended with rough simplicity.

Revie, who was in charge of the England side at a low ebb in their fortunes, following his own great years as manager of Leeds United, may have been offering an honest assessment of the likely outcome of an important match, based on his own considerable professional experience and knowledge of the opposing teams. More likely he was indulging in an unsettling pre-match foray against the Scotland manager, Willie Ormond. A little gamesmanship was not untoward under the circumstances: England needed to win.

Revie was bound to believe he could deliver a result with a decent, if not notably strong, England side that included Kevin Keegan, appearing at an early stage in his brilliant career.

Once the visitors had been accorded the courtesies of a polite and considerate host telling the world they were favourites to win, there was nothing in the rules of engagement that precluded taking advantage of their weakest link.

And with Scotland at Wembley, history suggested this was most probably the goalkeeper. On this unhappy occasion the man wearing the number one jersey was Stewart Kennedy, of Rangers, a relative newcomer to international honours, with only four previous caps to his credit. Wembley, 1975, the big one against England, the ultimate honour outside Hampden, was also his last.

On 24 May 1975, with at least 30,000 Scots helping to swell the Wembley crowd, the teams were: *England* – Clemence (Liverpool), Whitworth (Leicester), Beattie (Ipswich), Bell (Derby County), Ball (Arsenal), Channon (Southampton), Johnson (Ipswich), Francis (Queen's Park Rangers), Keegan (Liverpool). *Scotland* – Kennedy (Rangers), Jardine (Rangers), McGrain (Celtic), Munro (Wolverhampton), McQueen (Leeds), Rioch (Derby), Dalglish (Celtic), Conn (Tottenham), Parlane (Rangers), MacDougall (Norwich), Duncan (Hibernian). *Referee* – R. Gloeckner, East Germany.

In the course of a disastrous afternoon the first goal lost by the unfortunate Kennedy, as described by Geoffrey Green in the ultimate London paper, *The Times*, was 'a firmly hit rising shot to Kennedy's right side, but one surely within the scope of an international goalkeeper'.

That the Scotland goalkeeper failed to reach this opening salvo, struck after only five minutes of the match, from all of 20 yards by Gerry Francis, is history. Two minutes later, 'frozen in misjudgement, like a statue in the marketplace', wrote Geoffrey Green – the goalkeeper was completely out of position to deal with a Beattie header from a Keegan cross. The match was barely seven minutes old and Scotland were two goals down!

There was little chance now of the game developing into a serious contest which Scotland could win. An England side, playing at Wembley, was never likely to lose from such a commanding position.

In fact, by general consent, there was little difference between the two sides apart from the truly dreadful performance of Kennedy in the Scottish goal. Four minutes from half-time he compounded his earlier mistakes by leaving a large part of the goal area undefended. Bell, taking full advantage of his generosity, duly increased the home side's lead.

A penalty on half-time, given after Colin Todd handled, and competently converted by Bruce Rioch, offered Scotland the tiniest glimpse of hope going into the Wembley tunnel. Never much, given the state of the half-time scoreboard, it was soon obliterated by two more England goals, the first scored by Francis, off a deflection which did little to help Kennedy, the second by Johnson at the end of a desperate goalmouth scramble.

'It was all as simple as hopscotch,' according to Geoffrey Green in *The Times*.

Most people agreed with Geoffrey Green, although Alan Ball, the England captain, admired but unloved by Scottish supporters for the intensity of spirit he invariably displayed in matches against Scotland, insisted England didn't win easily. Ball also praised Scotland for continuing to attack long after victory was quite obviously beyond their reach.

Predictably, much of the blame for the final result settled on the goalkeeper, Stewart Kennedy. Perhaps unfairly, he never played for Scotland again, his career with Rangers withered, and he drifted into comparative obscurity.

Yet, nearly 20 years after his disastrous performance for Scotland against England, the name Stewart Kennedy continues to be remembered, alongside other Scots ghosts of Wembleys past, Fred Martin and Frank Haffey. Reserved only for goalkeepers who fail, it is a bleak sort of immortality.

CHAPTER ELEVEN

For almost half a century, some of the most memorable matches played at Hampden have featured neither the international side, nor the last two in the game's oldest, and most prestigious, competition, the Scottish Cup, a generally uplifting occasion well into its second century, most of it spent at the Mount Florida ground.

'The history of the league cup competition is one of the strangest chapters in the story of Scottish football,' historian Bob Crampsey suggested pointedly in *The First 100 Years*, published in 1990 to mark the centenary of the Scottish Football League. For a quarter of a century, starting with its inception during the war years, the league cup had been an outstanding success, Crampsey maintained. Then, for a whole decade, between 1967 and 1977, 'it increasingly lost its way, to such an extent that the tournament at one stage seemed scarcely viable'.

It may be all the more remarkable, therefore, that the final of the league cup – known in recent years, during the period of its greatest success, as the Skol Cup – is now one of the near-guaranteed highlights of the Hampden season.

Of course, any competition whose honours include Rangers winning no fewer than 17 times in 45 years, while losing disastrously on one occasion to their oldest rivals, Celtic, by six clear goals . . . as well as Partick Thistle, against all the odds, defeating a Celtic team that included three Lisbon Lions – Gemmell, Murdoch and Johnstone, with a fourth member of that wonderful team, Jim Craig, coming on as substitute for the injured Johnstone – by an amazing three-goal margin . . . and a match between Rangers and Aberdeen that is a certain starter in any contest to decide the most exciting match ever seen at the national stadium, excluding Real Madrid versus Eintracht Frankfurt in the 1960 European Cup final, probably, without question the all-time great game . . . is entitled to a special place in football history.

Since the war only ten clubs have won the right to see their names adorn the modern league cup. Rangers won it first, on 5 April 1947, defeating Aberdeen 4–0 in front of 82,584 spectators.

A year later not many more people, spread across two matches, saw East Fife defeat Falkirk by four goals to one, following a goalless draw in the final proper; the first of three wins registered at the same stage of the same competition by the remarkable little Methil club.

East Fife had been winners of the Scottish Cup in 1938, the year of the vain-glorious Empire Exhibition held at Bellahouston Park in Glasgow, and only a year before the SFA decided to abandon the competition until wider hostilities ceased to interfere with the conduct of organised football in Scotland. Kilmarnock, their opponents at Hampden, on 23 April 1938, had twice been winners of the Scottish Cup, as well as future league champions.

In the league cup, two years after their victory over Falkirk in season 1947–48, East Fife won again; defeating Dunfermline Athletic, another side from the wee kingdom, 3–0 in the final.

Then, on 23 October 1953, one of the largest crowds ever assembled for a league cup final at Hampden – 88,529 – was treated to five goals; with East Fife winning 3–2 against Partick Thistle, making their first appearance at the last stage of a competition they would one day galvanise.

Three wins in seven years by East Fife, in the second most important cup competition in the country, was a remarkable record by any standards. Only Rangers and Dundee, with two wins each, approached the Methil side's marvellous achievement.

The league cup was now eight years old and clubs such as Celtic, Hearts and Aberdeen were all waiting to see their names appear on the new trophy. Celtic and Hearts hadn't even made the final!

Hearts didn't achieve the first of their four wins in the competition until season 1954–55, when they defeated Motherwell, the 1950 winners, 4–2. Aberdeen, making their second league cup final appearance the following year, defeated St Mirren 2–1.

A year later, more than a little belatedly for a club of their stature, Celtic arrived at Hampden in the company of Partick Thistle. Forced to endure ten whole years without achieving even an appearance in the final of the league cup, there was a growing conviction among some Celtic supporters, and those who steered their thoughts, for their own advantage, in the sports pages of the newspapers, that this was one competition in which their appearance was somehow jinxed.

It had been eight years since a Glasgow club last won the league cup and Celtic manager Jimmy McGrory didn't treat the resulting offence lightly. Before the game McGrory conceded quietly: 'This is the only major trophy we haven't yet won. We'd like to take it and we'll be trying all we know.'

Gair Henderson was careful to remind readers of the *Evening Times* that, in season 1948–49, Celtic lost the Charity Cup to Thistle, 2–1. Henderson believed the present defences looked about equal, with the Celtic half-back line just that little bit stronger. 'But I reckon the final will be decided on forward power,' Henderson went on; a view, almost everyone agreed, that certainly favoured Celtic.

Thistle had been plagued with injuries as the day of the match approached and manager Davie Meiklejohn was unable to announce his team until shortly before kick-off. Celtic were at full strength and clearly determined to succeed where earlier Celtic sides failed, assorted teams with Scottish league champion-

Maurice Johnston scores his second goal for Scotland in a 1990 World Cup qualifying match against France at Hampden. Scotland won 2–0

Willie Miller suffered an ankle injury, and was later substituted, in this clash with Hansen of Norway during the 1990 World Cup qualifying campaign

Gary McAllister is at full stretch against Poland's Dziekanowski, with Stuart McCall and Murdo McLeod nearby

A fierce tackle by the Finnish player Petaja sends Gordon Durie flying during a match at Hampden

Argentina provided formidable opposition when they appeared at Hampden, in a pre-World Cup match, in 1990. Despite the attention of two defenders, Richard Gough heads for goal

Alex McLeish foils an attack as Scotland battle to save a crucial home point against Yugoslavia during the 1990 World Cup qualifying campaign

Despite injury, goalkeeper Ally Maxwell performed heroically for Motherwell against Dundee United in the 1991 Scottish Cup final. Motherwell won 4–3

The 1991 Skol Cup ended with an east coast final, Hibs against Dunfermline, which the Easter Road side won

Following the 1989 Scottish Cup final a jubilant Joe Miller – who scored the only goal of the match – and Celtic skipper Roy Aitken parade the trophy won against Rangers

The 1990 Scottish Cup final between Aberdeen and Celtic was decided on penalties. Aberdeen won

For more than a decade the Aberdeen defensive partnership of Willie Miller and Alex McLeish figured prominently for club and country at Hampden

Messrs Brown, Souness and Steven, aboard the Rangers team bus, keep a tight grip on the 1990 League Cup, won against Celtic

Bollan of Scotland powers his way past Al-Hammali of Saudi Arabia during the final of the FIFA Under-16 World Tournament played at Hampden on 24 June 1989. Saudi Arabia took the trophy on penalties after extra time

The Scotland team – who had been drawing 2–2 with Saudi Arabia after extra time in the final of the World Under-16 tournament, played at Hampden in 1989 – stayed behind to salute their supporters and applaud their opponents from the field

National coach Andy Roxburgh is capped by an enthusiastic fan after securing a place in the 1990 World Cup finals in Italy, with a draw against Norway at Hampden on 15 November 1989

Following a 1–1 draw with Norway at Hampden on 15 November 1989 these young fans can contemplate an unpredictable summer in Italy the following year

ships and victories in the Scottish Cup and Coronation Cup to their credit since the league cup started.

But on 27 October 1956, not many people bothered to watch them try. Either the majority of fans believed the result was a foregone conclusion or wet, miserable conditions kept them away. The crowd totalled 58,973, a considerable drop in numbers from those who watched the Maryhill side lose to East Fife three years earlier. The teams were: *Celtic* – Beattie, Haughney and Fallon; Evans, Jack and Peacock; Welsh, Collins, McPhail, Tully and Fernie. *Partick Thistle* – Ledgerwood, Kerr and Gibb; Collins, Davidson and Mathers; McKenzie, Smith, Slogan, Wright and Ewing. *Referee* – J.A. Mowat, Glasgow.

This was an era before substitutes were permitted and whatever hopes Partick Thistle entertained of repeating their eight-years-old Charity Cup success against the Parkhead side all but disappeared in the closing minutes of the first half. Two players, inside-right George Smith and centre-half Jimmy Davidson, both received injuries which thereafter reduced their contribution to the game to little more than an on-field presence: Smith could barely walk, let alone run, and a badly cut forehead, which required plaster, prevented Davidson heading the ball properly.

Gair Henderson reported: 'The man who looked as though he might win the game for Celtic was Bobby Collins, who lay deep right through the game and gave his other forwards enough good passes to win the game three or four times over.

'But the entire Celtic team must accept the blame for their failure to have the cup placed firmly on the Parkhead sideboard long before the end of the ninety minutes,' Henderson continued. 'Their shooting was lamentable and they never looked like beating the resolute Thistle defence by science.'

Events at Hampden on 27 October 1956 coincided with British troops landing in Suez. There was also a battle raging on the streets of Budapest where the Hungarian revolution was reported to have claimed the life of Ferenc Puskas. A report in the *Sunday Mail*, the day following the league cup final, claimed that Puskas came close to defecting in 1954, when the great Hungarian national side played Scotland at Hampden.

Polish born Czeslaw Muchniewski, who lived in Dumbreck, Glasgow, told the paper he met Puskas in a city department store on the Monday before the match and later for coffee. Puskas had been surprised to learn that top players in Scotland could earn as much as £15 a week. He also expressed an interest in playing for Celtic, it was claimed.

Puskas didn't die in the battle of Budapest. Happily, as time proved, Hampden and the rest of the football world, not least Madrid, hadn't seen the last of his marvellous skills.

Celtic supporters especially can only contemplate the havoc Puskas might have wrought on Partick Thistle – or, for that matter, any other Scottish club side – if he had been able to defect two years earlier; always assuming, of course, he managed to secure a place in the Parkhead side for Hampden that day!

However, no goals after extra time in the league cup final between Celtic and

Partick Thistle meant a Wednesday night replay. Tully replaced Walsh on the Celtic right wing, Fernie moved inside, and Mochan came into the side at outside-left; changes made by manager Jimmy McGrory from a position of strength.

On the other side of Glasgow, the Partick Thistle manager, Davie Meiklejohn, was forced to make changes from a players list wrecked by injury. Crawford replaced Davidson at the heart of the defence, Wright moved across to replace Smith, and Davie McParland, normally a winger, was named at inside-left.

Unchanged from the first match was the steely presence of the referee, Jack Mowat. Mowat was well known and feared for his strict interpretation of the rules. Between April 1950 and May 1960, his Hampden career included nine Scottish Cup finals, seven league cup finals and the European Cup final featuring Real Madrid and Eintracht Frankfurt. His appearance at the Mount Florida ground on the afternoon of Wednesday, 31 October 1956, guaranteed a no-nonsense approach to the game by the man in charge.

Thistle won the toss and kicked off for the benefit of all concerned, including a meagre crowd of 31,126, with the wind behind them. A dreary first half followed.

'Saturday was bad enough,' wailed one report. 'But that game at least carried the quality of nine men battling against eleven. The replay lacked even that.'

Writing in the *Evening Citizen*, George Aitken commented sorrowfully that lightning had struck the same place twice. Not one spark of genius lit the scene. And it would have taken several supermen to set the game alight, Aitken mused.

At least the second half produced some goals. Four minutes after the interval Billy McPhail pounced on a lob from Bobby Evans, as Tommy Ledgerwood, in the Thistle goal, and centre-half Willie Crawford both hesitated. Three minutes later Ledgerwood was again at fault when McPhail scored his second. Nine minutes later Bobby Collins scored from 18 yards.

An inept display by the Partick Thistle defence contrasted sadly with their courageous performance, against all odds, in the first game. But no-one who supported Celtic stopped to worry about that. A three-nil victory looked good in the record books. It also meant that the league cup, the one piece of silverware never before seen at the Glasgow east end ground, was on its way to Parkhead; where it remained for the next two years.

The fact that Celtic were able to retain the league cup, following their victory over Partick Thistle, wasn't in itself remarkable. Nor was it greatly significant that, the following year, it was Rangers who succeeded in securing the other final place.

The two great rivals were accustomed to encountering each other at some stage in the yearly struggle to achieve the game's highest honours; a tradition that has included more than a few cup finals! Until now the most important spoils have been shared almost equally. Rangers are ahead in the number of league titles won . . . Celtic enjoy a superior record in the Scottish Cup.

When the two clubs reached the final of the league cup in season 1957–58, neither side could boast much about their previous performance in this particular competition. Celtic were current holders, certainly, and appearing in the final for the second year running. Rangers, the reigning league champions, had been twice winners of the league cup and once losing finalists. But by their own exacting standards it wasn't much of a record, shared or otherwise.

Also of interest to anyone wishing to forecast the outcome of this latest encounter between the two sides: in two previous meetings that same season, Rangers defeated Celtic 2–0 in the Glasgow Cup and lost 3–2 in the league where it really mattered.

Neither side was destined to win the championship: that honour went to Hearts. But the bookies favoured Rangers to win the league cup, quoting 7–4 against Celtic. 'The odds seem to me like a most attractive proposition,' Gair Henderson mused in the *Evening Times*, 'and I am tempted to go right away and have a small nibble on Celtic.'

Forecasting the outcome of an Old Firm contest, especially a cup final, is always a tricky business. Gair Henderson believed the Parkhead side would win because they were the boys with the football craft and the ability to turn outfield play into goals.

On the afternoon of 19 October 1957, clear skies and an 82,293 crowd greeted the teams and match officials when they appeared from beneath the Hampden stand.

Neither side wished to contemplate defeat. Not winning was an unfavourable result against any opposition. But losing to one another in a major cup final was the worst possible result for either club. A single goal at the end of an otherwise splendid afternoon could mean the difference between total joy and absolute misery for thousands of fans.

Those who really cared, to the extent they were capable of working themselves into a frenzy of passion and despair over the result, would never accept an encounter between Rangers and Celtic was just another football match; only a game. Anyone who said so didn't know Glasgow with its dark undershift of screaming hate-filled sectarianism.

Newspapers based in Glasgow, not wishing to offend either side, usually contrived to make both look good: to do otherwise could have been bad for circulation. Considering the final result, however, those who claimed, in the interests of happy reading, that the sides about to contest the league cup final at Hampden on 19 October 1957 were well-matched, did nothing to enhance their own shaky credibility.

But, as *The Scottish Football Book*, in its review of the year, noted, on this occasion the critics felt there was little in it. A keen, tight match was anticipated. Rangers had started the season in great style, then slumped. Celtic, after a period of depression, were beginning to touch top form again. On the evidence of what transpired at Hampden, that much was certainly true.

However, if only on the grounds of basic humanity, when the time arrived to help one set of supporters prepare themselves for the worst day of their football lives, regular commentators on the great Scottish obsession didn't try hard enough. With referee Jack Mowat in charge the teams were: *Celtic* – Beattie, Donnelly, Fallon, Fernie, Evans, Peacock, Tully, Collins, McPhail, Wilson, Mochan. *Rangers* – Niven, Shearer, Caldow, McColl, Valentine, Davis, Scott, Simpson, Murray, Baird, Hubbard. *Referee* – J.A. Mowat, Rutherglen.

Bertie Peacock, the Celtic captain, a distinguished Irish international, had been a member of the league cup winning side the previous season. Ian McColl, who led out Rangers, was an Ibrox stalwart who played in two league cup winning sides and later managed Scotland. In terms of league cup final experience alone, however, the two captains were seriously out-ranked by the referee, Jack Mowat, who was taking charge of his seventh league cup final, including the previous year's replay, in six years. It was a remarkable record.

The two captains joined the referee in the centre circle to toss a coin and decide the direction of play. No-one knew it then, of course, but it was the last time any of them would appear in a league cup final at Hampden.

Mowat threw a coin in the air and the huge, familiar crowd, their numbers sufficient to populate a good-sized town, watched and waited as it rose and fell. There was satisfaction at the Celtic end when it was seen that this first exchange had been won by Peacock who elected to play with the wind.

The crowd shifted and growled. Everyone was impatient for the match to begin. But long before it finished more than half of those present were wishing it never happened.

The *Evening Times* match report, on sale later the same afternoon, confirmed for the benefit of those present, and all those who missed one of the worst days in Rangers' history, that the Ibrox side were in trouble right from the start – largely as a result of their half-back line failing to get into the game, according to the man from Buchanan Street. 'And with Mochan always the master of Shearer the Rangers rout was on,' his account continued beneath an enormous headline which proclaimed the almost unbelievable score in the league cup final at Hampden – Celtic 7 Rangers 1.

'Mochan was out on his own as the source of danger,' the *Evening Times* report, which would have been read aloud in certain city hostelries, prized as a souvenir of a famous occasion, and banned in others, within an hour of the match finishing, continued. 'He could run, he could shoot and he could cross the ball to precisely the right spot.'

Celtic were two up at half-time, and three ahead within ten minutes of the second half starting, with goals from Sammy Wilson, Neil Mochan and Billy McPhail.

With almost an hour played Billy Simpson scored for Rangers. It was a well-taken goal which began with Alex Scott cutting the ball to Ian McColl and the Rangers captain producing a perfect lob into the Celtic goalmouth where Simpson used his head to flick the ball past a previously idle Beattie.

But the reduction in Celtic's lead was soon restored. With astonishing speed and skill the Celtic attack quite simply destroyed the Rangers defence. Billy McPhail scored his second goal of the match after 68 minutes; seven minutes later the ebullient Mochan added his second; ten minutes from time McPhail completed his hat-trick with a *Boy's Own* effort which began with him heading the ball past Valentine deep in the Rangers half, before leaving the big centre-half stranded, collecting the ball as it dropped, and racing away on his own to push the ball past a flailing George Niven.

Then, to complete the Rangers' agony, in the very last minute of the game referee Mowat awarded Celtic a penalty after McPhail was brought down in the box.

There were many who thought, in all humanity, that the referee should have allowed Rangers the benefit of the doubt. Others feared the decision could, quite literally, cause a riot. Frustrated, angry fans had been fighting amongst themselves at the Rangers end, with women and children spilling on to the track to escape the danger, as police struggled to restore order.

But Willie Fernie, who had been one of the main architects in Rangers' destruction, wasn't paid to miss penalties. Pity for the afflicted didn't figure in his thoughts either as he put the ball past poor Niven who was reported, in all seriousness, to have complained wearily, 'Gosh, Willie, you might have left that one out.'

Gair Henderson, who was wise enough not to disclose any measure of personal gain at the expense of Rangers and the bookmakers' pre-match folly, later contemplated Rangers players, officials, and legions of light blue supporters licking their wounds. 'Every one of them must have died the death of a thousand cuts in the league cup final and they will be scarred for life by the seven horrible gashes which were inflicted at Hampden by a Celtic team merciless in their vast superiority,' he wrote.

His colleague, Cyril Horne, writing in *The Glasgow Herald*, thought the result was a comeuppance for all those who believed that results mattered more than method and encouraged players to indulge in a he-man type of game. 'Eleven players of Celtic Football Club did more in 90 minutes at Hampden Park on Saturday for the good of football than officialdom, in whose hands the destiny of the game lies, has done in years and years,' Horne contended. 'For with a display of such grandeur as has rarely graced the great, vast ground they proved conclusively the value of concentration on discipline and on the arts and crafts of the game to the exclusion of the so-called power play.'

It had been Rangers' worst-ever defeat, made doubly painful by the name of its perpetrators. There were those in Govan who might have been prepared to see a digit or two added to the 6–0 defeat their side suffered in the semi-final of the Scottish Cup at Hampden in 1954 rather than allow Celtic supporters the opportunity of a unique gloat at their expense.

On a clear autumn day at Hampden, Rangers had been humiliated beyond endurance by their oldest rivals. And there wasn't much consolation to be gained from all those pub historians who stared with glazed eyes at their drink and recalled, with what was left of their pride, how a Rangers side once defeated Celtic 8–1. That score didn't count as the occasion was a wartime southern league match, played at Ibrox, which wasn't included in official records.

During all the years the Glasgow clubs had been more or less posted missing from the final of the league cup, and East Fife in particular were establishing their marvellous record in the competition, winning three times, only one club produced a successful defence of the trophy: Dundee, who defeated Rangers 3–2 in 1951, and Kilmarnock 2–0 a year later.

Motherwell, Hearts and Aberdeen all posted wins in the first decade of the new competition. In future years Hibernian, Dundee United and Partick Thistle also added their names to the trophy.

Curiously enough, Dundee United, who have been twice winners of the league cup under the leadership of Jim McLean, have yet to win at Hampden. On the occasion of their first appearance in the final, against Aberdeen, in 1979, the first of two seasons when the tournament was known as the Bell's league cup, the first match, played at Hampden, ended in a draw and the replay was moved to Dens Park where the home town side duly won 2–0.

A year later, when Dundee United and Dundee both reached the final, the league management committee quite sensibly decided, for the sake of the fans, to stage the match at Dens Park for the second year running. With both clubs occupying grounds on the opposite side of the same street home advantage was minimal to Dundee. And any the club enjoyed was certainly not reflected in the result: Dundee United were ahead 3–0 at the finish, thus equalling their neighbour's record of winning in successive seasons.

The opportunity to make it three in a row, and bring themselves level with their neighbours' record of three wins in the competition, floundered at Hampden the following year when Dundee United lost to Rangers 2–0.

Once Celtic and Partick Thistle established the return of the Glasgow clubs in the dismal 1956–57 final, it took another seven years before the fans were treated to a last game in the competition which didn't feature one of the many clubs from Scotland's largest city.

At that time, in addition to Rangers and Celtic, Clyde, Partick Thistle and Third Lanark were all contenders for top honours. Yet, in the first ten years of the league cup competition, Glasgow teams featured in only four finals.

Following the devastation heaped upon Rangers by Celtic in the 1957–58 final it was the turn of Hearts to dominate the competition. The Edinburgh club were enjoying good times, with Tommy Walker in charge, and the remorseless Dave Mackay providing the power in midfield.

Hearts were reigning league champions when they arrived at Hampden on 25 October 1958 to play Partick Thistle in the final of the league cup. In a dress rehearsal at Tynecastle the previous week they had been able to dispose of the Glasgow side, comfortably enough, 2–0.

No-one really expected Thistle to offer the champions much in the way of discomfort; although, surprisingly, the Maryhill side had been responsible for the elimination of Celtic in their semi-final. With a crowd totalling 59,960 in attendance, the teams were: *Heart of Midlothian* – Marshall, Kirk and Thomson; Mackay, Glidden and Cumming; Hamilton, Murray, Bauld, Wardhaugh and Crawford. *Partick Thistle* – Ledgerwood, Hogan and Donlevy; Mathers, Davidson and Wright; McKenzie, Thomson, Smith, McParland and Ewing. *Referee* – R.H. Davidson, Airdrie.

The final score, 5–1 in favour of the Edinburgh side, neither flattered Hearts nor shamed Thistle. On their Hampden form Gair Henderson believed the Tynecastle side would have beaten almost any team in Britain. 'The inside forward play of Bauld and Murray was devastating,' he wrote, 'the generalship of Wardhaugh so inspired that the services of Hamilton and Crawford were scarcely needed.'

By general consent Thistle weren't helped any by the luck of the game. But according to R.E. Kingsley – the famous Rex – reporting for the *Sunday Mail*: 'The only time this looked like a real match – let alone a cup final – was for ten precious minutes shortly after the interval. At this point Thistle let their hair down, ignored the Bauld facts and staged a great rally that brought a great goal.'

Rex considered Thistle so heavy-footed at inside forward, so mediocre at half-back and so patchy at full-back that Hearts didn't have to pump very hard. 'But some of their moves were so confident and preconceived you got to enjoying something that had turned into an exhibition rather than a match,' he wrote.

The following year Hearts again made the league cup final, no longer league champions, but actually on their way to recovering the title which they lost to Rangers the previous year. Another of the Glasgow clubs outside the Old Firm – the once famous Third Lanark – were waiting to meet them in the final.

It should have been easy for Hearts. There was no point thinking otherwise. They were a full-time side playing a bunch of part-timers. Third Lanark, former league champions and twice winners of the Scottish Cup, was a much-loved south side club with a past and not much future.

The two sides who appeared at Hampden on 24 October 1959, with the attendance totalling 57,974, and Mr R.H. Davidson, of Airdrie, in charge for the second year running, were: *Heart of Midlothian* – Marshall, Kirk and Thomson; Bowan, Cumming and Higgins; Smith, Crawford, Young, Blackwood and Hamilton. *Third Lanark* – Robertson, Lewis and Brown; Reilly, McCallum and Cunningham; McInnes, Craig, D. Hilley, Gray and I. Hilley.

The fact that the Edinburgh side totally outplayed the men from Cathkin – the little ground on the other side of the hill from Hampden, also known as Hampden before Queen's Park moved to the present site, taking the name with them – didn't matter for most of the match. Because for almost an hour they were a goal down to their unfancied opponents.

In the Hearts goal Gordon Marshall totally misjudged a high ball which fell at the feet of Matt Gray who didn't stop to question his good fortune. The ball was immediately despatched to the back of the Hearts net. Time taken, about two and a half minutes. Hampden erupted!

Third Lanark supporters, unaccustomed to such excitement, watched in disbelief as their team played out the whole of the first half without losing a goal, thanks mainly to an amazing display by the goalkeeper, Jocky Robertson.

Hearts' supporters were equally dumbfounded. Their team did everything but score. On one occasion a header by Alec Young left Robertson, who was judged to be too small for the job by many senior clubs, including Hearts, stranded, hit a post and returned obligingly to nestle in the grateful goalkeeper's outstretched arms.

It couldn't last, of course; not really. And in all fairness, it would have been difficult to deny justice for Hearts. Twelve minutes into the second half Johnny Hamilton, advancing through the middle, tried a fierce shot from all of 25 yards. Left to himself Jocky Robertson, in prevailing mood, might have stopped it. But a deflection from a defender put the ball beyond his reach and into the net.

All afternoon the crowd had been treated to a courageous display by the little 'keeper. That, assisted by amazing good fortune, was the reason Hearts were behind. Now, through sheer persistence and an element of luck deserting the other side, the cup-holders were finally level.

And almost immediately, they went ahead. A long clearance by 'keeper Marshall reached Alec Young who managed to escape the attentions of McCallum, the Third Lanark centre-half. Robertson came out to meet him. But there was no stopping Young. As the ball settled in the back of the net, although more than half an hour of the match remained to be played, everyone knew the league cup would be returning to Tynecastle for another year.

George Young, newly appointed manager of Third Lanark, in succession to Bob Shankly, praised the courage of his part-time players. But he thought his side tired in the last 20 minutes. That was the difference between part-time and full-time players, the distinguished former captain of Rangers and Scotland explained matter-of-factly. But he didn't grumble. 'Hearts were a grand team,' the big man smiled.

Later the same evening two members of that grand team examined their winners' medals with quite different feelings of pleasure and relief. Gordon Smith, one of the greatest players Scotland ever produced, was appearing in his fourth Hampden final. Smith is the only man ever to have won league championship medals with three different clubs in Scotland – Hibs, Hearts and Dundee where he ended his career. But on that Hampden afternoon in 1959, when Hearts beat Third Lanark in the final of the league cup, two of these medals were high spots in an uncharted future career.

On three previous occasions with Hibs he had been on the losing side: once in the Scottish Cup against Aberdeen in 1947; once in the league cup against Motherwell in 1950; and, finally, in the Coronation Cup, against Celtic in 1953. Now, after almost two decades of trying, Smith was the proud possessor of a cup medal won at Hampden.

His young team-mate, Billy Higgins, at left-half for Hearts against Third Lanark, was playing in his first-ever cup-tie. However, if he was ever tempted to believe winning medals came easy, a word with Gordon Smith would soon put him right.

The first 14 years of the league cup, which ended with Hearts' victory over Third Lanark at Hampden, was curious in part because it produced only four victories, evenly shared, by the Old Firm.

The next 14 years was almost a mirror image of the first – Rangers and Celtic between them won the trophy 11 times. And one or other of the great duopoly featured in every final except one; a dangerous trend that didn't much improve with the years.

Hearts won again on 27 October 1962, defeating Kilmarnock 1–0 in the only league cup final to exclude either Rangers or Celtic in 19 years; a remarkable record by the two Glasgow clubs. In an amazing run, starting in season 1964–65, when they lost to Rangers 2–1 in front of 91,000 fans, Celtic appeared in 14 consecutive finals.

When the Parkhead team bus crawled to a halt outside Hampden on 24 October 1970, Celtic, the holders, were intent on achieving their sixth consecutive victory in the league cup final.

Their opponents, Rangers, who hadn't won a trophy in more than four years, were given no chance against a Parkhead side that could still call upon six of the Lisbon Lions, with Bobby Lennox on the subs bench in addition to those named to play from the start.

Willie Waddell, the Rangers manager, who had been back at Ibrox less than a year, paid no attention to the merchants of gloom, however. 'People could say what they liked, it didn't worry us one bit,' Waddell insisted later. 'I've yet to go into any game feeling the slightest bit inferior to the opposition.'

Rangers prepared for the match at Gullane, attacking the local sand-dunes, honing their fitness and learning to suffer, with all the energy and fervour they could muster, encouraged not to slack by the intimidating presence of their coach, Jock Wallace.

In addition to their dismal record of the previous few years, as the day of the match approached, Rangers' chief worry was the impending loss of skipper John Greig. Word of his illness was a closely guarded Ibrox secret for most of the previous week. But an hour before kick-off news of his absence reached the Rangers fans, adding to their gloom.

Greig was an inspiring captain and probably Rangers' key player. He would have been an automatic choice for a place in the final. His loss was a decision forced on manager Willie Waddell. But, for the Rangers fans in the 106,263 crowd, just as sensational as the enforced loss of their captain was the inclusion, quite deliberately, of another name on the Ibrox team-sheet. As the Rangers team was announced, and the absence of Greig confirmed, there was a low murmur of disappointment from the crowd on the west terracing. Then the name of the player designated to wear the number nine jersey for Rangers crackled from the Hampden loudspeakers. Johnstone!

Most of the huge Rangers support exchanged astonished glances. 'Johnstone? Derek Johnstone?' they inquired of each other, disbelievingly.

They recognised the name, of course. Derek Johnstone was a big, strong lad from the reserves who showed great promise as a goalscorer. Aged 16! He had played in the first team on only two previous occasions. And there he was, the youngest player ever to appear in a major British cup final, and easily the least experienced player on the park, preparing to do battle with a man who had subdued some of the best strikers in Europe, Billy McNeill.

Before the match, Jim Parkinson, in *The Glasgow Herald*, reported Rangers approaching the game on tip-toe, refusing even to name a panel of players. Guessing better than he knew a puzzled Parkinson suggested: 'It may be they intend to spring a tactical surprise.'

Johnstone, who last played in the first team in a league match against Cowdenbeath two weeks earlier, didn't expect a place in the final. 'Willie Waddell and Jock Wallace took me into the boot room after training on the Friday,' Johnstone recalled. 'The boss handed me a few complimentary tickets for the match and told me to go home and make sure I got a good night's sleep. That's when I knew I'd be playing.' He was also ordered to keep the news to himself. The Ibrox bosses wanted to surprise their old rival, Jock Stein.

The teams were: *Celtic* – Williams, Craig, Quinn, Murdoch, McNeill, Hay, Johnstone, Connelly, Wallace, Hood, Macari. *Rangers* – McCloy, Jardine, Miller, Conn, McKinnon, Jackson, Henderson, MacDonald, Johnstone, Stein, Johnston. *Referee* – T. Wharton, Glasgow.

It may have been due to the strength in their legs from all that work on the sand-dunes of Gullane, or quite simply the unbridled enthusiasm of youth, but once Johnstone kicked off for Rangers it was Celtic, and not Rangers, who found themselves on the receiving end of an attacking blitz.

Henderson, in particular, was inspired. Right from the start, he led Jimmy Quinn and the rest of the Celtic defence a merry dance. *The Scottish Football Book* reported: 'The first real chance in an incredible final came when Henderson, back to the form which had made him the hammer of English defenders, turned back a ball from the bye-line, caught the Celtic defenders on the wrong foot, but saw the inexperienced Johnstone hesitate and robbed before he had time to shoot.'

This was a critical period of the match for both teams. Jock Stein observed later: 'Some of our players obviously considered it would be too easy and surrendered the initiative.'

The goal that settled the match was scored after 40 minutes.

In his tussles with Billy McNeill for command of the Celtic penalty area, young Derek Johnstone had been winning a fair number of the aerial exchanges, justifying the wisdom of manager Waddell's decision to hand him the number nine jersey.

With five minutes left before half-time, Willie Johnston's cross from the right was perfect. His near-namesake rose to meet it. Two men, Billy McNeill and Jim Craig, who were winning glory in Lisbon barely a year after the Rangers youngster left primary school, were in a position to stop him. They didn't.

For Johnstone especially it was an unforgettable moment; literally, a schoolboy dream come true. 'You can imagine how I felt, just a lad, scoring the winning goal in a cup final against Celtic,' Johnstone recalled. 'But it wasn't until later in life I realised what that goal meant to the Rangers' fans.'

Lisbon Lions Billy McNeill and Jim Craig can't match Derek Johnstone, just 16 and the youngest player ever to appear in a major final, as he leaps to head the winner for Rangers in the 1970 League Cup final against Celtic

For the Ibrox side victory against Celtic in the 1970 league cup final at Hampden signalled the end of a nightmare period in the club's history.

'What we must do now is to consolidate on this win, to keep going after other trophies,' manager Willie Waddell announced truculently for the benefit of the Ibrox faithful. 'This has to be the start of something for this team,' Waddell went on. 'It is a beginning, a starting point, and more must follow before I am satisfied.'

It provided little comfort to supporters of the Parkhead side that, in the course of their amazing run in the league cup, mostly, when it came time to lose, they were beaten by Rangers who won four times; or that the Ibrox side continued to keep ahead of their rivals in the number of league cups won.

Hibernian, winning for the first time, Aberdeen and Dundee also added to their favourites' pain. But between season 1964–65 and 1977–78, it was the fourth name to appear on the league cup, in place of Celtic, that caused the greatest surprise. And hurt!

CHAPTER TWELVE

Not many, in a crowd exceeding 62,000 who gathered at Hampden on Saturday, 23 October 1971, for the final of the league cup, would have forecast with any great seriousness the outcome of the afternoon's events. Partick Thistle hadn't won a trophy in 50 years; Celtic were in the habit of winning almost everything in Scotland.

In a giddy six-year spell starting in 1966, they had been six times league champions, three times winners of the Scottish Cup and five times winners of the league cup. Even without their record in Europe their success rate was light years ahead of Thistle.

On a dull and dismal afternoon at the Mount Florida ground supporters of the Maryhill side hoped for a touch of the unexpected, perhaps even a goal from their own side, which would brighten their spirits and add interest to the afternoon, without straining their expectations too hard. Everyone else imagined Thistle would be fortunate not to find themselves cast as victims in some ritual Hampden slaughter.

'Our aim is to entertain,' manager Davie McParland announced bravely at the start. 'We'll go at Celts and no doubt they'll come at us. If we play as well as we can then it will be some game. As long as we play well that's all that matters.'

At least one good judge forecast an upset. Willie Ormond, then manager of St Johnstone, was happy to remind anyone with short memories that his team had beaten Celtic twice already that year – and lost to Thistle twice. 'Thistle will win,' the future Scotland manager declared mischievously. 'Davie McParland has the right idea – he is coming at you from the front, not the back.'

Malcolm Munro, a familiar figure on the streets of Maryhill, believed the danger to Thistle would be the loss of a quick goal; a Celtic speciality. 'We all know what Celtic can do,' Munro ventured cautiously in the *Evening Times*. 'None of us know what Thistle will do.'

It was true that Thistle were famously unpredictable. Their only other cup triumph, victory in the Scottish Cup final 50 years earlier, had been won at the expense of Rangers, the league champions. The prospect of defeating Celtic, the current league champions, in the final of the league cup, in the year they were entitled to celebrate the golden jubilee of their most famous victory, offered Thistle an opportunity not to be missed.

But if the coincidence of dates was a warning of sorts, few among the Celtic supporters arriving at Hampden bothered to read the signs. Or worry much about a view expressed by Malcom Munro who liked to be known as the heavyweight champion of the fans. 'On their game, on their free running, brave, very often daft game,' Munro insisted, wistfully, 'Thistle are capable of beating any team in Scotland – including Celtic.'

Not that Jock Stein was taking any chances. He never did. Billy McNeill, the Celtic captain, who had been suffering from a leg strain, was missing from the side. 'I can't afford to field players who are less than 100 per cent fit,' Stein explained firmly; demonstrating for the benefit of anyone who'd forgotten that he never took the outcome of any match, least of all a cup final, for granted.

Raymond Jacobs, in *The Glasgow Herald*, thought Stein was paying Thistle a real compliment by not risking McNeill. He also reported that Celtic were expecting great things from newcomer Kenny Dalglish, aged 20. Dalglish had been in great form the previous week, scoring three times against Dundee. 'A repetition of that sort of form would lead Celtic to their sixth victory in eight successive appearances in the final,' Jacobs added.

The two sides lined up for the start as follows: *Partick Thistle* – Rough, Hansen and Forsyth; Glavin, Campbell and Strachan; McQuade, Coulston, Bone, Rae and Lawrie. *Celtic* – Williams, Hay and Gemmell; Murdoch, Connolly and Brogan; Johnstone, Dalglish, Hood, Callaghan and Macari. *Referee* – W.J. Mullan, Dalkeith.

Celtic, for all their experience, didn't know what hit them. A goal after only nine minutes could be dismissed as typical Thistle. Everyone knew they were unpredictable. But another goal six minutes later was indulging the underdogs' well-known talent to amuse to a degree their illustrious opponents could easily do without.

'It was panic stations all the way when Thistle went forward,' Malcolm Munro reported. 'This so very experienced Celtic defence just did not know what to do with a team which kept going forward.'

Skipper Alex Rae scored first. Thistle, who had been attacking the Celtic goal right from the start, with good shots at Williams from Bone and McQuade, won a corner. The ball went to Rae on the edge of the penalty area. His right-foot shot hit the roof of the Celtic net with Williams nowhere. Bobby Lawrie scored next. A pass from Bone sent him on his way. 'Thistle were hungry for the ball,' the heavyweight champion of the fans enthused. 'They were, in fact, doing a Celtic on Celtic.'

The impeccable Kenny Dalglish, put in the clear by Gemmell, lofted the ball over the bar with only Rough to beat. 'This seemed to mirror what was happening to Celtic,' Munro confided.

Struggling to establish a grip on the game, the Parkhead side wasn't helped any by the loss of Jimmy Johnstone, with a leg injury, after only 17 minutes. The little winger was a proven match-winner at the highest levels of the game. Given time, and a chance to display his fabulous skills, who knows, but he might have been able to turn a nightmare afternoon in the champions' favour.

The Celtic substitute – another of the Lisbon Lions, Jim Craig – assumed his customary position at right-back. Davie Hay moved to midfield. Partick Thistle appeared not to notice.

Thirteen minutes after Celtic lost Johnstone the Maryhill side scored again. A corner-kick, taken accurately but unspectacularly by Bobby Lawrie, caused consternation in the Celtic defence. When the ball reached Denis McQuade in front of goal he accepted the gift with alacrity.

A total of 30 minutes had been played and Celtic were three down. Somewhere the earth moved.

A fourth goal, scored nine minutes from half-time by Jimmy Bone – with the Celtic defence again marked absent – simply reduced the Celtic support to a state of deeper shock. No – correction – deepest shock!

'As the interval approached, Thistle were actually toying with the champions of Scotland, the former champions of Europe. It was fantastic to see,' a bewildered Malcolm Munro reported with ill-concealed delight.

The second half was a different story, of sorts. Celtic, upbraided in the dressing-room by an angry Jock Stein, came into the game and Thistle tired. Glavin, who had been limping, was replaced by Gibson before the end. But a goal by Dalglish, 20 minutes from time, only chipped at the margin of their opponents' amazing superiority – on the day.

As the *Evening Times* reported, perhaps with an eye on future markets, there would be a tale to be told and retold around Maryhill for years to come. Celtic had been licked by a team of hungry, talented, unspoiled youngsters who, on the form they displayed at Hampden in the league cup final, could have licked any team in the country.

At one point Thistle, who went for every ball, had been too fast for the former European champions. 'And if this sounds ridiculous, it is nonetheless true,' the newspaper insisted. 'They were dynamic on the break and calm in defence.'

It seemed a total of twelve new names, including the manager, Davie McParland, now occupied a special place in an uncrowded Firhill firmament.

Epic matches involving the Old Firm against each other are part of the folklore of Scottish football. In recent years, however, in the hunt for major cup honours, two other clubs, Aberdeen and Dundee United, have featured every bit as prominently as the two Glasgow giants.

Hampden has proved a particularly happy hunting ground for the furthest travelled of the four, Aberdeen. During the past decade their record in the Scottish Cup has been outstanding: five appearances, five wins. While in the league cup, although they contrived only two victories out of four appearances in the final, the Eighties will be remembered mainly for three consecutive finals, Aberdeen against Rangers.

Curiously enough, in the chequered history of the league cup, which started as a makeshift wartime tournament organised by the old Southern League, the two clubs are linked inextricably.

The original version, encouraged by the wartime government, who recognised the need for mass entertainment, was designed to provide more football at a time when the number of league matches had been curtailed, and the Scottish Cup had been abandoned entirely due to hostilities.

Organised on the basis of four teams in four sections, playing each other home and away, with the section winners proceeding to the semi-finals, the entire tournament was dominated by Rangers. Out of six Southern League Cup competitions held between 1941 and the end of the war, the Ibrox club won four. A fifth final, against Hibernian, went against them when a corner count put the Easter Road side ahead at the finish, and the cup departed for Edinburgh. Then, in the very last of the wartime series, with Rangers securing their usual appearance at the last stage, Aberdeen put a stop to the expected celebrations in Edmiston Drive by winning 3–2.

However, by the end of the war, the Southern League Cup had been generally judged a great success and the Scottish Football League wasted no time building on its reputation, just as Rangers moved with maximum speed and wilful intent to revenge themselves against Aberdeen, the team that deprived them of victory in the last match of the original competition. When the two sides met at Hampden in the first final of the new – but same-style – competition on 5 April 1947, Rangers won convincingly. Four-nil ahead at the finish, they were able to claim the distinction of seeing their name inscribed first on a sparkling new trophy, the Scottish League Cup.

Almost an entire decade passed, during which Rangers also defeated Aberdeen in the final of the Scottish Cup, before the name of their opponents in that first league cup final joined the Ibrox club on that particular roll of honour.

The Fifties were long underway before a new generation of players was able to avenge the Pittodrie name against Rangers. For years early round matches in the league cup produced mixed results. However, in a semi-final of that other competition, the Scottish Cup, an amazing goal blitz by Aberdeen crushed the Ibrox side 6–0 as season 1953–54 neared its end.

The final, in front of 129,926 spectators at Hampden on 24 April 1954, was eventually lost to Celtic 2–1. But if Aberdeen needed to know, and demonstrate, that they were still capable of defeating Rangers in the closing stages of a major competition, season 1953–54 provided the proof.

Two years later, with so much history still to be written, Aberdeen were the reigning league champions, when against them, in the semi-final of the league cup, came Rangers.

For Aberdeen, at least, the result brought satisfaction far in excess of any goal difference, 2–1 in favour of the Pittodrie side. It also earned them a place in the final against St Mirren, their first appearance in a league cup final for more than eight years. The teams at Hampden on 22 October 1955 were: *Aberdeen* – Martin, Mitchell and Caldwell; Wilson, Clunie and Glen; Leggat, Yorston, Buckley, Wishart and Hather. *St Mirren* – Lornie, Lapsley and Mallan; Neilsen, Telfer and Holmes; Rodger, Laird, Brown, Gemmell and Callan. *Referee* – H. Phillips, Wishaw.

The biggest upset ever witnessed at Hampden occurred on 23 October 1971 when Partick Thistle defeated Celtic to win the League Cup. Alan Rough, in the Partick Thistle goal, watches the ball go wide. Kenny Dalglish and Lou Macari can see it isn't their day

Everyone concerned with the match was disappointed by the attendance which barely exceeded 44,000. At least one reporter thought Hampden itself was affected by the poor turn-out. Hugh Taylor wrote: 'The great ground seemed to wear a peeved expression – as it always does when it is not given the tribute it feels is its due.'

Taylor, writing in his annual review, blamed the absence of Rangers and Celtic. 'There are, alas, few football neutrals in the West of Scotland,' he explained. 'To pull in crowds of more than 90,000 it is essential that either Rangers or Celtic are featured.'

Few people thought St Mirren, who were making their one and only appearance in the final of the league cup, could do much to prevent an Aberdeen victory.

Following a non-scoring first half it required an own goal by Jimmy Mallan to put Aberdeen ahead. A diving header by Bobby Holmes at the other end earned the equaliser. Aberdeen faltered in attack and St Mirren looked to be in control of the game – until a shot by Graham Leggat, positioned not far from the touchline, executed a strange, hypnotic arc, seemingly mesmerised Lornie in the St Mirren goal, and finished in the net.

It hadn't been easy – but the league cup was on its way to Pittodrie, at last.

More than two decades passed before Aberdeen again reached the final of the league cup. Celtic, appearing in their 13th consecutive league cup final, occupied the other Hampden dressing-room as if by right. But it wouldn't have escaped the notice of the ebullient Ally MacLeod, who was in charge of Aberdeen, that in the previous 12 years Celtic won only on six occasions. And there was always something ominous about the number 13.

MacLeod, a man whose later brief career as Scotland manager sometimes demonstrated a remarkable capacity for optimism in the face of overwhelming odds, was entitled to believe the fates might be on his side on this occasion.

On a dismal day at Hampden, on 6 November 1976, with a crowd totalling 69,268, the teams at the start were: *Aberdeen* – Clark, Kennedy, Williamson, Smith, Garner, Miller, Sullivan, Scott, Harper, Jarvie, Graham. *Celtic* – Latchford, McGrain, Lynch, Edvaldsson, MacDonald, Aitken, Doyle, Glavin, Dalglish, Burns, Wilson. *Referee* – J.W. Paterson, Bothwell.

With his team playing well, the Aberdeen manager, a splendidly resilient character by nature, would have been able to cope easily enough with the small matter of them losing a penalty after only 12 minutes. Kenny Dalglish, then at the height of his powers for Celtic, was the player brought down when edging towards a scoring chance with typical outrageous flair. But Dalglish didn't frighten easily either. As skipper, he elected to take the kick himself.

A moment later, to no-one's great surprise, the ball hit the back of the net – and the crowd was treated to that familiar joyous smile which greeted each of the hundreds of goals Dalglish was destined to score in the course of his marvellous career.

Ally MacLeod, from his seat in the dugout, grinned ruefully. With customary bravado, he could have been thinking: an early Celtic goal at least allowed his own players plenty of time to equalise.

Thirteen minutes later – 13 again, and the beginning of the end for Celtic – Arthur Graham swung the ball to Harper who clipped it to Jarvie who headed into the net.

For most of the first half Aberdeen stormed the Celtic penalty area and more goals seemed certain. 'Play was brilliant, with an abundance of fine, thrilling football, exciting challenges and narrow escapes,' *The Scottish Football Yearbook* recalled.

But following the interval Celtic played like a team transformed. Only good fortune, in support of Aberdeen, and a splendid performance by Bobby Clark, playing with a broken thumb, prevented the Parkhead side taking the lead. Miraculously, at the end of 90 minutes the match remained level.

During the second half Tommy Burns had been replaced by Lennox for

Celtic and Robb came on for Aberdeen in place of Jarvie. Bobby Lennox, as everyone expected, added power and pace to the Celtic attack. But it was Davie Robb who made the most significant contribution to the match. Soon after the start of extra time, with few present able to believe Aberdeen could long continue to withstand total collapse, Robb scrambled a cross from Scott into the net.

For a moment, on the west terracing, the large Aberdeen support couldn't believe they were ahead. There was a moment of quiet; a small hush which became a gasp, then a roar!

As inspiration it worked. Following the goal the Pittodrie side played with all the vigour and endeavour of a team reborn. As it was in the first half, so it became in extra time. Aberdeen played like a team possessed. Celtic never stopped trying but the match was lost.

'If you don't put the ball in the net, you don't win,' a disappointed Jock Stein mused afterwards. 'That's the sad truth. Aberdeen scored and we didn't. There are no excuses from us.'

Next day more than 20,000 supporters packed the Aberdeen ground to welcome the victors home and, hopefully, obtain a glimpse of a trophy that had been last seen in the granite city several years before many of them were born.

Everyone appeared to sense they were on the verge of great things. But it would have been difficult for anyone, including the resourceful Ally MacLeod, to imagine that, by the time of their series of epic league cup final duels with Rangers, the men from Pittodrie would be an established football power – not just at home but abroad.

The following year marked the end of an amazing league cup final run by Celtic: 14 finals in a row is a record which will be hard to beat. But again the Parkhead side lost in extra time. On this occasion their opponents at Hampden on 18 March 1978 were Rangers who won 2–1.

Parkhead interest in the competition faltered thereafter: four appearances in a dozen years hardly compared with their previous achievements. Similarly, it is interesting to recall that, although they appeared in four finals of the league cup between 1979 and 1991, the Parkhead side won only once. In the same period, during which they qualified for ten finals, Rangers lost just twice.

When the total performance of the two clubs in the league cup is examined, across more than 40 years of its existence, the same record of wins and losses is reflected. Between 1947 and 1991, Rangers appeared in 23 finals, winning 17; while the name of Celtic, with only three fewer finals to their credit, appears nine times. There is also little comfort for Celtic fans who inquire about the outcome of league cup finals involving the two sides. The first 46 years of the league cup has produced eleven Old Firm finals. The score so far? Rangers 7 Celtic 4.

Since season 1984–85 the league cup competition has been known to one and all as the Skol Cup, a straight knock-out competition from the early rounds through to the final. Judged by the standard of play produced at Hampden in recent years, as a marriage of sport and sponsor it appeared a union made in heaven and many people were surprised when it ended.

Remarkably, considering its huge appeal, only six clubs featured in the first eight finals: Rangers, Dundee United, Aberdeen, Hibernian, Celtic and Dunfermline.

It all started, quietly enough, at Hampden on 28 October 1984, when a crowd of 44,698 saw Rangers defeat Dundee United by a single goal. The following year, an even smaller crowd watched as Aberdeen destroyed Hibernian 3–0. A year later, when Rangers and Celtic met for the first time in a Skol Cup final, the attendance jumped to 74,219, a record for the competition.

Rangers, who were beginning a great new lease of life with Graeme Souness in charge, and sometimes playing, faced Celtic without the benefit of Souness's commanding on-field presence: a thigh injury suffered against Boavista Porto in a UEFA Cup qualifying round kept the manager sidelined. Still, the Ibrox side, laying the foundations of a significant trend, won 2–1.

A year later Rangers again reached the final. Aberdeen, the only other winners of the Skol Cup, were their opponents at Hampden. Everyone expected a memorable match. In fact, by general consent, a crowd of 71,961, plus a huge audience watching the match live on television at home, were treated to one of the greatest games ever seen at Hampden. It was also the first in a series of epic matches featuring the same two clubs at the same stage of the same competition: Rangers against Aberdeen in the final of the Skol Cup.

Rangers would be without Chris Woods in goal, skipper Terry Butcher and player-manager Graeme Souness, all suspended. Before the match Souness confided to reporters: 'I've had my share of finals but you can never get enough of them. I'm sad to miss out. There may not be too many more finals for me at my stage in the game.'

For different reasons, Aberdeen-born Nicky Walker, in the Rangers goal, didn't expect to participate in many more matches at this level of competition either. Pre-match testimony, freely given, that he hadn't once played in a winning side against Aberdeen with any of his clubs, including the reserves, did little to calm the nerves of Rangers supporters worried about his ability. Walker himself appeared unconcerned. 'I'm going to enjoy the experience,' the far-from-reluctant-goalkeeper-substitute announced cheerfully. 'I know I will be going back into the reserves no matter what happens.'

Ian Porterfield, probably best remembered as the man who scored the only goal of the game for Sunderland against Leeds in the 1973 FA Cup final at Wembley, had been appointed manager of Aberdeen in succession to the highly successful Alex Ferguson. Showing steel on his first appearance at Hampden as manager of Aberdeen, Porterfield discounted any suggestion his team might have it easy, facing a weakened Rangers side. 'Any team who can go two goals down in an Old Firm match in which they have only nine men on the park and still get a point has to know quite a bit about fighting spirit,' the new manager insisted shrewdly, reminding those with short memories of occurrences at Ibrox the previous Saturday.

When the two sides lined up at Hampden on Sunday 25 October 1987 for the final of the Skol Cup three of those present were survivors from the last time Rangers met Aberdeen in a League Cup final eight years earlier. Davie Cooper, for Rangers, and Willie Miller and Alex McLeish all played in an ill-tempered match at Hampden on 31 March 1979. Rangers won 2–1; but only after Doug Rougvie had been ordered off and his Aberdeen team-mates Drew Jarvie, Gordon Strachan and Joe Harper were all booked, together with Tommy McLean and Alex Miller of Rangers. The referee on that somewhat frantic occasion was Mr I.M.D. Foote of Glasgow. No doubt hoping for a quieter time, the man in charge of this latest encounter was Mr R.B. Valentine, of Dundee.

The teams started as follows: *Rangers* – Walker, Nicholl, Munro, Roberts, Ferguson, Gough, McGregor, Fleck, McCoist, Durrant, Cooper. *Aberdeen* – Leighton, McKimmie, Connor, Simpson, McLeish, Willie Miller, Hewitt, Bett, Joe Miller, Nicholas, Falconer.

An important football match, one with much at stake, a cup or a league decider, even simple pride, or jealous rivalries, which concentrate the minds of old protagonists wonderfully, usually begins long before play actually starts. Expectancy among the fans, on the terracing and in the stands, is high, of course. Although experience dictates caution, everyone hopes that this time they will be treated to a match to remember.

There is never less than serious tension surrounding the players, their managers, the match officials, even the police. For football is a game of passion as well as skill. More often than not, perhaps, the end result, the game itself rather than the final score, is disappointing for the majority of those present.

But whatever the circumstances, whenever a match transcends all expectations, no-one can deny the excitement it generates, or the beauty and skill of the game at its heart. All those present at Hampden Park, Glasow, on Sunday, 25 October 1987, were treated to such a match. It was a thriller right from the start.

In its early stages the match appeared to be swinging in favour of Aberdeen as Bett, Nicholas and Simpson, for Aberdeen, and Ferguson, Cooper and Durrant, for Rangers, battled for control of the midfield.

Ten minutes into the match a pass from Miller found Falconer in the box. Nicky Walker, anxious and inexperienced, brought him down. Penalty! Bett scored with ease.

Mike Aitken, writing in *The Scotsman*, reported: 'It was all Aberdeen at this stage and had they been able to show a lethal touch in front of goal Rangers might not have been able to force their way back into contention.'

Another 12 minutes passed before a foul by Miller on McCoist, on the edge of the Aberdeen penalty box, provided an uncertain means of entry. But a wondrous free-kick by Davie Cooper, worthy of the great Brazilian masters of the art, which would have been enough in itself to make any match memorable, brought Rangers level.

Given the marvellous quality of Cooper's equaliser it was hardly surprising that Rangers immediately commenced to play like a team inspired. Three minutes from half-time Durrant and McCoist tore the Aberdeen defence apart with a dazzling exchange that finished with Durrant, well on his way to becoming the sponsor's man of the match, sweeping the ball away from Leighton into the net.

At the end of a pulsating first half Rangers probably deserved to be ahead; just! Given points for the order in which the two sides scored, the second half might have been judged in favour of Aberdeen.

First Hewitt thrashed an 18–yard shot past Walker to earn the equaliser. Then, ten minutes from time, a chipped ball from Bett found Falconer who headed into the net. For the second time in the match, and with time running out, Aberdeen were ahead. But the Ibrox side never stopped trying. This wasn't a match anyone wanted to lose.

Four minutes of the match remained when the tireless Durrant, running endlessly, passed to Fleck. As Mike Aitken noted later: 'In a game full of heroes no-one influenced the final result more than Durrant. His attacking play from midfield was a sheer delight throughout.' However, as the ball settled in the back of the net behind Leighton, it was Fleck's shot that sent the match soaring into extra time; and delayed the presentation of the Skol Cup for at least another half hour.

Rangers might have won in the additional spell of normal play. They were the better side during that period of the game. McCoist, for example, could have made better use of a pass from the irrepressible Durrant. Scorer of 20 goals for Rangers already that season, his shot went high.

Neutrals present, who believed they were strong enough to endure the agony of a penalty-kick shoot-out in exchange for the highly-charged atmosphere penalties could be relied upon to provide, probably didn't mind. People who dislike this method of deciding an important match, especially a cup final, are usually more vociferous than those who consider it as good a way as any of achieving a tie-break in football. It can be hard on the players, and especially cruel when the moral victors end up losing – but the same could be said of many games decided in normal time.

One thing in its favour, certainly: a more gripping, exciting, nerve-wracking method of separating the winners from the losers, and conveying the difference between triumph and tragedy at the end of a match, would be difficult to find.

Appropriately enough, after both teams failed to score during extra time, and Welsh international Peter Nicholas missed in the penalty shoot-out, the goal that won the 1987 Skol Cup for Rangers was delivered with the last kick of a momentous afternoon by Ian Durrant, a week short of 21, and easily the man of the match. 'Tremendous!' said Souness.

Ian Porterfield thought the afternoon had been a great advertisement for football. 'It was how the game should be played. I'm just disappointed we lost the third goal which pushed the game to penalties,' he said.

'It was a great game and a great team performance by Rangers,' the winning manager, who admitted sympathy for Aberdeen losing on penalties, observed proudly. 'I hoped for a classic and we got it.'

Having won three out of four Skol Cup finals Rangers were allowed to keep the trophy. The delighted sponsor, whose name had been associated with one of the greatest cup finals in living memory, also provided a special award for the losers.

Alex Cameron, writing in the *Daily Record*, thought the game at Hampden had been 'one of the truly finest finals this great sporting acreage has hosted. A great game and all of it a very pleasant memory,' Cameron concluded happily.

It would have been a brave and contentious soul who dared prophesy more of the same a year later.

But on 23 October 1988, Rangers and Aberdeen contested the Skol Cup final for the second year running. And again the fans were treated to a riveting clash between two of the most exciting, and determined, sides in the country.

Aberdeen, looking back to the previous year, could have been forgiven wondering what happened to all the able and familiar figures they faced on that momentous occasion. The team from the north showed three quite modest changes in personnel from an occasion now fixed in the public mind as the penalty kick final: Theo Snelders, David Robertson and Davie Dodds replacing Jim Leighton, Joe Miller and Willie Falconer.

However, under the command of Graeme Souness, for many players, these were often fleeting, as well as challenging, days at Ibrox. The Rangers side which emerged from the Hampden tunnel included only two players who made the same short walk a year earlier – Richard Gough and Ally McCoist.

Those missing from the Rangers side included the man who set the previous year's final alight, Ian Durrant. It was thought the little midfielder's whole career had been threatened following a horrendous clash with Neil Simpson, of Aberdeen, less than ten minutes into a league match at Pittodrie a fortnight earlier. An emergency operation on shattered ligaments in his knee, lasting four hours in a Glasgow clinic, followed by protracted treatment in the United States and elsewhere, was required before the player could return to first-team duty three years later.

Some good judges thought Aberdeen manager Alex Smith would be wrong to risk playing Simpson in the Skol Cup final because of the hostile crowd he was certain to face at the Rangers end at Hampden. Smith himself appeared unworried. 'Neil is a big honest type of player who has been put under a lot of pressure but has been bearing up well. Players respond either in a positive way or not to jeering of the type we can expect at Hampden. Aberdeen are full of experienced men who have been over this kind of course before and I would anticipate them coping well,' said Smith.

Graham Roberts, who captained Rangers in the Skol Cup final the previous year in place of the suspended Terry Butcher, hoped the Rangers fans would be fair to Simpson. Now with Chelsea, following a celebrated row with manager Souness, he told the *Daily Record*: 'Bad tackles and bad injuries are part of the game and players accept this. I hope the Ibrox fans, the best in the world, give Simpson a chance. No-one likes to see a fellow professional treated badly. Off the park Simpson is a nice lad.'

But fears that the 1988 Skol Cup final could degenerate into a grudge match were on everyone's mind. 'If either side, on the pitch or the terracings, gets bogged down balancing old scores, they will deserve to lose,' the highly experienced Alex Cameron, writing in the *Daily Record*, warned sombrely.

Ian Paul, whose readers probably included a substantial majority of local lawyers, also ventured a pre-match opinion. 'Footballers may not have a reputation for daunting intellect,' he proposed cautiously, perhaps for the benefit of a different breed who bought *The Glasgow Herald*, 'but I would be astonished if an Aberdeen or Rangers player is foolish enough to attempt any viciousness during a final which will be scrutinised by the great Scottish public – and those further afield – for any sign of illegal nonsense.'

Alastair MacDonald, writing in the *Press and Journal*, printed and published in Aberdeen, took a different view. He warned against people approaching the game expecting trouble. 'That would be a case of the thought being father to the deed and would produce an atmosphere in which trouble would be even more likely to develop,' Macdonald insisted.

Not that trouble was any kind of stranger at meetings between the two sides. Any match involving Rangers and Aberdeen was expected to produce quality football. But there was also another side – a harder side – to their image, reflected in the not inconsiderable number of times players from both sides were on the receiving end of red and yellow cards in matches involving each other.

Statistics covering the previous decade revealed a catalogue of crimes and misdemeanours. Before the 1988 Skol Cup final, with feelings running particularly high because of the injury to Durrant, the two clubs met in a total of 50 matches across a ten-year period and ended with 15 players ordered off – ten from Rangers and five from Aberdeen – plus 148 bookings, 84 accumulating to the Glasgow club and 64 to their northern opponents. Only a scant five matches appeared trouble-free, reaching a conclusion without a player from either side seeing his name go into the referee's little black book.

More than anyone, probably, Graeme Souness was aware of the dangers facing his players if they allowed personal feelings, and any notion of vendettas, to intrude on the match. In his book, *A Manager's Diary*, written with Ken Gallacher, the former Rangers manager recounts how, before the 1988 Skol Cup final against Aberdeen, problems generated by Durrant's injury had been eating away at him. At a pre-match dressing-room meeting with his players Souness emphasised the need for restraint. 'I told them that the greatest favour we could do Ian Durrant was lifting the Cup for the third year in succession,' he wrote. 'I told them that we had to make sure that this was a game to match the one everyone saluted last year,' Souness continued. 'And I warned them that if anyone did get involved in any kind of revenge action then they would be letting down themselves, the Rangers Football Club and Ian Durrant.'

At the start of the match, which attracted a crowd in excess of 72,000, an increase of 161 from the previous year, despite the continued presence of live television, those under the kind of scrutiny envisaged by Ian Paul were: *Rangers* – Woods, Stevens, Brown, Gough, Wilkins, Butcher, Drinkell, Ferguson, McCoist,

Cooper, Walters. *Aberdeen* – Snelders, McKimmie, Robertson, Simpson, McLeish, Miller, Nicholas, Bett, Dodds, Connor, Hewitt. *Referee* – G.B. Smith, Edinburgh.

Rangers, who had been last to score when the two clubs met in the final of the same competition a year earlier, went ahead first in much the same fashion as they finished then – with a goal from the penalty spot. Almost a quarter of an hour into the game a throw-in by young David Robertson, despatched carelessly in the general direction of his own goalkeeper, was intercepted by Drinkell. Snelders, unable to reach the ball, brought him down. McCoist scored.

Six minutes later Aberdeen equalised. Hewitt took a corner, Woods misjudged the cross and the ball cannoned off Dodds into the net.

One-all at half-time, Rangers went ahead again, ten minutes into the second half. A throw-in from Stevens reached Ferguson who crashed the ball into the net.

At the other end, with just over an hour played, Nicholas passed to Bett who crossed to the far post. In the right place at the right time once again, Davie Dodds' header was perfectly judged: 2–2!

As everyone expected, for as long as he was on the park, and anywhere near the ball, Neil Simpson was given a rough time by a large section of the Rangers support. Having substituted him in the second half because of injury, his manager commented: 'Many people wouldn't have been able to handle the situation. He took responsibility and I'm proud of him.'

With less than five minutes remaining of normal time, and the match and the crowd settling to the prospect of extra time, and the threat of yet another penalty shoot-out if neither side scored, the whole of Hampden went wild.

'No fewer than five great chances were made but only one was taken,' an enraptured Ian Paul reported. 'It was a tie within a tie, four minutes of the most pulsating and enthralling drama, the kind that encapsulates all that the people's game can be.'

It started with Dodds setting up a chance for Bett who beat Woods, only to see his well-struck shot go inches past the post. Next Drinkell nodded down to McCoist who blasted the ball wide. Gary Stevens, running down the right, skipping tackles, was straight on target. A good save by Snelders knocked the ball for a corner. Over it came, taken by Walters, and this time McCoist made no mistake. With only two minutes left for play, Rangers were ahead!

But, still, as everyone acknowledged, Aberdeen didn't stop trying. First a shot by Bett was blocked. Then, from six yards, Dodds struck at goal. And groaned as the ball hit Stevens and bounced clear.

For the second year running there was little justice in seeing one side win and the other lose. But nobody argued about the quality of the match as entertainment. 'Rangers felt they deserved to win,' wrote Ian Paul in *The Glasgow Herald*. 'Aberdeen felt they were unlucky not to win. Maybe they are both right.'

By general consent, both teams produced another great final. And with it another not inconsiderable bonus: the kind of on-field mayhem so many people feared in advance of the match didn't occur.

Souness made sure there was also a medal for Ian Durrant, which was sure to please just about everybody, not least the unfortunate player.

A year later, to no-one's great surprise, considering the two sides appeared to enjoy some exclusive rights in the competition, Rangers and Aberdeen reached the Skol Cup final for the third year running – and again, contrary to all the odds, produced yet another match to remember.

Mischievously, it must be assumed, some people suggested Rangers should be given Aberdeen to keep if they won again. A 3–1 defeat by Hearts in a league match a week before the final also suggested the Pittodrie side might have trouble achieving their best form at Hampden.

Not that Graeme Souness was ever likely to allow a single result to cloud his judgement for the match ahead. 'If that had happened to us we would be at our most dangerous,' he professed. 'It's safe to assume that's exactly the way it applies to Aberdeen.'

Most of the players chosen to appear at Hampden on 22 October 1989, together with the referee, Mr G.B. Smith, from Edinburgh, were survivors from the previous year's final. The two sides lined up at the start as follows: *Rangers* – Woods, Stevens, Munro, Gough, Wilkins, Butcher, Steven, I. Ferguson, McCoist, Johnston, Walters. *Aberdeen* – Snelders, McKimmie, Robertson, Grant, McLeish, Miller, Nicholas, Bett, Mason, Connor, Jess.

In the course of their epic struggle for supremacy in the Skol Cup final, throughout much of its existence, serious infringements which the referee thought worthy of a penalty cost both clubs important, and sometimes crucial, goals. On Sunday, 25 October 1987, Walker, in goal for Rangers, fouled Falconer of Aberdeen: Bett scored. A year later, on Sunday 23 October 1988, the Aberdeen goalkeeper, Snelders, fouled Drinkell of Rangers: McCoist scored.

It was hardly surprising, therefore, and in line with established tradition, on 22 October 1989, when referee George Smith awarded a penalty at a crucial point in the match.

Ally McCoist, of Rangers, and his international team-mate, Willie Miller, of Aberdeen, had been engaged in a determined struggle for the ball when both players fell inside the penalty area. Many people, not at the Rangers end, and in the stand, thought referee Smith was harsh to penalise Miller.

McCoist, with five league cup medals to his credit, four of them in the Skol Cup, was well known for his insatiable appetite for goals. But on this occasion he deferred to Mark Walters, who put the ball into the right-hand corner of the net as Snelders went left. After 34 minutes, Rangers were level.

Twenty-two minutes into the match Aberdeen had taken the lead when Paul Mason, a young Englishman purchased from the Dutch side Groningen for a bargain £160,000, scored. 'Aberdeen's goal was scored at a time when their play was not carrying any great threat,' one report noted.

'But following the penalty, players such as Bett and the central defensive partnership of Miller and McLeish began to tap their deep reservoir of experience to hold the team together.'

Bett, the man of the match, assumed a visionary role in midfield, with surging runs deep into Rangers' territory, according to James Traynor, writing in *The Glasgow Herald*. The same writer also suggested: 'It is never a straightforward encounter when Rangers play Aberdeen at the national stadium and many might have felt short-changed had they been denied extra time.'

That they weren't was clearly due in large part to referee George Smith's first-half decision to side with Ally McCoist against Willie Miller on the question of the disputed award of a penalty to Rangers.

Twelve minutes into the additional period Mason added to his score with the goal that finally took the cup to Aberdeen. A corner, taken by Robertson, was headed down by van der Ark, who had replaced Brian Grant late in the second half. Nicholas squared the ball to Mason who immediately snapped it past Woods in the Rangers goal.

'It was now nerve-fraying stuff,' the winners' home-town paper, the formidable *Press and Journal*, reported excitedly. 'Could Aberdeen hold on or would Rangers, with their traditional fighting fervour, get the equaliser?'

They certainly came close. Ally McCoist and Maurice Johnston both almost scored. At the final whistle, however, Aberdeen were still ahead. And no-one could say they weren't there on merit.

Devoting the whole of its main leader to the local team's marvellous achievement, the *Press and Journal* could barely conceal its excitement. 'It is never easy to go to Glasgow and win what is always a home match for Rangers, given the intimidating and hostile atmosphere their huge support can generate,' a leading article, no less, observed.

There was no hiding the paper's pride or its delight in the result. The leading article noted happily: 'Aberdeen, once again, are a force to be reckoned with and it is marvellous that the many loyal thousands who made the long trek to Glasgow have been rewarded.'

A considerate Alex Smith, the Aberdeen manager, not unused to success at Hampden – he was in charge of the St Mirren side that won the Scottish Cup, with a goal by Ian Ferguson, in 1987 – offered some small consolation to his beaten rivals. 'It takes two teams to make an entertaining final and Rangers deserve sympathy because I know how we felt last year,' said Smith.

Graeme Souness, having become used to victory in the Skol Cup final, sounded stoical in defeat. He thought Rangers were ahead in the first half; with Aberdeen the better side in the second half. Aberdeen also got a bit of luck, Souness thought. 'But maybe we had that last year,' he conceded generously. 'I have no complaints.'

It was a fine note on which to end an intriguing and always exciting series of matches. Play lasted the best part of six hours and produced 22 goals, 11 of them from the penalty spot, including three in the course of normal play.

And those who questioned the closeness of the contest could also reflect that, across three games, excluding the penalty shoot-out, both sides finished level on goal average.

CHAPTER THIRTEEN

Few people recognised the signs then, of course, but, as the 1980s approached, the days of the British championship and serious matches between Scotland and England, home and away at Hampden and Wembley, were numbered.

As a competition the British championship, which was first staged in 1883, served the four home associations well for more than 100 years. Increasingly, however, new priorities imposed by the growing importance of the World Cup and the European Nations' championship served to reduce its value.

Two world wars hindered the development of international football in Europe. For years the two leading home football associations were unable to play serious foreign opposition, such as Germany, Austria, France, Italy, Czechoslovakia and Hungary. But there was also a feeling, widespread in Britain for many years, that foreign sides weren't quite good enough to compete on equal terms against Scotland and England.

In the British championship, throughout the first half of the present century, Wales and Northern Ireland provided only an occasional threat to the supremacy of Scotland and England. The most imposing opposition the two leading home countries could expect to face each year was one another, either at Hampden or at Wembley.

But there was probably never a time when the fixture didn't generate greater interest in Scotland than in England. Whether it was played at home or away, to the vast majority of Scottish supporters, the annual match with England always amounted to something more than a football match. Scotland was different from England: historically, socially, politically. For years, at Hampden especially, football and politics intermingled dangerously.

Scottish supporters usually divided into two main groups. The majority, possibly, would have been among the first to agree football and politics could be a dangerous mix. They wanted Scotland to win against England largely because victory was usually preferable to defeat, whatever the opposition. As England was our oldest rival on a football pitch it was not unreasonable to admit a win over England was a peculiarly enjoyable experience.

For a start it demonstrated for all to see that Scotland, despite its size, quite often surpassed its larger neighbour in general achievement. If this was the cause of any embarrassment to the defeated English, good! There was even a possibility those of an arrogant and complacent disposition might benefit from the experience, or so those of a reasonable and tolerant nature among the large body of Scottish supporters present at matches against England liked to imagine.

Others on the terracing and in the stand who supported Scotland demonstrated a noisier, darker, more dangerous side to the national psyche. Most of them actively disliked the English for reasons they found difficult to articulate but largely because for centuries, they believed, with a passion it was impossible to disengage, England had been the dominant and domineering force in a union they didn't want and couldn't change.

It was never fair on the players involved, including several who were happy to be conscripted to the flag, that they were made to carry the burden of a nation's hopes, dreams, aspirations, anger and frustration.

Notoriously, when the London transport trade unions made it impossible for Scots fans to travel, by bus or train, from the centre of London to Wembley Stadium, claiming they feared for the safety of their members, as many as 30,000 tartan-bedecked supporters completed the long march to Wembley in support of their heroes, and in open defiance of anyone who tried to stop them.

That this was the Wembley of poor Stewart Kennedy, and a crushing defeat for Scotland didn't make the dispiriting trek back to the city centre any easier. But neither did it succeed in seriously impairing the Scots' dream of future glory – of next year, when England were due at Hampden, and the day's events could be consigned to the debit side of history.

Which, not surprisingly, is exactly what happened at Hampden a year later, on 15 May 1976, when 85,165 spectators saw a new and vigorous Scotland side rise from the ashes of the Wembley fiasco.

Both teams showed major changes from the previous year. They lined up as follows: *Scotland* – Rough (Partick Thistle), McGrain (Celtic), Donachie (Manchester City), Forsyth (Rangers), Jackson (Rangers), Rioch (Derby County), Dalglish (Celtic), Masson (Queen's Park Rangers), Jordan (Leeds United), Gemmill (Derby County), Gray (Leeds United). *England* – Clemence (Liverpool), Todd (Derby County), Mills (Ipswich Town), Thompson (Liverpool), McFarland (Derby County), Kennedy (Liverpool), Keegan (Liverpool), Channon (Southampton), Pearson (Manchester United), Francis (Queen's Park Rangers), Taylor (Crystal Palace). *Referee* – K. Palotai, Hungary.

Scotland had been enjoying a good season with two wins over Denmark, a draw against Rumania and victories over Switzerland, Wales and Northern Ireland to their credit.

But terracing hopes, high at the start, were almost shattered in the opening minute. An awkward ball skidded on the wet surface in front of the Scotland goal. Fumbling to control it, Alan Rough smarted as the ball caught him full in the face. Some in the crowd exchanged nervous glances, and gasped, as the ball bounced clear.

It had been an uneasy moment, precursor, perhaps, of other uneasy moments; dreaded, but half-expected, in the course of the afternoon.

When it came to excitement, this was a contest that set its own rules of engagement. And rarely failed to generate its own peculiar sense of tragedy – and drama. As most of those present realised to their cost, Rough's near-gaff was typical of what happened when Scotland played England at Hampden.

However, on this occasion at least, the young goalkeeper's early encounter with fate wasn't accompanied by the loss of an early goal; although, as events soon proved, there was nothing unusual about England looking outplayed and scoring first. In particular, an early header by Kenny Dalglish, after Scotland settled quickly, forced the best from Clemence to keep England level.

Then, with the match barely 11 minutes old, Roy McFarland, the England centre-half, instituted a raid on the Scotland goal. With the Scottish defence floundering, McFarland despatched a dangerous-looking ball across the face of the Scottish goal. Channon reached it first. His header was too much for Rough. Scotland were a goal down.

The large crowd had been contemplating the huge and happy sound that would fill the Hampden air when Scotland scored. Now they sighed and shuffled, and glanced at their neighbours, muttering and cursing disconsolately; fearing the worst.

'Credit Scotland with skill and courage,' *The Scottish Football Book* enthused later. 'There was furious reaction to that dent to their pride.' Seven minutes after Channon scored Scotland equalised, Don Masson heading the ball into the net from an Eddie Gray corner. The crowd, who had been responding with verve and clamour to the non-stop nature of the Scottish assault on the England goal, went wild.

A disallowed penalty might have helped Scotland to a half-time lead. As the players headed for the dressing-rooms the home side probably deserved to be a goal or two in front. Scotland a goal or two ahead at half-time was a circumstance rarely encountered at Hampden, or anywhere else Scotland played, and regular supporters would have been delighted to sample the experience.

But even the most obdurate, zealous and anxious follower of the national side, someone, for example, who'd spend decades following Scotland's fluc-tuating international fortunes, who was privileged to be present at Hampden on 15 May 1976, or happened to be watching the match live on televison, could have been persuaded to trade a comfortable half-time lead for the stuttering, solitary goal which decided the match in Scotland's favour. It happened some-thing like this.

Four minutes into the second half Joe Jordan crossed from the left. Kenny Dalglish, deep inside the England penalty area, avoided a sliding tackle from Mick Mills. Only one man stood between him and the England goal, Ray Clemence.

The crowd roared. This was a good scoring chance. Given to Kenny Dalglish! Nobody better! Given half a chance, Dalglish was usually lethal in front of goal. On this occasion, however, the ball was only half hit. And a huge groan of disappointment from the noisier elements in the Hampden crowd was all this particular effort looked likely to attract.

Ray Clemence, a world-class goalkeeper who played 61 times for England, with Liverpool and Spurs, dropped to his knees to gather the ball – and fell

Kenny Dalglish celebrates the cheekiest goal ever scored in a major match at the national stadium. Playing against England on 15 May 1976 a half-hit shot trickled between goalkeeper Ray Clemence's legs and into the net

England goalkeeper Ray Clemence can't believe his misfortune. His blunder brought Scotland outright victory in the British championship for the first time in nearly a decade

forward on to the grass, covering his face, as it slipped from his grasp, through his legs and trickled into the net.

There was a moment's stunned silence from the Hampden crowd, followed by a gasp of disbelief, and then laughter, as Dalglish, arms stretched high, his face a picture of wondrous delight, accepted the amused, but thankful, congratulations of his team-mates. It was a goal, someone remarked, more suited to Glasgow Green than Hampden Park. Not that anyone cared. It was good enough to beat England.

There would have been little welcome in Scotland for the realisation that Ray Clemence's blunder, which helped Scotland to an outright win in the British championship for the first time in nearly a decade, also provided Scotland with their very last win against England at Hampden in the near-century-old competition.

Even as its detractors continued to undermine the fixture, in the face of wider competition, and the demands made on players whose regular employers expected them to produce top form in lucrative club competitions involving European sides, matches between Scotland and England continued to attract sizeable crowds and generate considerable public interest, in Scotland at least. Most people would have been forced to confess some interest in the result. Indifference was hard to find and difficult to justify.

Following the game against England at Hampden in 1976 there were only four more matches in the British championship, involving the same two countries, played at the Mount Florida ground.

Victory at Wembley in 1977 by the odd goal in three helped Scotland retain the British title. But it was the last good cheer for Scotland against England for quite some time. Between 1978 and 1980 England notched another hat-trick of wins against Scotland; two of them at Hampden. Thereafter, before the British championship came to a sad, but predictable, end, the best Scotland could manage in the competition against England was a one-goal victory at Wembley in 1981, and a 1–1 draw at Hampden in 1984.

There was not a lot memorable about that last match except, once and for all, it brought to an end the island mentality of those who steered and governed Britain's ailing football fortunes; although many people felt sorry for Wales and Northern Ireland who, with the loss of the British championship, had been deprived of their main source of income.

Both countries made a significant contribution to the development of football as Britain's national game. They also produced their share of great players, among them, from Wales, John Charles, Ivor Allchurch, Ronnie Burgess, Cliff Jones and Ian Rush; with Northern Ireland providing star names across the years like Peter Doherty, Danny Blanchflower, Bertie Peacock and Phil Jennings, not forgetting the man many good judges considered the greatest player of his generation in the world, George Best.

It was somehow typical of football that, having rid themselves of the perceived burden of the British international championship, the SFA and the FA showed themselves unwilling to abandon their own exclusive little earner: matches played against each other at Hampden and Wembley.

158

Right from the beginning, in 1883, there had been a legitimate national pride, and a true sporting purpose, to the British international championship. But there was only one real point to the Rous Cup, which followed the British championship, and that was to ensure people in large numbers continued to part with their money for the benefit of the SFA and the FA, instead of some other less worthy pursuit.

It could be argued, of course, that the two governing bodies would have been historically unwise, and commercially foolish, to abandon the ancient fixture. Scotland against England, whether at Hampden or Wembley, generally provided an exciting, and usually meaningful, finale to any season; a fact of history which was bound to please a majority of fans. It was their interest which ensured the fixture was also highly profitable; and, in pursuit of income, the SFA and the FA rarely demonstrated a liking for profligacy.

So, for the first two years of its brief and perhaps future life, only two countries competed for the Rous silverware – Scotland and England. In 1985, only a year after the British championship ended, England returned to Hampden and lost by a single goal. The following year Scotland travelled to Wembley and lost 2–1.

Supporters were assured the new tournament would eventually develop to include one other country, with Italy, France, Germany, Holland, or some other leading continental nation, invited to make up the numbers each year; even alternating, from year to year, with one of the great South American sides on a fact-finding mission to Europe. But it was always hard to imagine this happening in any meaningful, truly competitive sense. There was enough to occupy the minds of those legislators with a real interest in the outcome of the World Cup, or the destination of the European Nations championship, without adding the Rous Cup to their labours.

It always seemed the best the Rous Cup could hope to achieve was the continuation of the annual match, home and away, between Scotland and England; and, possibly, the sight of some especially gifted foreign practitioner appearing at Hampden in a superior friendly.

Brazil, on a blooding tour of Europe in 1987, aimed mainly at giving younger players some experience of European conditions and playing styles in advance of the 1990 World Cup in Italy, were the first foreign side to accept an invitation to compete in the Rous Cup.

There was a growing suspicion, propagated in Scotland at least, that the Football Association didn't want the new tournament to continue, never mind prosper; although it had been named after one of English football's most famous administrators, a former president of FIFA, Sir Stanley Rous.

In a crowded international calendar that now rolled on, inexorably, from one season to the next, the European Nations tournament augmented the already demanding World Cup.

There were also the demands of European club competitions, in which clubs from England and Scotland figured prominently until the Heysel stadium disaster in 1985 put an end to England's participation, temporarily, to consider; plus a bloated league fixture list, on both sides of the border, that left the men who really mattered, the players, exhausted.

It wasn't long before Alex Cameron, one of Scotland's most experienced football watchers, complaining about the Rous Cup's lack of a competitive edge, felt obliged to warn readers of the *Daily Record*: 'Fans are being conditioned to the idea that end-of-season internationals are an inconvenience football could do without.'

To date only three teams from overseas have appeared in the Rous Cup. None came from Europe: South America, incongruously, provided all three.

Brazil was the first to appear. Scheduled to arrive in Glasgow only three days after England, supporters, gluttonous for excitement, were expecting a football treat.

After watching the Brazilians draw with England at Wembley in midweek, Andy Roxburgh, not long in charge of the Scottish team, was optimistic about Scotland's chances of regaining the Rous Cup. 'Hampden is the kind of stage our players should relish. England and Brazil drawing gives us a chance of winning the trophy,' Roxburgh declared; demonstrating he could touch the heart of the Scottish character.

In other words, if the national coach and his chosen team could simply master England and Brazil, in the space of a remarkable four days at Hampden, the Rous Cup would be returning to its rightful place at Park Gardens, home of the SFA. Nobody was asking very much of the Scotland team; except, perhaps, the impossible.

Roxburgh had been put in charge of the national side following the World Cup in Mexico and the planned departure of Alex Ferguson who took temporary command following the death of Jock Stein. Roxburgh preferred the job description 'national coach' to the more familiar title of 'team manager'. His credentials as a coach were impeccable and respected worldwide. However, nearer home, on the dubious grounds he was an SFA insider who never performed at the highest levels as a player, his appointment was viewed with suspicion by many people.

Of course, Roxburgh wasn't the first Scotland team boss to be the subject of constant scrutiny and often unfair criticism; although, in view of his achievement in steering his players to the finals of the World Cup in Italy in 1990 and, uniquely, the European finals in Sweden two years later, until now, he is the last!

Shortly before his first encounter with an England side managed by the highly experienced Bobby Robson, the new man ventured hopefully: 'It should be quite a game and one that should bring out the best in us. It is a huge occasion for all of us and for me, personally, it is the highlight of my career so far.'

Most people agreed Roxburgh had been wise not to consider any player from Dundee United, exhausted and disappointed following two cup final defeats in less than a week.

For more than a decade, Dundee United, managed by Jim McLean, had been one of the most consistent sides in Scotland. One league championship, two Bell's league cups, and an appearance in two finals of the Scottish Cup in the last eight years was evidence of their high success rate.

However, during the same period, different teams dressed in tangerine also demonstrated a tendency to stumble, with a major trophy almost within their grasp. They had been beaten once by Rangers, following a replay, and once by Celtic in finals of the Scottish Cup; as well as losing twice to the Ibrox side on the last day of the Skol Cup.

As they were already into the final of the 1987 UEFA Cup against Gothenburg, and only trailing by a single goal from the away leg in Sweden, it was hardly surprising most people rated Dundee United ahead of St Mirren to win the Scottish Cup for the first time in their history.

This was only the third of five Scottish Cup final appearances by Dundee United in a ten-year period starting in 1981. Sadly, for Jim McLean and the teams he built, they all ended in defeat.

At Hampden on 16 May 1987, a crowd totalling 51,782 saw a goal by Ian Ferguson, scored in extra time, take the trophy to Paisley. The teams at the start were: *St Mirren* – Money, Wilson, Hamilton, Abercromby, Winnie, Cooper, McGarvey, Ferguson, McDowall, Hamilton, Lambert. *Dundee United* – Thomson, Holt, Malpas, McInally, Hegarty, Narey, Bannon, Gallacher, Paatelainen, Ferguson, McKinlay. *Referee* – K.J. Hope, Clarkston.

Four days later, in the second leg of the UEFA Cup final, played on their own ground, with the whole of Scotland hoping their luck would change, courage and determination weren't enough: Gothenburg finished 2–1 ahead on aggregate and Dundee United saw another great prize snatched from their grasp.

In different circumstances, Maurice Malpas, David Narey, Jim McInally and Paul Sturrock might have been included in the side to play England at Hampden on Saturday, 23 May 1987. Their absence, and other problems over team selection, at least meant the usual large army of Scotland supporters arrived at Hampden unburdened with customary expectations – always exaggerated! – of victory.

Of more immediate concern, especially to the vast majority of the population with only a passing interest in what happened on the playing surface at Hampden, was the rumoured arrival in Glasgow of an army of thugs from England, intent on causing trouble before, during and after the match against Scotland.

Scotland supporters had been earning a reputation for good behaviour wherever the national team travelled: no coincidence, perhaps, that this was in direct contrast to the shameful tales of violence that accompanied the English national side on trips abroad.

It would have been difficult to orchestrate, of course, but good behaviour was a weapon too. If it helped embarrass their oldest foes, even among the sturdiest Scottish supporters, it was one worth employing. However, nobody believed the admirable standards of behaviour set by Scottish supporters during the last two decades were entirely immune from provocation.

Although the football authorities were once again blameless, the game itself

Referee Kenny Hope resists an appeal by David Narey, Jim McInally and Ian Redford, of Dundee United, following an incident in the 1987 Scottish Cup final against St Mirren. A goal by Ian Ferguson, in extra time, settled the match in favour of the Paisley side

was unlikely to emerge unscathed from any riot: one of the most exciting and enduring contests in the history of British sport was clearly under threat.

Most of the 5,000-strong visiting England support were given a police escort to and from Hampden. Inside the ground they were confined to a section of the uncovered east end terracing, well away from the large army of Scots fans in the 64,713 crowd, occupying what was left of Hampden.

Following the game trouble did spread from the area of the ground to the surrounding streets of normally peaceful Mount Florida and King's Park, before erupting, finally, in the city centre. A determined response by Strathclyde police filled cells to overflowing.

Those with the best interests of Scottish football at heart were pleased to note that most of the troublemakers gave addresses outside Scotland.

The teams at Hampden on 23 May 1987 were: *Scotland* – Leighton (Aberdeen), Gough (Tottenham Hotspur), Miller (Aberdeen), McLeish (Aberdeen), MacLeod (Celtic), Aitken (Celtic), McStay (Celtic), Wilson (Leicester City), Simpson (Aberdeen), McClair (Celtic), McCoist (Rangers). *England* – Woods (Rangers), Stevens (Everton), Pearce (Nottingham Forest), Hoddle (Tottenham Hotspur), Butcher (Rangers), Robson (Manchester United), Beardsley (Newcastle United), Hateley (AC Milan), Hodge (Tottenham Hotspur), Waddle (Tottenham Hotspur). *Referee* – D. Pauly, West Germany.

Nobody expected much from a depleted Scotland side. There should have been more on offer from England, however.

In fact, it was a dull match with hardly any excitement for the fans to enjoy for any part of the 90 minutes; and, for only the third time in the history of the fixture, no goals. Bobby Robson, the England manager, blamed tired minds and tired legs, at the end of a long, hard season, for his team's poor display. 'I'm glad it's all over. We could all use the rest,' Robson sighed.

Andy Roxburgh praised his players on their commitment against England. 'A lot of people south of the border were rubbing their hands, thinking we were going to get a doing. Well, we didn't,' Roxburgh declared.

With the Brazilians due at Hampden in three days' time, the Scotland squad couldn't afford to relax.

Carlos Albert Silva, the Brazilian manager, was quick to reassure anyone who believed his players, average age 23, would be treating the match with Scotland less than seriously. 'To play against Scotland is something very special for them,' Silva insisted.

Nothing short of victory at Hampden would please the fans back home in Brazil, the manager explained. 'If we can beat Scotland then we can win a trophy against England and Scotland which will give our supporters a great lift,' Silva said.

In previous years Brazil never really planned for the World Cup, Silva continued, going on to admit: 'It was our arrogance that we always felt we had good players and that everything would come right on the day.' Now the World Cup was changing, people who expected Brazil to keep on winning were losing patience with the national side. 'I just hope the Scottish fans like what we are trying to build,' the manager added seriously.

James Traynor, reporting for *The Glasgow Herald*, refused to be fooled by the relative youth of the Brazilian players. He acknowledged the current batch might lack the charisma which clung to their predecessors – no Pele, Garrincha, Rivelino or Socrates, although his little brother, Rai, might play at Hampden. However, afforded hero status back home they were 'still good enough to bamboozle most teams stupid enough to give them time and space to perform', Traynor warned.

'Morale is high, never better,' coach Roxburgh told reporters. 'We're going into the game feeling we can win.'

'If only it were that simple,' James Traynor appeared to reply. 'If only we were so well endowed with the skilful and flamboyant types that we could feel genuine confidence about taking on the masters of technique and flair.'

With crowd numbers totalling only 41,384, the teams at Hampden on 26 May 1987 were: *Scotland* – Goram (Oldham), Gough (Spurs), MacLeod (Celtic), Aitken (Celtic), McLeish (Aberdeen), Miller (Aberdeen), McStay (Celtic), McInally (Dundee United), McCoist (Rangers), Wilson (Leicester City), Cooper (Rangers). *Brazil* – Carlos, Josimar, Geraldao, Ricardo, Douglas, Nelsinho,

Muller, Mirandinha, Edu, Valdo, Rai. *Referee* – L. Angolin, Italy.

In the first few minutes of the match, Davie Cooper, who, in a different life, wouldn't have looked out of place practising his own marvellous skills on Copacabana beach, demonstrated that the Brazilians weren't the only people on the park with technique and flair. Having won a free kick against Josimar, the Rangers' winger proceeded to demonstrate his speciality, delivering the kind of ball that would discomfit any side, even Brazil. The visitors were fortunate that Richard Gough, on the receiving end, miskicked and Roy Aitken headed over. But it was an encouraging start for Scotland. The crowd, small in numbers but appreciative, roared encouragingly.

'The Scots were given licence to kill by the tactics of the Brazilians. The visitors passed the ball accurately but they didn't want to know anything physical,' the *Daily Record* reported.

Before half-time Scotland missed several good chances. Richard Gough and Alex McLeish, in particular, both squandered golden opportunities; while a thunderous shot by Willie Miller from 35 yards was well held by goalkeeper Carlos.

Scotland were making their presence felt in the match but only for as long as Brazil cared to let them, it seemed. A mistake by Goram, early in the second half, let Rai open the scoring, to be followed soon after by Valdo who made it 2–0.

To the delight of the Hampden crowd, who were always prepared to tolerate Scotland losing to Brazil, once settled in their lead the visitors set about tantalising the opposition with a display of skills Scotland couldn't equal. 'Brazil gave Scotland a reminder of how soccer should be played,' the *Daily Record* reported. 'It was a superb exhibition of passing and holding the ball.'

Nobody grudged Geraldao the honour of collecting the Rous Cup; or the entire Brazilian team their lap of honour, to an accompaniment of Scotland supporters applauding them hugely, at the end.

'Once again our fans were a credit to their country,' Jim Reynolds informed readers of *The Glasgow Herald*. 'The players, although beaten, didn't do themselves any harm either.' Reynolds, who ventured the opinion Scotland did better against the South Americans than against England, thought the real losers were those fans who stayed away from Hampden. 'They missed a real treat,' he declared.

Showing no great surprise at the result, the Scotland coach, Andy Roxburgh, admitted later: 'It's all down to goal scoring or, in our case, not goal scoring. We just did not take our chances and that has been the problem for a long time.'

Roxburgh paid tribute to the Brazilians' superb mastery of the ball. 'We must concentrate on this with our boys.'

Carlos Albert Silva, pleased with his team's performance, beamed. 'We could feel the warmth of the Scottish admiration for our players,' he said.

Asked by a visiting journalist how he assessed the young Brazilians, Roxburgh deadpanned, 'I think one or two of them have a future.'

Colombia and Chile who participated in the last two tournaments, staged in 1988 and 1989, were never likely to attract the same crowd appeal as their neighbour Brazil.

A goalless draw against Colombia, and a 2–0 victory over Chile, did little for Scottish morale, considering England won again in consecutive years. However, if these unfancied South Americans were the most interesting foreign opposition the SFA and the FA could attract to Hampden and Wembley, the Rous Cup, as a three-nation spectacle, was almost certainly doomed.

With or without some foreign ingredients, and despite its shortcomings as a serious competition, in the absence of a British championship, the Rous Cup at least allowed dedicated supporters of Scotland and England to pursue their century-old rivalry beneath a different banner. If 22 players, dressed in the colours of Scotland and England, never again appeared at Hampden or Wembley the loss to the game, in emotional terms at least, would be incalculable.

CHAPTER FOURTEEN

An element of farce, bordering on madness, has been known to attend the efforts of various Scotland squads sent in pursuit of football's biggest prize, the World Cup.

However, those players, and their managers, who pursued a long and difficult road to limited glory by qualifying for five consecutive finals between 1974 and 1990, could be forgiven thinking people were a mite fickle.

Qualifying for the finals – almost always dangerously! – made them heroes. Their chances of proceeding beyond the first round of the finals – when the serious business of winning the World Cup begins in earnest – occasionally appeared good; especially to those of their countrymen who were quite capable of ignoring the strength in depth of any task force ranged against them. Certainly, in Germany, Argentina, Spain, Mexico and Italy, the uncritical optimism of many fans did little to prepare them for the players' ultimate failure against superior, and, not infrequently, inferior, opposition.

The lessons for Scottish football of more than four decades' proximity to the World Cup are gloomy: the national side could never really justify the fans' loudly proclaimed pretensions that they were the favoured representatives of a world football power. Those who disagree should ask themselves, if the World Cup was starting now, would Scotland be offered a virtual bye into the finals in order to ensure their presence?

Yet that is exactly what happened when the World Cup was relaunched following the Second World War. Typical of the collective foolishness attendant on some of our subsequent adventures in pursuit of the great prize, the offer was refused.

For nearly three decades, following the First World War, Scotland, England, Wales and Northern Ireland all elected to remain outside the world football community represented by FIFA. The decision deprived the four home countries of an invitation to compete in three World Cup tournaments, held in Uruguay, Italy and France, between 1930 and 1938.

It also helped extend by several years the fanciful, and certainly questionable notion, as it was largely untried, and never the subject of rigorous examination, that British football generally – Scotland and England especially! – couldn't be equalled anywhere in the world.

However, long before regular exposure to the demands of the World Cup, and the European Nations tournament, provided the means of testing the national side's capabilities outside the narrow demands of the home international championship, there was evidence to suggest the game in Scotland was weaker than many of its followers imagined.

The sight of Scotland obliged to face opposition from outside the United Kingdom, and struggling to compete against the best sides in Europe, is a relatively new experience. During the early part of this century continental travel, although sometimes conducted in the grand manner, could be difficult and uncertain. Two world wars, and the general disruption of Europe, didn't help. But for years the home football associations showed little enthusiasm for the rigours involved.

There was also a general feeling – an unwarranted complacency – that the continentals weren't quite good enough; an attitude to life hindered by the stifling Scottish assumption that beating England was all that mattered.

The twentieth century was almost three decades old before Scotland first ventured abroad. But in the summer of 1929 a three-nation tour of Europe produced a satisfactory crop of results.

On 28 May, in their first match against a country from outside the British Isles, a Scottish side defeated Norway 7–3 in Bergen. According to one eye-witness account the home side displayed a sound knowledge of the game but 'fore and aft Scotland did well'.

Four days later, in Berlin, there was a crowd of 45,000 for the game against Germany – more familiar numbers to members of the Scotland party than the sparse 4,000 who watched them play in Bergen. However, there was also a noticeable difference about the quality and attitude of the opposition in the German capital, as the Scots soon discovered!

In the words of one report: 'The Germans let themselves go. They stood not on ceremony. Our fellows had to strain every nerve to keep up their end.' A goal by Germany early in the second half wasn't matched until three minutes from the end. But everyone agreed it was a fair result. 'Although the contest was hard and fast,' SFA secretary George Graham commented later, 'it was fought out in thoroughly sportsmanlike fashion.'

One member of the touring party, Rangers chairman, Bailie James Buchanan, confessed himself much impressed 'by the fairness of the Berlin crowd. When we were leaving the stadium they gathered round our car and, raising their hats, gave us a hearty cheer.'

The tour ended happily with a 2–0 victory over Holland in Amsterdam. According to the Press Association 'the Scottish players did not expose themselves to the reproach so frequently levelled against visiting British teams on the continent. They gave of their best and showed no lack of enthusiasm and dash from start to finish.' However, according to another eye-witness: 'In technique the Scots were only slightly superior to the Hollanders.' But not everyone interested in the continued good health of Scottish football noticed or agreed with this assessment. SFA secretary, George Graham, told reporters on his return:

'Norwegian, German and Dutch papers are unanimous in praise of our football.' Another senior official admitted he thought the continental game was progressing. But he also ventured the opinion that 'everybody was endeavouring to cultivate the Scots style'.

A visit to Paris the following year, which produced a 2–0 victory over France, appeared to consolidate this view.

Certainly, the nation was ill-prepared for the trauma of Scotland's second major European tour – to Vienna and Rome, the capital cities of Austria and Italy, concluding with a visit to Geneva, for a match against Switzerland, in the summer of 1931.

A 2–0 victory over England at Hampden failed to secure the home international championship outright. Points squandered against Wales and Northern Ireland obliged Scotland to share the British title with England, a not uncommon occurrence.

The absence of players from some of the top clubs, including Rangers, Celtic, Motherwell and Third Lanark, who were all otherwise engaged, pursuing the business of football for gain in other parts of the world, meant the selectors were forced to recruit a makeshift side.

There was the usual litany of complaint, familiar down the years, that it was folly to undertake a tour of this importance at a time of year when the players were 'tired and fed up with the game, and the future of football demands they should be resting'.

People generally were apprehensive about the tour. Following the opening match against Austria in Vienna on 16 May 1931, one leading reporter, Waverley of the *Daily Record*, informed his readers darkly: 'I have warned the SFA and our players by letters from continental Scots friends what to expect over there.'

One thing no-one expected – even the brooding Waverley at his gloomiest could be discounted – was a 5–0 drubbing. 'Fancy Scotland, the home of soccer, sending out an international team to be beaten five goals to nothing,' wailed Waverley; adding bleakly: 'Couple this with England's 5–2 defeat in France the other day and think what a tasty morsel this is for Gaul and Austrian. What a knock out for our perfervid Scots and Saxons who never cease telling the foreigners with whom they live that the Gael and Saxon are the world's top footballers. How they will have to hide their diminished heads.'

However, as a report in the same newspaper made plain: 'The Austrians were the better team and thoroughly deserved their victory.' The same report continued: 'Right from the start Scotland was in difficulties. The Austrian forwards swung into their game at once and the 37,000 crowd was roused to the pitch of excitement by the manner in which the Scottish defence was beleaguered.'

Another reporter thought 'the Austrians were vastly superior in strength, in speed, in combination, above all in purpose. In the end they were doing as they liked with the ball and they became too lazy to shoot any more goals. The crowd began to laugh and then, in time, melted away.'

It was left to Waverley to voice the hopes of the nation. 'We may do better on Wednesday against Italy in Rome and on Saturday against Switzerland in Geneva. But even if we do ever so much better we cannot atone for Saturday's debacle.'

But in Rome, with Benito Mussolini beaming and waving to the crowd, mostly comprising 30,000 noisy Latins, and the British ambassador seated beside Il Duce, struggling to conceal his embarrassment, Scotland were once again humiliated; beaten 3–0 on this occasion, a narrower margin than the one suffered in Vienna – but no less crushing.

'In splendid weather, and on a dry, fast ground, the Scots were no match for the continental side,' was the bleak view contained in one dispatch.

A mood of black despair descended on the Scottish camp. Everyone was praying for better luck in Geneva. With no great insight, Ivan Sharpe, editor of *Athletic News*, informed the *Daily Record*: 'If they are to succeed they must improve much. So far they have certainly failed to cover themselves, or their country, with glory. Rather the reverse has been the case.'

In the event the tour ended scrappily with an unsatisfactory 3–2 win against Switzerland in Geneva on Sunday, 24 May. The match was played in torrid conditions in front of 20,000 spectators and offered little joy to the dispirited tourists. As described in one report: 'The Swiss were not of the same calibre as the Austrians and Italians. But your Scots won and, really, we are thankful for small mercies.'

Yet, despite the national humiliation suffered in Vienna and Rome in the summer of 1931, when viewed across the Thirties as a whole, Scotland's record against continental opposition, home and away, appears good; certainly one any modern manager might envy. A total of 12 matches involving France, Holland, Italy, Germany, Switzerland, Austria, Czechoslovakia and Hungary provided eight wins, two draws and two defeats.

Following their performance in Rome on 20 May 1931, and prior to the outbreak of the Second World War in September 1939, Scotland enjoyed an unbeaten run of eight matches against continental opposition.

Having beaten France 2–0 in Paris in 1930, Scotland retained the same margin of superiority on a second visit two years later; winning what another set of opponents of the period, Germany, would help ensure was the last match between the two countries for more than 16 years, 3–1.

But it was the winter of 1933 before home fans could judge the burgeoning quality of foreign opposition at Hampden first hand. No-one questioned the importance of the occasion – a return match with Austria.

'We have that five goals Vienna defeat to avenge,' thundered one leading scribe. 'We have the prestige of Scottish football to re-establish on the continent of Europe. Our fellows must lay the proud Austrians low.'

Anyone who believed continental football lacked vision and ambition wasn't listening to the pre-match words of Herr Hugo Meisl of the Austrian FA. It was his greatest dream, he told reporters, that one day all the nations of Great Britain and the continent would co-operate in an international league or cup competition. 'That would be great fun!' Herr Meisl insisted presciently.

Of immediate concern was the match at Hampden on 29 November 1933. An anxious Waverley confided to readers of the *Daily Record*: 'While there is none of the Bannockburn touch about today's match which attaches to a Scotland-England battle, I say we are equally keen to win.'

On the occasion of Scotland's ill-fated 1931 European tour, the selectors had been denied the services of players from several top clubs due to commitments elsewhere. Now they contrived to include five new caps, four of whom – Kennaway, Watson, Ogilvie and Bruce – never played for Scotland again. Macfadyen, the other new cap, was marginally more fortunate; extending his international career, with an appearance against Wales, later the same year.

But career stagnation, affecting nearly half a team, suggests a lack of judgement, or a marked contrariness, on the part of those responsible for national team selection at the time. It also confirms the vicissitudinous nature of selection by committee.

Of course, by present-day standards, before matches against foreign opposition became commonplace, it was impossible for even the most distinguished, and favoured, players to accumulate a large number of international honours. For example, the team selected to play Austria at Hampden on 29 November 1933, which fairly bristled with transitory new caps, also included one of the country's most experienced players, the centre-half and captain, Davie Meiklejohn.

In the course of a long and distinguished career Meiklejohn won 11 league championship medals and five Scottish Cup medals with Rangers. One recent club history names him as possibly the greatest Ranger of all time. Willie Thornton, another Ibrox great, thought him 'the greatest player I ever saw'. Bob McPhail, with 70 years' experience, also testified, in his biography, that he never saw a centre-half who could improve on Meiklejohn. But between 1922, when he won his first cap against Wales at Wrexham, and the match against Austria at Hampden in 1933, Meiklejohn played only 15 times for Scotland; and always, except for his last appearance, against home opposition.

On the occasion of their first Hampden encounter with a foreign side Scotland lined up as follows: Kennaway (Celtic), Anderson (Hearts), M'Gonagle (Celtic), Meiklejohn (Rangers), Watson (Blackpool), Brown (Rangers), Ogilvie (Motherwell), Bruce (Middlesbrough), Macfadyen (Motherwell), McPhail (Rangers), Duncan (Derby County).

In addition to welcoming the men from Austria, a good-sized Hampden crowd, totalling around 60,000, was treated to the unfamiliar sight of a Belgian referee. At least one reporter thought M. Langelus, who was dressed in cap, jacket and tight-looking breeches, looked ready 'to go cycling or shooting rather than refereeing'.

Austria looked dangerous from the moment play began. One reporter noted admiringly: 'They concentrate on constructive football. The backs pass to a half-back or a forward rather than kick hard or out of play.'

Another confirmed: 'The half-backs co-operated with the forwards who played the game along the front and on the floor as often as not. Their sense of position was always, or nearly always, in evidence.'

Presumably one such aberrant moment, when an Austrian player failed to position himself correctly, occurred seven minutes into the match: a Meiklejohn free-kick, assisted by a deflection, put Scotland ahead.

It was a lucky beginning which the home crowd found encouraging; although Austria appeared untroubled by this early misfortune and their introduction to the famous Hampden roar. Instead, as one reporter noted, they continued to involve all 11 players 'in cultured, intelligent combination'.

It proved a sensible way to proceed. Shortly before half-time, the visitors equalised. Few disagreed that, at this stage of the game, a draw could be considered fair.

Then, soon after the second half started, Scotland again took the lead. This time the ball dropped to Macfadyen after Ogilvie headed against the bar following a cross by Duncan.

Eight minutes into the second half the score was 2–2. And from then until the end of the match neither side scored again.

Writing in praise of Austria's goals Ivan Sharpe declared each of them a gem. 'That the Austrians could twice draw level by the highest class of football was a tribute to their ability that all must acknowledge,' wrote Sharpe. It was a view echoed by the experienced Waverley who thought the home side had been taught an object lesson by the Austrians; adding wryly: 'They played the game pretty much as we were in the habit of playing it, once upon a time.'

Hampden Park had been the SFA's favoured venue, and the established home of the Scottish international side, for almost 30 years. However, following the visit of Austria, and before the outbreak of the Second World War, three of the most important fixtures played against foreign opposition were staged at Ibrox. In a dizzy two-year spell between October 1936 and December 1938 with the national frontiers of Europe about to crumble, Scotland played host to Germany, Czechoslovakia and Hungary – and dealt convincingly with all three.

It was hardly surprising, given the explosive nature of European politics in the autumn of 1936, that many people thought the SFA had been foolish to arrange a match against Germany. The appearance of a German national side on British soil clearly presented Hitler with an excellent propaganda opportunity.

One reporter claimed to have seen German supporters, arriving at Queensferry, presenting cartons of food to unemployed workers they met in the street. Glasgow corporation, headed by Patrick Dollan, refused to honour the visitors with a civic reception – a decision which the SFA condemned as 'an insult to the association and to Scottish football'. An anonymous member of the SFA was alleged to have told reporters: 'We are not concerned with Germany's political beliefs. We are meeting as sportsmen. Football is a bond between nations.'

The response from Scotland's capital, as expressed by *The Scotsman*, appeared to support this sanguine view of the occasion. Someone writing anonymously from North Bridge was of the opinion that the German chancellor, Hitler, and his

171

propaganda minister, Goebbels, 'have accomplished few things to more purpose in their efforts to foster friendship between their people and those in this country than by their assent to the football match between representative teams of Scotland and Germany at Ibrox'.

A swastika-emblazoned aircraft brought the visitors from Cologne to Renfrew where the welcoming party included the German consul in Glasgow. Once ensconced in the Central Hotel, Glasgow, they attended an evening performance at the Pavilion Theatre. There the entertainment on offer included Herschel Henlere – who gave 'a delightful pot-pourri of old and new favourites', according to one view from the stalls – and Teddy Foster and his Kings of Swing – 'a red hot rhythm combination which put across their music with plenty of pep'.

On the day of the match the Union Jack and the Swastika flew side by side from the Ibrox stand.

The German players arrived at the main entrance in Edmiston Drive stripped and ready to play. But they were also late, due, in large part, to the presence of a large, enthusiastic crowd which blocked their route from the city centre.

No-one appeared to mind the match starting 18 minutes late. As *The Glasgow Herald* reported: 'A great wave of applause greeted the German players as they came on to the field. It was a disciplined entrance. The captain, Szepan, led them out, in single file, at a quick march. They made straight for the centre and lined up as if on parade.

'In this fashion they posed for newspaper and newsreel cameramen,' the same paper went on. 'They raised their right arms briskly towards the main stand. Then, turning about, they repeated the salute.'

The teams were: *Scotland* – Dawson (Rangers), Anderson (Hearts), Cummings (Aston Villa), Massie (Aston Villa), Simpson (Rangers), Brown (Rangers), Delaney (Celtic), Walker (Hearts), Armstrong (Aberdeen), McPhail (Rangers) and Duncan (Derby County). *Germany* Jakos, Mucnzcnbcrg, Munkert, Janes, Goldbrunner, Kitzinger, Elben, Gellesch, Siffling, Szepan, Urban. *Referee* – Mr H. Nattrass (England).

Not long into the match, with a glum-looking Jerry Dawson clearly beaten, the visitors appeared to be on the verge of achieving a major upset in the bright, breezy conditions. It seemed a perfectly good goal to most people watching. However, fortunately for Scotland, it was judged off-side by the referee, Mr Harry Nattrass. And, with a sigh of relief, the vast majority of those present were content to accept his unexpected beneficence.

According to the *Evening Times* match report – which, unusually, also carried an account in Germany alongside for the benefit of 700 fans who travelled from Hamburg for the match! – 'The Scots forwards all had clever touches but the keen tackling of our visitors prevented combined action.' There was little more than 20 minutes left for play when Scotland finally opened the scoring. 'In a fast attack Armstrong's shot struck a defender and Delaney, darting into the centre of the goal, shot cleanly to the net.'

Five minutes from the end it was Delaney again: a courageous effort, to judge by one account. 'It was daring to speed past the back's tackle and more than brave to face the oncoming 'keeper's rush. Delaney did both. Got knocked out inevitably, but got his well-earned reward.'

In its account of the match *The Scotsman* was barely lukewarm in its praise of the home performance. Scotland were really seldom dangerous as an attacking force and deserved their win principally on account of territorial advantage. 'The Germans might well have created a sensation in European sport had they not had fatal weaknesses at centre-forward and in goal. But for these the score might well have been reversed,' the paper claimed.

Czechoslovakia, another nation with its sights set on securing a place among the future giants of the game, arrived in Britain towards the end of 1937, and proceeded to give one of the best England teams in years the fright of their lives.

Playing at White Hart Lane, London, a week before they were due in Glasgow for the match against Scotland at Ibrox, the little known Europeans impressed everyone with their dribbling and short passing skills.

In a match which England finally won by the odd goal in nine the visitors also showed great resilience. Twice in the course of the afternoon England went two goals ahead and each time the unfancied Czechs succeeded in drawing level. Only a brilliant left-foot shot from Stanley Matthews, who was in marvellous form, securing his third goal of the match five minutes from time, salvaged the home side's pride.

However, as *The Glasgow Herald* noted: 'Not until the last kick was taken in darkness could the crowd feel sure that England had retained their supremacy over all continental visitors.'

The Czechs were only the third national side from continental Europe to visit Scotland. But a draw against Austria and a win over Germany meant Scotland could also claim an unbeaten record at home against strong continental opposition.

Only those with a dreamer's view of Scotland's place in the world game believed they could continue to win against an influx of foreign opposition. But, for as long as it lasted, everyone agreed it was a small distinction worth preserving.

For the match against Czechoslovakia at Ibrox on 8 December 1937, the Scottish selectors were obliged to depend on a side which didn't include their first-choice goalkeeper, Jerry Dawson, and their regular captain, Jimmy Simpson, both of Rangers. Instead a crowd of 41,000 welcomed: Waugh (Hearts), Anderson (Hearts) and Cummings (Aston Villa); Robertson (Kilmarnock), Johnston (Sunderland) and Brown (Rangers); Buchan (Chelsea), Walker (Hearts), M'Culloch (Brentford), Black (Hearts) and Kinnear (Rangers).

The side included no fewer than six new caps. But to almost everyone's surprise, considering the form which the visitors demonstrated against England only the previous week, Scotland completely out-played and out-manoeuvred the Czechs, thanks to what *The Glasgow Herald* described as 'a brilliant exhibition of wing half-back and inside-forward co-operation'.

173

'By the second half the forcing work of Brown and Robertson, and the swinging passes of Black and Walker to the wings, had the poor Czechs' defence overrun,' the same newspaper continued.

'The Brown-Black-Walker triangle was delightful to watch, and with Kinnear and Buchanan rounding off their movements with accurate crosses into goal, the spectators enjoyed a football treat.'

But even the most optimistic supporters, hoping for victory, encountered some difficulty in absorbing the final scoreline – 5–0 in favour of Scotland, with the opening goal scored almost straight from the kick-off.

'We are disappointed but not despondent,' was the philosophical view from the Czech camp afterwards. 'Scotland had a good team and deserved to win.'

Davie Meiklejohn, the former Scotland captain, who viewed the match as a journalist, thought the Czechs possessed football ability aplenty. What they lacked was a show of fire in their play, Meiklejohn maintained. The same good judge also counselled: 'If Scotland has not yet a great team, they have the makings of a good one.'

Almost exactly one year later, on 7 December 1938, a Hungarian national side arrived in Glasgow for the first time. Through no fault of its own the occasion eventually acquired an unfortunate distinction in the history of Scottish football: it was the last time Scotland appeared against continental opposition in advance of the Second World War.

The prevailing mood before the match is easily gauged from the opinions expressed by an anonymous correspondent in *The Glasgow Herald* whose attitude would be consistent with the majority British view of continental football at that time. Although his knowledge of the visitors was probably scant, the man from *The Herald* didn't doubt Scotland would triumph. 'So far as the result is concerned the match ought to be in Scotland's pocket,' he declared solidly, before further dismissing the importance of the Hungarian presence at Ibrox with a warning to the men who appeared for Scotland. 'The manner of the victory, if one may presume thus far, will be noted by the selectors, who have this last chance of seeing a representative side in action before the match with England in April. Our players therefore will do well to be on their toes from the kick-off if they are to leave a lasting impression on the selectors' minds.'

In the interests of caution, however, the same writer also observed: 'It might be as well to strike a warning note. If the Hungarians are anything like their close neighbours, the Austrians, in ball control and manipulation, they will be harder nuts to crack than we may think. Indeed, Austria, in their three engagements with Scotland, twice had the satisfaction of drawing.'

From this, it would appear, the Austrians weren't much interested in winning. Or else, in some quarters, the memory of that 5–0 thrashing inflicted on Scotland in Vienna in 1931 had been conveniently forgotten!

This time Scotland lined up as follows: Dawson (Rangers), Anderson (Hearts) and Beattie (Preston North End); Shankly (Preston), Baxter (Middlesbrough) and Symon (Rangers); M'Spadyen (Partick Thistle), Walker (Hearts), M'Culloch (Derby County), Black (Hearts) and Gillick (Everton).

The match itself was disappointing. Scotland were forced to play for the whole of the second half without Black who was injured, but throughout the whole of the 90 minutes there was a distinct lack of international atmosphere, and little sustained action to maintain crowd interest, according to most reports.

'One shudders to think what England – and Matthews in particular – would have done to this Scottish team,' *The Glasgow Herald* reflected gloomily.

'Certainly the namby-pamby play of the Hungarians, who were obviously unhappy on the heavy, greasy turf, did not encourage the Scots to put a deal of ginger into their work. But for all that one did not expect to see so much defensive slackness, loose passing, and deplorably weak shooting from members of an international team,' the same paper continued.

However, as witnessed by Davie Meiklejohn, the 'Hungarians certainly showed us the value of finding your man with the pass. In this phase of the game they were 18 carat.' The former Scotland skipper believed the visitors lost because of poor positional play in defence. 'However, let's hand it to our boys for once again keeping Scotland's flag flying.'

CHAPTER FIFTEEN

A year after the Second World War ended, when the four British associations rejoined FIFA after an absence lasting since 1920, it was understood they would all compete for a place in the first post-war World Cup due to be held in Brazil in 1950.

But so anxious was FIFA to ensure British participation in the reborn tournament, all four home countries were excused playing preliminary round matches against foreign teams. Instead, it was agreed that whoever won the 1949–50 British championship would qualify automatically for Brazil.

Considering they only played each other once, instead of home and away, as was normal in qualifying rounds of the global tournament, Scotland, England, Wales and Northern Ireland were being offered a much easier route to the World Cup finals than any of their foreign rivals.

But no matter how attractive these conditions might seem now, in an age of hazardous, highly competitive qualifying groups, they were further improved by FIFA offering to provide a place in Brazil for the top two countries in the British championship.

A near-bye into the World Cup finals wasn't a bad arrangement. If ever they had the chance, in view of their fluctuating fortunes in future years, it is something all four associations must regret not negotiating on a continuing basis; like post-empire Britain's permanent membership of the United Nations Security Council!

With two matches, against Wales and England, due to be played at Hampden, the Scots looked a near-certainty for the finals. Having defeated Northern Ireland 8–2 at Windsor Park, Belfast, in October 1949, and Wales 2–0 a month later at Hampden, skipper George Young and other Scottish stalwarts of the period, such as Jimmy Cowan of Morton, Sammy Cox and Willie Waddell of Rangers, Billy Liddell of Liverpool, Lawrie Reilly of Hibs, and Billy Steel of Derby County, could have been measured for their tropical gear and advised to order the suntan oil a good seven months before the World Cup finals were due to begin.

Except, in its wisdom, the SFA decided Scotland wouldn't compete in the World Cup finals unless they first won the British championship outright.

Traditionally, the home international championship was decided on points, regardless of goal difference. Thus, when England defeated Wales 4–1 in Cardiff,

SFA secretary George Graham didn't want Scotland competing in the World Cup finals except as British champions

and crushed Northern Ireland 9–2 at Wembley, the match with Scotland at Hampden on 15 April 1950, became more than a simple championship decider, of little interest to anyone outside Britain.

England proposed to make the long journey to South America regardless of the result against Scotland. But if England won at Hampden, and Scotland remained indifferent to the additional place offered by FIFA, the World Cup finals would be a team short with only a few weeks left in which to find a replacement.

It is easy to imagine what the Scots' intransigence meant to the organisers, charged with arranging the various groups. The men who ruled FIFA could have been excused thinking Sir George Graham, secretary of the SFA, and the rest of the Carlton Place power élite, weren't quite sane.

But in the weeks before England were due at Hampden, all attempts to coax, or coerce, the Scots into changing their minds, failed. 'The players were desperate to go,' George Young recalled years later. 'It was the chance of a lifetime. But nothing we said would make the officials change their minds.'

Scots fans, generally, weren't all that bothered. Following a convincing 3–1 victory at Wembley the previous year, they expected the national side to continue the good work on their return to Mount Florida; a cheery assumption unsupported by recent Hampden history. Discounting wartime internationals, and the unofficial Victory international four years earlier, the last two full internationals played between the two countries at Hampden, in 1939 and 1948, had been won by the visitors.

But most people in the 134,000 all-ticket crowd at Hampden on 15 April 1950, confident of their God-given right to a place in the World Cup finals, probably didn't realise the extent to which they were participants in a unique experience that would become commonplace: Scotland struggling to make the most of a last-gasp opportunity, against serious odds – including a tendency to self-destruct – in the World Cup.

As future generations of supporters, players and officials learned to their cost, at this level of competition Scotland was under-resourced, in some cases to the point of national embarrassment.

During the home international championship in season 1949–50, a total of three matches which also counted as Scotland's first attempt to reach the finals of world football's most prestigious competition, the selectors permutated no fewer than 18 different players.

Jimmy Cowan, of Morton, his former club-mate Billy Steel, who was then with Derby County, together with George Young, Sammy Cox and Willie Woodburn, all of Rangers, played in every match. Another famous Rangers name, Willie Waddell, distinguished himself by making two appearances and scoring twice. As a sign of the selectors' fickleness of purpose, however, a crop of eight players made only one appearance, including the unfortunate Willie Moir of Bolton Wonderers.

In the row that followed his inept performance in the crucial last game against England, when the senior players' hopes of a trip to South America were crushed

George Young welcomes England captain Billy Wright to Hampden for the match that decided Scotland's 1950 World Cup fate. The pensive-looking referee is Mr R. J. Leafe of England

by a single goal, it emerged that some of the selectors never saw Moir play before bestowing his one and only cap.

For the match between Scotland and England at Hampden on 15 April 1950, the teams lined up as follows: *Scotland* – Cowan (Morton), Young (Rangers), Cox (Rangers), McColl (Rangers), Woodburn (Rangers), Forbes (Arsenal), Waddell (Rangers), Moir (Bolton), Bauld (Hearts), Steel (Derby County), Liddell

179

Scots defender Sammy Cox and goalkeeper Jimmy Cowan are unable to prevent Roy Bentley scoring the goal that kept Scotland away from Brazil and the 1950 World Cup finals

(Liverpool). *England* – Williams (Wolves), Ramsey (Tottenham), Aston (Manchester Utd), Wright (Wolves), Franklin (Stoke), Dickinson (Portsmouth), Finney (Preston North End), Mannion (Middlesbrough), Mortensen (Blackpool), Bentley (Chelsea) and Langton (Bolton Wanderers). *Referee* – R.J. Leafe, England.

The goal that kept Scotland out of the 1950 World Cup finals was scored after 63 minutes by Roy Bentley, of Chelsea, with a shot from 12 yards, which Cowan touched but couldn't stop. 'We should not now be too proud to learn; we are no longer the masters,' *The Glasgow Herald* opined sadly. Most sensible observers were prepared to concede that, on this occasion at least, Scotland had been defeated by a superior England team; although this didn't stop FIFA continuing to plead for a Scottish presence in Brazil.

By then it was too late, however, although there was general agreement that the men who governed Scottish football from offices overlooking the Clyde at Carlton Place should have been glad of an opportunity to compete against the best in the world. Their antics over their refusal to accept an invitation to play in Brazil made them look foolish. But a change of mind at this late stage, following

Despite their obvious commitment to the cause, the girls in the picture failed to inspire Scotland to a win against England and thus gain a place in the 1950 World Cup finals

the result of the match against England, would do nothing to restore their shaky credibility in anyone's eyes. Mistaken pride ruled; Scotland didn't travel.

Of course, in the end, for many xenophobes who believed the next best thing to Scotland acquitting themselves well in a tournament was the prospect of England doing badly, events in Brazil offered a large measure of unexpected joy. On 25 June 1950, England began their first, much-trumpeted, visit to the World Cup finals with a 2–0 win against Chile in Rio de Janeiro.

In some quarters, mostly located in pubs around London, they had been judged favourites, alongside Brazil. So the result against Chile was the least their supporters expected. It was the outcome of their next match, played at Belo Horizonte four days later, which caused a sensation; although it was welcomed in hundreds of hostelries around Scotland with wicked grins, and wild cries of celebration.

Put simply, in faraway Brazil, with Scotland not competing for reasons understood by few people outside the SFA hierarchy, an England team had been defeated 1–0 by the soccer might of the USA!

Even non-partisan witnesses insisted it was a fluke result. For most of the match, everyone, with the exception of the England goalkeeper, Williams, was fully occupied in the vicinity of the US goal, to no good purpose, as England viewed the outcome. In the course of a rare US attack, a header from centre-forward, Joe Gaetjens, which left the unfortunate Williams clutching the air, settled everything.

Their experience at Belo Horizonte stunned the England team, their management and supporters around the world. No-one could doubt it was English football's darkest hour; aggravated a few days later when skipper Billy Wright and his bewildered troops suffered a second defeat against Spain. A single goal was all that separated the teams at the finish. But it was enough to send England home, dejected.

Bright and shining hopes of glory, in their first World Cup, had been shattered by the reality of their experience. Nor did it help English pride when Spain, who finished winners of their group, were subsequently crushed 7–1 by Brazil at the next stage of the competition.

In their final match against Uruguay, in the Maracana Stadium, filled with a hugely partisan crowd, the hosts required a draw to finish ahead of Uruguay on points and win the World Cup. Few people thought they would fail, and Brazil scoring first, with a goal by Friaca, heightened their supporters' already highly developed sense of joyous expectation.

The huge stadium thundered to the intimidating sound of the maracanoes' drums. But even the highly-charged atmosphere of their own national stadium, in a match which would decide who took possession of the coveted Jules Rimet trophy, couldn't save Brazil. In the end it was Uruguay, with goals by Schiaffino and Ghiggia, who won.

Uruguay had been host to the first World Cup, and winners, in 1930. Now, on the occasion of the tournament's post-war rehabilitation, they were once again supreme in the world.

Anyone in Britain, with a serious interest in the continuing development of world football, could hardly ignore the danger signs. The four British associations' long-cherished notion of themselves as world football powers, each in their own right, well-nigh invincible, was no longer sustainable.

Yet, despite their apparent fall from grace, when arrangements for the 1954 World Cup finals in Switzerland were announced, the presence of two teams from Britain figured prominently. Again, although the system of qualifying was clearly unfair, FIFA continued to decree that these two places would depend solely on the outcome of the home international championship.

This time, however, there was no talk of Scotland refusing to participate other than as outright winners in Britain. The rancour and criticism aroused by their refusal to compete four years earlier could have been the main cause of the SFA's change of heart. Certainly, they couldn't have been encouraged in the view that Scotland might perform well in Switzerland on the basis of recent results against foreign opposition. For Scotland had been experiencing a chastening time during the previous four years; starting with a match against their old enemies, Austria, at Hampden on 13 December 1950.

Almost 20 years earlier Austria had been the first foreign team to defeat Scotland outside Britain. Now they became the first foreign side to beat Scotland at Hampden. And no-one seriously believed they would be the last!

Of course, on paper, 1–0 might be judged close. Scotland could always claim a narrow result and a degree of misfortune; hardly a disaster, apart from the loss of their precious home record against foreign opposition.

Except, in the space of five months, when the two countries met for a return match in Vienna on 27 May 1951, the difference between them could be seen to have widened to worrying proportions – Scotland conceding four goals while scoring none.

Next it was Sweden's turn to play host to an offshore island country which showed little sign of wishing to become wise in the ways of the continent. This time the venue was Stockholm. The date was 30 May 1952. And Scotland duly lost 3–1. It was a result which the previously unfancied Swedes came close to repeating on a visit to Hampden the following year. This time they won by the odd goal in three.

In the home international championship, which would decide the two British places in the World Cup, Scotland were fortunate to beat Northern Ireland 3–1 in Belfast: according to most neutral observers the result flattered the visitors.

Typically, the selectors responded to criticisms of the team's performance by dropping the entire forward line for the match against Wales at Hampden on 4 November 1953. Out went Willie Waddell (Rangers), Charlie Fleming (East Fife), John McPhail (Celtic), Jimmy Watson (Huddersfield Town), and Jackie Henderson (Portsmouth); together with centre-half Frank Brennan (Newcastle United), who lost the number five shirt to Willie Telfer (St Mirren).

Wales always presented a serious threat to Scotland at Hampden. Three matches at the Mount Florida ground since the war all produced winning scores,

183

with Wales ahead on two occasions. The teams lined up as follows: *Scotland* – Farm (Blackpool), Young (Rangers), Cox (Rangers), Evans (Celtic), Telfer (St Mirren), Cowie (Dundee), M'Kenzie (Partick Thistle), Johnstone (Hibs), Reilly (Hibs), Brown (Blackpool), Liddell (Liverpool). *Wales* – Howells (Cardiff City), Barnes (Arsenal), Sherwood (Cardiff City), Paul (Manchester City), Daniel (Sunderland), Burgess (Tottenham), Foulkes (Newcastle), Davies (Newcastle), Charles (Leeds), Allchurch (Swansea), Clarke (Manchester City). *Referee* – T. Mitchell, Lurgan.

Much of the pre-match interest centred on the appearance of John Charles, then aged 21, and already on his way to enjoying a remarkable career. Many of his admirers believed Charles was the best centre-forward then operating in Britain; others claimed he was an even better player when allowed to function at centre-half. Nobody argued he was an exceptional talent.

Most observers thought Willie Telfer, who never won another cap for Scotland, played as well as could be expected against the big Welshman. Charles treated the 71,000 spectators to a brilliant display, scoring twice, given only two real chances, including the first for Wales and a goal two minutes from the end which deprived Scotland of a well-earned victory. Ivor Allchurch had been Wales' other scorer; while Allan Brown, Bobby Johnstone and Lawrie Reilly all scored for Scotland.

The result kept both countries' World Cup hopes alive for another few months at least. Wales were due to play Northern Ireland at Wrexham at the end of March, and Scotland could look forward to welcoming England to Hampden on 3 April. If Wales defeated Northern Ireland four days before Scotland were due to play England at Hampden, the Scots would be under some pressure, needing at least a draw against England to ensure a place in Switzerland. Fortunately for Scotland they were never put to the test. The previously unlucky Irish defeated Wales 3–1.

Scotland were bound for Switzerland and the World Cup finals. But first there was a small matter of a match against England at Hampden to consider. Whoever won at Hampden would be seeded in Switzerland; always a distinct advantage in the final stages of the World Cup.

Scotland's recent record, in full international matches against England at Hampden, was deplorable, however. It had been 17 years since Scotland last won on their own ground against their oldest opponents. The last full match between the two countries before the start of the Second World War had been won by England, who also finished ahead on the last three occasions they visited Scotland during the home international championship. Victory on this occasion would make it five Hampden wins in a row for England; a bitter blow to Scots pride.

The teams lined up as follows: *Scotland* – Farm (Blackpool), Haughney (Celtic), Cox (Rangers), Evans (Celtic), Brennan (Newcastle), Aitken (Sunderland), McKenzie (Partick Thistle), Johnstone (Hibernian), Henderson (Portsmouth), Brown (Blackpool), Ormond (Hibs). *England* – Merrick (Birmingham), Staniforth (Huddersfield), Byrne (Manchester United), Wright (Wolves), Clarke (Tottenham), Dickinson (Portsmouth), Finney (Preston), Broadis (Newcastle),

Allen (West Bromich Albion), Nicholls (West Bromwich Albion), Mullen (Wolves). *Referee* – T.J. Mitchell, Scotland.

Fierce winds and heavy rain didn't deter 134,000 spectators from attending the match, including a large contingent from England who were accustomed to winning at Hampden.

On this occasion, however, England, who fielded four new caps, started badly and Scotland, given an early lead, should have taken command of the match. The opening goal by Allan Brown, after only eight minutes, certainly raised Scottish hopes.

Anyone who cared about the national predicament was entitled to believe an end was in sight to the long years of misery which had been inflicted on Scotland, appearing on their own home ground, by various teams sent from England. Or so it seemed to those supporters of Scotland who happened to be at Hampden, on that wet and windy afternoon, on 3 April 1954; for a while, at least.

Another seven minutes passed before England equalised. The goal, by Ivor Broadis, surprised many people – not least George Farm in the Scotland goal. Farm was forced to confront an unstoppable shot from the elegant Englishman after Sammy Cox and the rest of the Scotland defence failed to contain him.

Scotland, who had been playing comfortably until then, collapsed. For most of the second half Tom Finney was in charge. Six minutes after the interval he outwitted Cox and crossed for Nicholls to score. Twenty minutes later Allen put England further ahead. Then, with about eight minutes left for play, Mullen put the match beyond Scotland's reach.

An own goal by Roger Byrne, in the closing seconds, might have been credited to Willie Ormond. Winning the first of his half dozen caps, the little Hibs winger, and future World Cup manager, crossed a harmless-looking ball into the England goalmouth where Byrne and Merrick both went for it, became entangled, and watched, disbelieving, as the ball slithered over the line.

The difference between Scotland's performance in the opening minutes of the match, when they appeared to be taking command, and the team's maladroit display following the equaliser, didn't go unnoticed, of course.

'To fall to such a moderate English side was mortifying beyond words,' one veteran reporter, Sandy Adamson, observed witheringly. His colleague, Hugh Taylor, also writing in the Glasgow *Evening News*, quite clearly despaired of Scotland's closing performance. 'It was agonising. Scotland gave up almost without a fight,' Taylor wailed.

The forthright Taylor, who didn't blame the selectors for the day's fiasco, but the men on the park, also warned: 'Unless there is a terrific improvement, more fighting spirit and injection of devil in the forward line, the fares to Switzerland will be money thrown down the drain.'

Countries were entitled to nominate a pool of 22 players for the final stages of the World Cup. Scotland, with no previous experience at this level, unseeded, and drawn against Uruguay, the holders, and Austria, who could be expected to provide a serious threat to anyone's chances of progressing beyond the opening round, thought 13 would be enough.

185

Those invited to take part were: Fred Martin and George Hamilton (Aberdeen); Willie Cunningham and Tommy Docherty (Preston North End); John Aird (Burnley); Doug Cowie (Dundee); Allan Brown (Blackpool); Jimmy Davidson and John McKenzie (Partick Thistle); Willie Ormond (Hibernian); and Bobby Evans, Neil Mochan and Willie Fernie (Celtic).

Defying any prospect of injury, illness, or simple loss of form, the final pool included only one goalkeeper, Fred Martin of Aberdeen, preferred in place of George Farm, who had been discarded after playing in all three qualifying matches.

There was also a distinct lack of international experience about the squad. Prior to the 1954 finals, the players concerned could claim a total of only 63 appearances for Scotland. But discount 17 caps won by Bobby Evans, of Celtic, and 12 awarded to Allan Brown, of Blackpool, and the rest were left with a share in about half the total number.

The most glaring omission concerned George Young, a national hero, who had been captain of Scotland on numerous occasions, and first choice for the right-back position since 1947. The popular Rangers player was a man of considerable geniality and warmth who demonstrated high leadership qualities throughout a long and successful career.

Following the fiasco surrounding Scotland's failure to compete in Brazil, when Young, as the established captain, wanted the SFA to take part, Switzerland appeared to be offering him one last chance of a place in the World Cup finals; or so it was thought at the time. In fact, Young continued as a Scotland stalwart for another four years and his international career finally ended with Scotland fighting to survive another dangerous World Cup campaign. The circumstances surrounding his departure then were brutal and rancorous. But everyone accepted it was the end of a great career.

His absence from the squad for the World Cup finals in Switzerland appeared to confirm the popular view that it was time to replace the selectors with an experienced, full-time professional. The selectors defended their position by claiming that Young was unfit and not available for inclusion. Young, who had been missing from the game against England for the first time in eight years because of injury, insisted otherwise, however. He later declared: 'I was fit and ready to play if the selectors wished to include me.'

But, although the squad appeared weak, Scotland could now boast the services of a part-time manager, Andy Beattie. A former international player with seven caps for Scotland to his credit, Beattie was currently in charge of Huddersfield Town, then the proud possessors of a place in the English First Division.

His appointment appeared to suggest that the SFA, recognising their own shortcomings, perhaps, were embarked on a new approach to the demands of the modern game. The view from the dressing-room was something less than supportive, however. Many of the senior players disdained the manager's role. They believed the business of playing, and tactics, was a matter for them and the captain. The manager was simply an extension of the administration; a bag-carrier to the stars.

In fact, with Bobby Evans injured, unable to play, and George Hamilton out of favour with the selectors for the duration of the tournament, there wasn't much Andy Beattie could accomplish in Switzerland. Still, his resignation, half-way through the tournament, came as a shock to Scotland.

Before the manager's surprise departure, the chairman of the SFA selection committee, Mr Tom Reid, was committing Scotland to a hard, no-nonsense approach to the World Cup. 'Our boys are not the least worried about the much ballyhooed opposition,' Mr Reid, who was also chairman of Partick Thistle, proclaimed proudly. He also confided to reporters that, knowing from experience continental sides disliked coming from behind, the Scottish forward line had been instructed to go all out for an early goal.

For their first appearance in the World Cup finals Scotland lined up as follows: Martin (Aberdeen), Cunningham (Preston), Aird (Burnley), Docherty (Preston), Davidson (Partick Thistle), Cowie (Dundee), McKenzie (Partick Thistle), Fernie (Celtic), Mochan (Celtic), Brown (Blackpool), Ormond (Hibs).

It would have been forgivable if everyone associated with Scotland thought of Austria as a bogey team. Three victories, twice by a considerable margin, and a pair of draws, all earned home and away, were proof of their clear superiority over more than two decades.

Meeting in Zurich, on the occasion of the 1954 World Cup finals, there was little to choose between the two sides. But again Austria won.

A goal by Probst after 35 minutes decided the match. Most people thought Scotland were unlucky to lose and deserved a draw. In his post-match analysis, W.G. Gallagher, who wrote as Waverley in the *Daily Record*, offered an epitaph for broken dreams which suited Scotland perfectly: 'No team could have fought harder,' he declared.

There was a belief in some quarters that Uruguay, twice winners of the World Cup, in 1930 and 1950, and Scotland's next opponents, might somehow fail to adapt to European conditions. At least one experienced observer, the much-travelled English reporter, W. Capel Kirby, thought Scotland could upset the world champions. 'I fancy Scotland to take the bounce out of the Uruguayans, big, tough, confident as they are,' he mused.

At best, it was a heady hope, an impossible dream, which the world champions, in devastating form, quickly set about destroying in the sweltering heat of the Basle stadium.

'We left the dressing-room, and were kept waiting out on the park for about quarter of an hour before the game started,' Neil Mochan recalled. 'It must have been at least 100 degrees, and getting warmer all the time.

'We were shattered, but the Uruguayans loved the heat. The warmer it got, the better they played.' The former Celtic winger shrugged ruefully. 'They simply annihilated us that day,' he declared.

The final score remains Scotland's worst-ever World Cup defeat; no goals scored, seven lost.

'We are old in the game and we played like old men,' a dispirited W.G. Gallagher informed his readers later. 'It was a hot day, a very hot day, the type of day absolutely foreign to our own soccer season. But that is no excuse. Our opponents were immeasurably superior in every branch of the game,' Gallagher insisted.

The third World Cup in which Scotland took an active interest was held in Sweden in the summer of 1958. It would be remembered in later years as the tournament which introduced a 17–year-old wonder player to soccer's greatest stage – Edson Arantes do Nascimento, otherwise known as Pele.

By his own admission, when he appeared for the first time in the 1958 World Cup finals, Pele was a skinny little black boy who could have been mistaken as 'either the team mascot or the son of a friend of the coach; I can't be the son of the coach because the coach is white'.

The 50,928–strong crowd, who saw Brazil play Russia in Gothenburg on 15 June 1958, contained a number of people who were 'probably outraged that as important an event as a World Cup match should be reduced to parody by having an infant on the field'. For the benefit of readers of his book, *My Life and the Beautiful Game*, Pele, with ill-concealed amusement, also reasoned: 'The more sentimental, however, probably felt pity for a team so reduced in talent as to face the need to bring children along with them. The entire Brazilian team is young as teams go; everyone knows that – but this is ridiculous!'

Sweden provided the venue for the first of Brazil's three World Cup triumphs to date. Pele, who was virtually unknown in Europe when the tournament started, played in four matches including the final. His name didn't appear on the score-sheet against Russia. But he scored the only goal of the match against Wales in the quarter-finals, three against France in the semi-finals, and twice against Sweden in the final which Brazil won 5–2.

Pele was in tears at the end. 'As the whistle blew, ending the game and the tournament, I had a strange feeling that I was going to faint,' he wrote.

In celebration of his amazing performance, with the King of Sweden waiting to greet the winners of the World Cup, the boy who had been Edson Arantes do Nascimento, from the small town of Tres Coracoes in the State of Minas Gerais, and was now called Pele, was lifted shoulder high and carried round the field by the rest of the Brazilian team.

It was a moving and generous tribute, from a remarkable group of players, to a precocious and prodigious talent already reaching beyond the top. In time the skinny little black boy of his own description would become the greatest footballer in the world.

However, long before the 1958 World Cup ended in Stockholm and the name of Pele was familiar to anyone with the slightest interest in soccer, it had been made clear that FIFA no longer wished to provide the United Kingdom with two final places, or even one, automatically.

Worldwide exposure on television in 1954 helped generate enormous interest in the new tournament, a heartening development which also caused problems for the organisers, FIFA. An increased demand for places in the qualifying rounds from countries outside the magic circle, represented by Europe and South

America, was an immediate prospect. Africa and Asia, especially, were desperate to compete.

There could be no more favours for the game's oldest participants: in future each of the four home football associations would be required to play home and away against whatever foreign opposition the qualifying draw decreed.

Foreign interests who sought a single combined British entry in the World Cup probably hoped exposure to the skills of other countries at the qualifying stage might reduce, or even eliminate, the UK presence. In fact, by diverse means, which included the hurried recruitment of Wales to compete in a play-off against Israel, after countries from Africa and Asia objected to playing in the Jewish state, Scotland, England, Northern Ireland and Wales all qualified for Sweden!

Scotland's road to Sweden, and a second appearance in the World Cup finals, began at Hampden Park, Glasgow, on 8 May 1957, with Spain providing dangerous opposition.

It was the first international match between the two countries and the expert view favoured Spain to win easily; an odd assumption considering the Spaniards' recent loss of a precious point to the unfancied Swiss in Madrid.

The Spaniards had been described as the greatest team in the world and Scotland were expected to face them feeling inferior. Asked what he thought of Scotland's chances, skipper George Young's comment was cheerful and to the point. 'If we are to believe all reports, we are asked to meet a team of supermen,' he grinned. 'Take it from me, we will go out at Hampden with just one thought: we are as good, if not better, than the senors,' said Young.

A crowd of 89,000 saw the teams line up as follows: *Scotland* – Younger (Liverpool), Caldow (Rangers), Hewie (Charlton), McColl (Rangers), Young (Rangers), Docherty (Preston North End), Smith (Hibernian), Collins (Celtic), Mudie (Blackpool), Baird (Rangers), Ring (Clyde). *Spain* – Ramallets, Olivilla, Garay, Verges, Campanal, Zarraga, Gonzales, Kubala, di Stefano, Suarez, Gento. *Referee* – A. Dusch, Germany.

There was only one survivor in the Scotland team from those who played against Austria and Uruguay in the 1954 World Cup finals in Switzerland – Tommy Docherty.

Spain, with a point dropped against Switzerland in Madrid, were already in trouble. A Scottish victory at Hampden, followed by a win over Switzerland in Basle in two weeks time, meant Scotland could lose the return match against Spain in Madrid later the same month and still qualify for the World Cup finals. But the men selected to represent Scotland were at least in charge of their own destiny and weren't seeking any favours. It was a condition to be cherished, as future generations of Scottish footballers, and their managers, would testify.

On this occasion, for all the world to judge, skipper George Young and his men didn't falter, winning 4–2 against the reckless Spaniards.

'That some of the Spaniards were not ordered off before half-time was proof that the safest field in football on which to misbehave is the international field,' one reporter complained.

In its front page report of the match the *Daily Record* trumpeted its pride in the 11 players who brought Scotland an unexpected and glorious victory. 'They showed Spain – and Europe – that we can still play football despite the knees, boots and the elbows that the senors brought into the game,' it claimed.

Their own savage bad temper, and a mistaken belief in the monotonous pre-match publicity which insisted they were invincible, probably cost Spain the match. In addition, according to Waverley, the home side won by remaining calm in the face of Spain's rough play. 'They were not slow to rumble that they had the opposition in a state of mental duress and they played on it by producing cool and calculating football,' he wrote.

Jackie Mudie, of Blackpool, who scored a hat-trick was the undisputed man of the match. 'From the very outset he was eager, enthusiastic and hard-working and an inspiration to his mates,' Waverley enthused.

Kubala and Suarez scored for Spain. Scotland's other goal was scored by John Hewie from a penalty kick, awarded shortly before the interval when Olivilla exercised his talent for violence with a trip on Tommy Ring which the German referee considered worthy of a hard response. Following the penalty, one reporter noted: 'Some of the Spanish players went berserk and even the retaliatory tactics of such as Docherty, Collins and Baird were mild behaviour in comparison.'

Switzerland followed, with George Young still in charge. According to Young the match was a battle of tactics. An early goal put Switzerland ahead. 'Many in the crowd thought that they would march away to victory,' skipper Young recalled later. 'It was then that I pulled our wing-half backs into the middle of the pitch to watch the inside men, while I directed our full-backs to keep on the toes of the wingers,' Young explained.

The final result was a 2–1 win for Scotland who thus continued on course for Sweden.

Before leaving Scotland there had been reports that George Young, who had been left out of the squad for the previous World Cup finals in Switzerland, proposed retiring from international football after the match with Spain in Madrid. Young didn't need to be told that the selection committee might take exception to the presumptious nature of these reports. 'I had a hunch the selectors might feel slighted,' he wrote.

With a total of 53 full caps to his credit – a Scottish record that lasted well into the modern era – Young enjoyed the status of a national football institution in the years following the war. In his first public statement on the affair Young denied fuelling speculation concerning his intentions. 'The thought had crossed my mind that I'd like to say farewell to soccer in sunny Madrid,' the player admitted. 'But to think such a thing and publicly announce I was going to play my last game in Madrid are two totally different things.'

If the selectors were annoyed, or some of them actually believed there had been a challenge to their authority, or, just as likely, they no longer required George Young's services, whatever the truth, no-one expected the extraordinary, and bitter, end to his international career that followed the match with Switzerland in Basle.

Following the match with Switzerland, and before Scotland were due in

Madrid on crucial World Cup business, a friendly match had been scheduled against the world champions, Germany, in Stuttgart.

Young, who had been nursing a groin strain from the match against Spain at Hampden a fortnight earlier, didn't play against Germany and Tommy Docherty assumed the captaincy. Most people thought Young would return to the side, and reclaim the captaincy, for the match against Spain. 'To play in that match, and lead Scotland on to the field in Madrid, was my great ambition,' he recalled.

But if he wasn't selected to play against Spain the long-time captain of Scotland was entitled to expect a dignified end to his international career. From his own version of what happened in Spain, it was evident the selectors didn't agree. Young confided in his memoirs: 'I was literally tossed overboard, stripped of my captaincy, and from no official was there a word of sympathy or explanation.'

For the match against Spain, with the familiar figure of George Young no longer a commanding presence at the heart of the Scottish defence, Bobby Evans assumed the centre-half position.

In front of their own fans the Spaniards kept their tempers in check, produced some brilliant football, and duly won 4–1. Only some superb goalkeeping by Tommy Younger, and a splendid performance by Bobby Evans, in the opening minutes of the match, saved Scotland from a rout.

Six months later an unedifying 3–2 win over Switzerland at Hampden earned Scotland boos from the crowd as well as a place in Sweden. The teams were: *Scotland* – Younger (Liverpool), Parker (Falkirk), Caldow (Rangers), Fernie (Celtic), Evans (Celtic), Docherty (Preston North End), Scott (Rangers), Collins (Celtic), Mudie (Blackpool), Robertson (Clyde) and Ring (Clyde). *Switzerland* – Parlier, Kernan, Morf, Grobety, Koch, Schneiter, Chiesa, Ballaman, Meier, Vonlanden, Riva. *Referee* – R. Leafe, Nottingham.

'The Swiss were immeasurably more skilful, more artistic, more methodical, more intelligent players, and produced an understanding of one another, a cohesion in team-work that the Scots never showed,' W.G. Gallagher insisted gloomily. Gallagher, a man of strong opinions, wanted Scotland to withdraw from the World Cup finals. 'They will be made to chase shadows,' he warned.

Scotland's performance in Sweden, against Yugoslavia, Paraguay and France, is generally forgotten; although a dismal pattern was beginning to emerge. As in future years, the second final stage was beyond Scotland's reach. Out of three matches played in the opening exchanges the first ended in a draw and the remaining two were lost. For the second time running, in the early stages of the World Cup finals, Scotland finished bottom of their group and were eliminated.

CHAPTER SIXTEEN

In the years that followed Scotland often played well, but generally fared badly, in the qualifying stages of the World Cup. A decade of maximum disappointment somehow contrived to coincide with the appearance of some of the greatest names the sport has known in Scotland. But that simply made their lack of success all the more dispiriting.

The 1962 campaign started happily enough with a 4–1 win over the Republic of Ireland at Hampden on 3 May 1961, followed by a 3–0 victory in Dublin four days later.

Everyone expected tougher opposition from the third team in the group, Czechoslovakia. But it would have been hard to imagine, and painful to accept, the 4–0 annihilation job which the Czechs administered on an unhappy Scots side a week later in Bratislava. It was one of Scotland's worst-ever World Cup defeats, matched only by events in Switzerland in 1954, when Uruguay won 7–0, and in Lisbon in 1993 when Portugal won 5–0.

A point from the second match, four months later, would guarantee the Czechs a place in Chile the following summer. A crowd gathered at Hampden on 26 September 1961, hoping to see them fail. But few would have been prepared to bet on the home side achieving a result. *Scotland* – Brown (Tottenham), MacKay (Celtic), Caldow (Rangers), Crerand (Celtic), McNeill (Celtic), Baxter (Rangers), Scott (Rangers), White (Tottenham), St John (Liverpool), Law (Turin), Wilson (Rangers). *Czechoslovakia* – Schrolf, Novak, Bomba, Bubernik, Popluhar, Masopust, Pospichal, Scherer, Kadraba, Kvasnak, Masek. *Referee* – L. Gulliksen, Norway.

Scotland attacked strongly from the start but it was Czechoslovakia who scored first. A fierce shot by Kvasnak gave goalkeeper Bill Brown no chance. His goal was clearly against the run of play. But the ease with which the Czechs outwitted the Scotland defence during their first real attack, suggested they could score any time they wanted. There was a raw feeling in the Hampden crowd that the humiliation suffered in Bratislava was about to be repeated, with all of them there to see it, and without the comfort of distance to console them.

Hampden, whatever its history, was never meant to be the scene of Scottish despair. A goal by Ian St John raised everyone's hopes. At half-time the teams were level.

A goal by Scherer, early in the second half, put the visitors ahead again. Scotland responded with a goal by Law. The SFA had been obliged to insure Law for £200,000 before the player's Torino masters would agree to let him travel for the match. The premium was money well spent. Law had been closely involved when St John scored Scotland's opening goal. The second, which exploded into the net from six yards, was all his own work.

It wasn't his fault Czechoslovakia appeared to be heading for the World Cup finals.

But, with only seven minutes left for play, a draw looked the likely result, giving Czechoslovakia the point they needed to qualify. It was then Law took a pass from John White, evaded two defenders, drew the goalkeeper out of position, and scored the winner.

An anonymous writer in *The Glasgow Herald* noted Law's supreme confidence and his ability to make and to take chances. 'What a pity this player is lost to British football,' he complained. 'His acceleration from a standing start is amazing, his ball control phenomenal, and his swift assessment of a situation probably unequalled.'

But a third match was now needed to decide who would qualify for Chile. The Heysel stadium, in Brussels, was the chosen venue and the match was scheduled for 29 November 1961.

Scotland were without goalkeeper Bill Brown, centre-half Billy McNeill and both wingers, Alex Scott and Davie Wilson, all injured the previous Saturday, from the team that performed so courageously at Hampden. 'It is no disrespect to the players who took their places to say that Scotland were considerably weakened by their absence,' Denis Law argued later. Law himself was unable to repeat the form he'd shown at Hampden. 'I just couldn't get going,' Law admitted.

Scotland were leading 2–1, with only 11 minutes left for play, when Czechoslovakia equalised with a goal which many people thought never crossed the line. The referee thought it good enough to ensure the match went into extra time, however.

'The Czechs were a much bigger and physically stronger side than Scotland, and, on the heavy, muddy pitch, they wore us down,' Law recalled.

The final score was 4–2 in favour of Czechoslovakia. But, as events proved, Scotland hadn't been disgraced. Czechoslovakia could claim a distinguished record in the World Cup. They had been beaten finalists in 1934, when Italy won, and quarter-finalists in 1938. Following their momentous three-match struggle with Scotland, they also performed splendidly in Chile. The men Scotland almost matched defeated Spain, drew with Brazil, and lost unexpectedly to Mexico in the opening stages before registering wins against Hungary and Yugoslavia, in the quarter-finals and semi-finals, on their way to a losing final against Brazil.

Denis Law couldn't help wondering. 'Would Scotland have done as well had they qualified?'

The three matches against Czechoslovakia in 1961 represented the epic highlight of Scotland's wilderness years in the World Cup.

Four years later there was the excitement of beating Italy at Hampden. John

John Greig, who kept Scotland's World Cup qualifying hopes alive with a memorable last-minute goal against Italy at Hampden on 9 November 1965, is congratulated by his delighted team-mates

Greig's winning goal, scored in the closing seconds of the match, is deservedly part of the nation's football folklore.

But the odds in favour of Scotland qualifying for the finals in England never really looked good following a 2–1 defeat by Poland at Hampden a few weeks earlier. A draw in Poland in May had been a satisfactory result. And the 107,550 Hampden crowd was entitled to believe the match on 13 October 1965, would end in their favour, especially after Billy McNeill headed the opening goal, from a Henderson corner, after only 14 minutes.

The teams were: *Scotland* – Brown (Tottenham), Hamilton (Dundee), McCreadie (Chelsea), Crerand (Manchester United), McNeill (Celtic), Greig (Rangers), Henderson (Rangers), Bremner (Leeds), Gilzean (Tottenham), Law (Manchester United) and Johnston (Rangers). *Poland* – Kornek, Sczepanski, Oslizio, Anczok, Gmoch, Nieroba, Sadak, Szoltysik, Liberda, Poh, Faber. *Referee* – H. Carlsson, Sweden.

Before the game Jock Stein, who had been released by Celtic to take part-time charge of the international squad in the qualifying matches, told reporters: 'If we have erred we have erred on the side of safety. We just couldn't take any chances in such an important game.'

194

Everyone expected Scotland, on their first-half form, to add considerably to McNeill's early goal. 'We should have killed them,' Denis Law recalled many years later. 'We were one up when we should have been leading by five.'

But for most of the match Billy McNeill's well-directed header was all that separated the two sides. And for most of the 70 minutes that followed it would have been fair to admit Poland didn't deserve to be a goal down. Raymond Jacobs thought the second half provided 'a simple, yet deadly, demonstration of what modern football is all about. In the process they revealed that Scotland haven't yet reached 11–plus standard.'

Six minutes from the end justice triumphed. Poland, who had been the better team and paced the game more astutely, according to one observer, equalised. Then, two minutes later, to the horror of the Hampden crowd, they went ahead.

'From a first half of pace and interest and enthusiasm Scotland tumbled to a level of incompetence, and a condition of total ruin, which were incredible to see,' wrote Raymond Jacobs.

The wrath of the crowd, and the boos which accompanied Scotland from the park, were predictable. A dispirited Jock Stein could only remark: 'I have nothing to say.'

A month later, as his side, showing several changes, prepared to face Italy, the big man told them: 'You've some job on your hands. But it isn't impossible. Fight till you drop.' His words weren't lost on the players. Following the match John Greig confessed he was about ready to drop when the 'goal came along to make us forget our tiredness. It was a real last-gasp effort.'

Greig, who was playing out of his normal club position at right-back, also admitted: 'If the ball had broken the other way, and the Italian winger got possession, I would never have had the strength to catch him.' Instead, with little more than a minute left for play, Greig and Jim Baxter exchanged passes, Greig ran to the middle of the park, took the ball from Baxter again, and whacked a marvellous left-foot shot past the Italian goalkeeper, Negri.

The 101,293 crowd, which no doubt included many of that unhappy number who watched the game against Poland from a similar position the previous month, was ecstatic. It was the first time the SFA ever agreed to pay their players a bonus for winning: £100!

The teams were: *Scotland* – Brown (Tottenham), Greig (Rangers), Provan (Rangers), Murdoch (Celtic), McKinnon (Rangers), Baxter (Sunderland), Henderson (Rangers), Bremner (Leeds), Gilzean (Tottenham), Martin (Sunderland), Hughes (Celtic). *Italy* – Negri, Burgnich, Facchetti, Guarneri, Salvadore, Rosato, Lodetti, Bulgarelli, Mazzola, Rivera, Barisson. *Referee* – R. Kreitlein, West Germany.

On paper, at least, Scotland could still qualify for a place in the finals of the 1966 World Cup. A draw against Italy in the second match, due to be played in Naples in December, would ensure a play-off in a neutral country.

A cheerful fantasy, the dream fuelled extravagant notions of national glory, and lasted all of four weeks. Sadly, but to nobody's great surprise, Italy won 3–0

Billy Bremner and Silva swap jerseys following the first-ever match between Scotland and Brazil at Hampden on 25 June 1966. Pele, clutching his own souvenir of the occasion, heads for the dressing-room. Brazil were preparing for the 1966 World Cup finals and happy to settle for a one-each draw

in Naples. The finals of the World Cup in England would proceed without Scotland. It could have been England's gain.

Scotland were never offered an easy route to the World Cup finals following the privileged days of the early 1950s. Failure against Czechoslovakia and Italy had been suffered honourably and was no disgrace. West Germany, in a lengthening line of quality opposition, arrived next.

The qualifying stages of the 1970 World Cup started encouragingly enough for Scotland when Austria visited Hampden in November 1968, and lost 2–1.

Matches involving Austria were never easy for Scotland. In fact, the record showed they could be downright disastrous. Ten previous meetings between the two countries, starting with their first match in 1931, finished with the Austrians ahead on five occasions, level on three, and behind only once, in Vienna in 1955, when Scotland won 4–1.

The tenth time the two countries met, at Hampden on 8 May 1963, nobody won; although Scotland were ahead 4–1 when the referee, Mr James Finney of England, abandoned the match with 11 minutes left for play. Although the match was officially described as a friendly, meaningless except in terms of the players' national and professional pride, there was little goodwill on display at Hampden.

The Austrians appeared intent on turning the match into a brawl. Some in the colours of Scotland were unaccustomed to turning the other cheek when provoked and might have been tempted to oblige. Fortunately, they weren't. As one report noted: 'They held themselves in check throughout and to their credit showed complete composure.'

The Austrians were reduced to nine men after one of their number, Nemec, spat at the referee, following a goal by Davie Wilson, and another, Hof, was ordered from the field for a foul on Willie Henderson. Austrian officials surrounded referee Finney to demand Hof stay. Mr Finney refused. Hof, ordered to remain on the field by Austrian team manager, Karl Decker, wouldn't quit.

A total of 10 Austrian players were gathered close to the Hampden centre circle, waiting defiantly for the match to continue, when the referee decided enough was enough. Mr Finney could be forgiven thinking anarchy and mayhem threatened. However, as he walked resolutely from the field, few people understood the match had been abandoned.

Nobody lightly deprived a Hampden crowd, totalling around 95,000, their occasional pleasures, not least the sight of a Scotland eleven dismantling serious continental opposition.

The men who appeared at Hampden that night were: *Scotland* – Brown (Tottenham Hotspur), Hamilton (Dundee), Holt (Hearts), Mackay (Tottenham Hotspur), Ure (Dundee), Baxter (Rangers), Henderson (Rangers), Gibson (Leicester City), Miller (Rangers), Law (Manchester United), Wilson (Rangers). *Austria* – Fraydl, Kolarik, Hasenkopf, Koller, Glenchner, Gager, Linhart, Hof, Nemec, Fials, Rafreider. *Referee* – J. Finney, England.

Before the 1970 World Cup qualifying match against West Germany, at Hampden on 16 April 1969, Scotland could actually claim a modest ascendancy in matches played between the two countries, home and away. Two earlier contests, in 1957 and 1959, had been won by Scotland and a third, in 1964, had been drawn. Beyond that, in the World Cup especially, Scotland's record was dismal by comparison.

West Germany didn't know what it was like to lose a World Cup qualifying match. They had been surprise champions, at their first attempt, in 1954, semi-finalists in 1958, quarter-finalists in 1962 and runners-up in 1966.

Bobby Brown, the Scotland manager, was pursuing a policy of trying to establish a settled squad. 'I don't want players going back to the days when they couldn't feel their international place was secure because of a single bad game,' Brown explained.

When the West Germans announced their side for Hampden on 16 April 1969, Brown was entitled to feel envious: it included six of the men who lost to England at Wembley three years earlier. The teams were: *Scotland* – Lawrence (Liverpool), Gemmell (Celtic), McCreadie (Chelsea), Murdoch (Celtic), McKinnon (Rangers), Greig (Rangers), Johnstone (Celtic), Bremner (Leeds), Law (Manchester United), Gilzean (Tottenham), Lennox (Celtic). *Germany* – Wolter, Schnellinger, Vogts, Beckenbauer, Schulz, Patzke, Doerfel, Haller, Muller, Overath, Held. *Referee* – J. Gardeazabal, Spain.

No-one questioned the awesome task facing Scotland. But there was no sign, as the match progressed, of the players lacking the necessary skill, courage and pace to produce a major upset.

Not unusually, in matches involving Scotland at Hampden, chances were squandered in the opening stages which made the home fans groan. Similarly, few in a crowd totalling 90,000, who were familiar with a pattern of play established by generations of different players over many years, would have been greatly surprised when West Germany scored first.

Six minutes from half-time, as he settled on a harmless-looking free-kick from Beckenbauer, the small matter of time shared in the match so far would be of little concern to Gerd Muller, the West German striker. Cleverly eluding the combined attentions of McKinnon and the rest of the Scottish defence, he swept the ball into the net from 12 yards, beating Lawrence at his left-hand post.

A feeling of hurt resignation overwhelmed the huge Hampden crowd. Muller's goal was almost entirely against the run of play. It was Scotland who deserved to be ahead. There was little justice in life and none in football. They just couldn't win!

However, as the match edged towards the finish, and the beginning of another long spell of national despair, occasioned by their failure to qualify for the finals of the World Cup, no-one could say Scotland stopped trying. And, as usual at the national stadium, for as long as the players were willing to work hard and commit themselves totally, whatever bleak prospect affected their chances of lasting success, the crowd provided wholehearted support.

When the two sides lined up for the second half the West German goalkeeper, Wolter, had been replaced by Sepp Maier. The change didn't appear to affect West Germany's composure or Scotland's chances of drawing level. Time and again attacks were contained, or frustrated, by the pace and skill of the West German defence where the commanding figure of Franz Beckenbauer provided an always vigilant presence.

The equaliser, which kept Scotland's hopes of qualifying for the World Cup finals alive – just! – could be credited to a feeling of massive determination, inspired in large part by skipper Billy Bremner. He simply refused to accept that

Scotland were beaten and out of the World Cup. His opinion was hugely optimistic, of course. Until a goal, five minutes from the end, confirmed his wildest hopes.

The goal which kept Scotland's interest in the 1970 World Cup alive began and ended with Bobby Murdoch, with some assistance from Charlie Cooke who had been introduced to the action as a substitute for Bobby Lennox. Cooke was capable of teasing and dominating any midfield. Accepting the ball from Murdoch, he judged his moment to perfection. A neat return pass helped Murdoch to evade Patzke. The shot that followed, into the top corner of the net, was unstoppable. Scotland were level!

Nearer the finish Billy Bremner almost earned the sensational result his never-say-die approach deserved. But just as the little red-head, as captain, had been an inspiration to Scotland throughout the whole of the 90 minutes, so it was left to Franz Beckenbauer, captain of West Germany, to save his side in the last few moments; heading clear on the line from Bremner with the goalkeeper clearly beaten.

Scotland weren't out of the World Cup – yet. For all practical purposes, the return group match against West Germany, in Hamburg six months later, provided the final exit. To be defeated 3–2 by West Germany, at the end of a hard-fought match, was hardly a bad performance. In Mexico the West Germans defeated England by a similar margin and eventually finished third, behind Brazil and Italy, who were also competing for outright possession of the Jules Rimet trophy.

Most people in Scotland with an interest in football were happy when the Brazilians won. It didn't bother them when England lost. England qualifying for the quarter-finals didn't count for much north of Carlisle, except as a spur to Scotland.

After nearly four decades of increasing success, everyone agreed the World Cup was important. Not being there, Scotland felt deprived.

There are days and nights in football, like life itself, people remember with joy and others they simply want to forget. Wednesday, 26 September 1973, is probably the most important night in the history of Scottish football.

Everyone at Hampden Park, Glasgow, to witness a qualifying match for the 1974 World Cup finals, who wished Scotland well, must cherish the memory. Not just because the match was won. But because the nation regained its pride – and with it a clearer idea of what football meant to the majority of its citizens.

The victory margin was 2–1 against a good side from Czechoslovakia. The Czechs had been favourites to win, or at the very least draw. 'My heart tells me Scotland, my head insists that Czechoslovakia will draw this evening and kill us off in Bratislava,' was the pre-match view expressed by Ian Archer.

Scotland had been having a lean time under the command of a new manager, Willie Ormond. He had been in charge of the national side ever since the previous manager, Tommy Docherty, accepted the golden challenge presented by Manchester United in need of help. Ormond had been manager of St Johnstone before accepting the Scotland job. But he was probably best known as a player with Hibs where he was one of the Famous Five. As manager of Scotland he had been having a bad time: six matches played, five lost, only three goals scored.

Czechoslovakia presented Ormond, and Scotland, with a desperate challenge. Scotland hadn't qualified for the World Cup finals since 1958. A whole generation of supporters had been denied the excitement – and the misery – of seeing Scotland compete against the cream of world football. Ormond, who enjoyed a reputation for plain speaking, acknowledged he could be in trouble. 'This is a match we must win,' he said.

Everyone expected Czechoslovakia to play for a draw. Vackla Jezek, the manager, made no attempt to conceal his intentions. 'At all costs we want to make the game in Bratislava mean something,' he explained.

The teams were: *Scotland* – Hunter (Celtic), Jardine (Rangers), McGrain (Celtic), Bremner (Leeds United), Holton (Manchester United), Connolly (Celtic), Morgan (Manchester United), Hay (Celtic), Law (Manchester City), Dalglish (Celtic), Hutchison (Coventry City). *Czechoslovakia* – Viktor, Pivarmik, Samek, Zlocha, Bendle, Bicovsky, Adamek, Kunn, Nehoda, Stratil, Panenka. *Referee* – H. Oberg, Norway.

Three of the men playing for Scotland were due a special handshake even before the match started out. George Connelly and Tommy Hutchison were new caps; while Denis Law could finally lay claim to 50.

Law never accumulated the full number of international caps his prodigious talent deserved. Between 1967 and 1972 he rarely figured in a Scotland side, due to injury or because the selectors preferred to proceed without him. In mid-career there was also a perception among certain journalists that he was unwilling to follow orders and wasn't a good team performer. Nonetheless, with his 50th cap, he was only the second player, after George Young of Rangers, to be honoured by Scotland so often.

When the match kicked off the opening exchanges were an exercise in pointless aggravation, with a foul every few seconds, mostly directed against Scotland. It would have been foolish, and under-informed at this level, to imagine Scotland could be intimidated. 'I think they tried to make us lose our temper and get involved in a physical battle,' skipper Billy Bremner explained at the finish. 'It was to the credit of all the lads that they didn't succeed.'

But just as Czechoslovakia wanted the match to end in a draw, Scotland were geared to attack, although it was the Czechs who scored first, from a poor shot by Nehoda which Hunter misjudged. Eight minutes later Scotland equalised. Hutchison, who was making a huge impression in his first international, took a corner on the left and big Jim Holton rose above the Czech defence to score. 'I'd started to come up for any dead ball situations,' a delighted Holton explained later. 'We thought we'd get a goal in the air and that's how it worked out.'

Billy Bremner thought the Czechs played some good possession football. 'If they had concentrated on that – on the way they played for a spell just after half-time – instead of trying to kick us out of the game, then it would have been a more difficult game for us to win,' Bremner argued.

With the teams still level, and time running out for Scotland, manager Willie Ormond decided to replace Kenny Dalglish with Joe Jordan. 'I was told to play up alongside Denis Law and look for the ball in the air,' said Jordan.

With about 12 minutes left for play Scotland were awarded an indirect free-kick inside the penalty area. Morgan played the ball short to Bremner who shot hard against the foot of the post. When the ball rebounded to Morgan he chipped it to Jordan. All it needed then was courage and timing. His header was perfect. 'I got it just right,' Jordan grinned later.

When the referee ended the match with Scotland still ahead the whole of Hampden was already celebrating with a joy and fervour that hadn't been seen in years.

Scotland would be returning to the World Cup finals after an absence of 16 years. Denis Law, whose international career began the year after Scotland's last appearance, could scarcely believe it. 'I have never been happier at any time in my life,' he declared.

Willie Ormond, rescued from the solitude of the dressing-room by his captain, Billy Bremner, was carried round a delirious, still-packed Hampden on the shoulders of his players. As witnessed by Ian Archer, for the benefit of readers of *The Glasgow Herald*, 'No-one remained unmoved or unemotional. It was a great and glorious night, a watershed.'

Wasn't it just!

To the delight of the Hampden brigade Scotland were back in the finals of the World Cup where, according to the dictates of popular mythology, they belonged.

In the years that followed the self-styled Tartan Army no longer marched on London: now a whole series of strange-looking maps was required to locate Dortmund and Frankfurt, Cordoba and Mendoza, Malaga and Seville, Nezahualcayotl and Queretaro, and, finally, Genoa and Turin where, on 20 June 1990, it all stuttered to an unhappy halt against Brazil.

Days and evenings of unbridled joy, centred on the professional activities of whichever group of players happened to be representing Scotland at the time, could be counted on the fingers of one hand. Yet the experience of Scotland participating in five World Cup finals in a row was exhilarating while it lasted.

The results were generally disappointing and quite often defeat was wrought from victory. Players were sometimes burdened beyond their modest allocation of talent by supporters harbouring dreams of vicarious glory and a longing for Scotland to be recognised among the great little nations of the world. But for nearly two decades players with Scottish names, and Scottish forebears, competed against some of the best footballing practitioners on the world stage. Occasionally, it appeared, Scotland came tantalisingly close to matching them. And then, always, the dream shattered.

With typical Scottishness much was made of what happened to the squad assembled by Willie Ormond in 1974. Unbeaten, and eliminated on goal difference because they didn't hammer Zaire, Ormond and his men returned home to a heroes' welcome which couldn't have been more ecstatic if they'd

Scotland qualified for the World Cup finals, for the first time in 16 years, with victory against Czechoslovakia at Hampden on 26 September 1973. Manager Willie Ormond, skipper Billy Bremner, David Hay and Willie Morgan acknowledge the cheers of an emotional crowd

actually qualified for the second final round in West Germany. Their reception, in the event of further heady progress to the quarter-finals, the semi-finals or the final itself, is impossible to imagine.

Four years later, with a new manager, Ally MacLeod, in charge of Scotland's fortunes, thousands took their place at Hampden, and lined the road to Prestwick to watch the squad depart, long since convinced by the ebullient MacLeod that they were heading for glory in Argentina.

In fact, securing a place in the final 16 for Argentina had been a shaky business, highlighted most dramatically by the final qualifying match with Wales at Anfield in October 1977.

A month earlier, Hampden had been the scene of a glorious win against Czechoslovakia, the reigning European champions. It was easily one of the most exciting nights, involving Scotland, ever witnessed at the old stadium.

The visitors wanted the match delayed for 24 hours, claiming the players were exhausted following an all-night rail trip from London, imposed because of an airport strike. FIFA refused their request and, on 21 September 1977, in front of a crowd totalling 85,000, the match went ahead as planned. The teams appeared as follows: *Scotland* – Rough (Partick Thistle), Jardine (Rangers), McGrain (Celtic), Forsyth (Rangers), McQueen (Leeds United), Rioch (Everton), Dalglish (Liverpool), Masson (Queen's Park Rangers), Jordan (Leeds United), Hartford

Smiling happily, Ally MacLeod, the man who encouraged everyone to believe Scotland would win the World Cup in 1978, is treated to a guard of honour at Hampden before the squad's departure for Argentina. Judged solely on results, MacLeod's record in Argentina stands comparison with his succesors in Spain, Mexico and Italy

(Manchester City), Johnston (West Bromwich Albion). *Czechoslovakia* – Michalik, Paurik, Capkovic, Dvorak, Geogh, Dobia, Gajdusek, Moder, Pollak, Masny, Nehoda. *Referee* – F. Rion, Belgium.

The visitors displayed little sign of tiredness as a result of their experience with British Rail, although it was soon clear this would be Scotland's night.

After only 18 minutes Scotland went into the lead, Jordan scoring with a header from a Johnston corner. The amount of time which had been necessary to obtain the opening goal was repeated, almost exactly, on two further occasions: Hartford adding goal number two after 35 minutes, and Dalglish taking the score to a less-than-familiar three for Scotland with 54 minutes played. For the humbled Czechs there was only the merest consolation when Gajdusek outwitted Rough shortly before the finish.

Sharing a group with the European champions looked a huge hurdle for Scotland when the draw was announced. Now they were clear. The large crowd lingered, demanding a lap of honour. Manager Ally MacLeod, rarely a reticent and unresponsive man, refused. 'We'll do that when we qualify for the World Cup finals,' he promised.

At least 30,000 Scottish supporters travelled to Anfield for the final match with Wales. A packed Hampden couldn't have provided Scotland with a more vociferous or loyal support. Goals by Masson and Dalglish settled the match for Scotland.

The teams at the start were: *Scotland* – Rough (Partick Thistle), Jardine (Rangers), Donachie (Manchester City), Masson (Queen's Park Rangers), McQueen (Leeds), Forsyth (Rangers), Dalglish (Liverpool), Hartford (Manchester City), Jordan (Leeds), Macari (Manchester United), Johnston (West Bromwich Albion). *Wales* – Davies, R. Thomas, J. Jones, Mahoney, D. Jones, Phillips, Flynn, Sayer, Yorath, Toshack, M. Thomas. *Referee* – R. Wurtz, France.

Most people thought afterwards that the French referee erred when he awarded Scotland a penalty: television evidence appeared to show it was Joe Jordan, and not one of the Welsh defenders, who knocked the ball down with his hand. Don Masson, who was captain for the night, elected to take the penalty himself – and, in the cauldron of tension that was Anfield that night, scored with great style.

For what remained of the match, and long after, Wales continued to feel aggrieved, although no-one could possibly question the quality of Dalglish's goal, a marvellously timed header from an inch-perfect cross by Martin Buchan of Manchester United, who was playing instead of Jardine. Television commentator Arthur Montford couldn't conceal his delight. 'Argentina here we come!' he cried.

A few days before the official departure Scotland contrived to lose to England, who hadn't qualified for the finals of the last two World Cups, by a single goal at Hampden. It was a poor omen but Scotland allowed themselves a lap of honour anyway. Argentina beckoned dangerously.

That time in Argentina is generally considered Scotland's worst-ever football experience. Nothing seems to compare a decade-and-a-half, and three World Cup finals, later.

Humbled by Peru, quarter-finalists in 1970, and humiliated by Iran, the so-called no-hopers of the group, Ally MacLeod, the happy extrovert who kept on saying Scotland would win the World Cup, is forever remembered as the villain-architect-in-chief of the nation's foolish expectations. MacLeod was considered guilty of not much planning, indifferent team selection, poor tactics and generally held responsible for the awful disappointment which followed the collapse of Scotland's challenge in Argentina.

A thoroughly deserved victory against Holland in the same tournament – with the Dutch on their way to the final against the host country – could be dismissed on the grounds it didn't count for much, apart from offering Scotland a degree of salvaged pride. However, for those who liked the idea, Scotland beating Holland added something to a dangerous myth which many people appeared to enjoy and helped perpetuate. The preposterous notion that Scotland could only function properly against the best in the world, in a meeting of equals, was never likely to prove helpful to any manager conducting a World Cup campaign.

In fact, judged solely on results, Ally MacLeod's record in Argentina stands comparison with those of his successors in Spain, Mexico and Italy.

Jock Stein, who was different in almost every respect from his flamboyant predecessor, Ally MacLeod, didn't permit any foolish talk about Scotland winning the World Cup when he was in charge. Stein believed qualifying for the World Cup finals was a major achievement for a country with Scotland's limited resources: thereafter it would be enough for him and the players concerned to concentrate their minds on winning a place in the second final round.

Stein led Scotland to Spain in 1982. There had been the usual worries about qualifying from a group which included Portugal, Sweden and Northern Ireland.

A poor performance in Tel Aviv, where Scotland struggled to defeat Israel 1–0, wasn't encouraging. Forced to share points with both Portugal and Northern Ireland at Hampden was another bad omen. Finally, however, Stein and his men mustered enough points to justify a place in Spain among the world's footballing élite.

It would have been unrealistic to expect much from a squad which experienced a difficult time qualifying. Yet, with Stein in charge, Scotland almost succeeded. Despite scoring first, they were beaten comprehensively by Brazil. But it was two needless goals, conceded against a raw New Zealand side, and a careless draw with the USSR, which put them out.

Nothing about Scotland's march on Mexico four years later could overshadow the shock of Jock Stein's death in Cardiff. He had been a titan of the Scottish game for more than three decades. Now he was gone.

Stein was the first Scotland manager to continue from one World Cup campaign to the next. And, just as he steered Scotland to a place in the 1982 World Cup finals in Spain, his last stewardship brought several of the same squad to the brink of qualifying for Mexico in 1986.

In his last campaign Stein was invited to overcome the usual dangerous and difficult mix; namely Spain, Wales and Iceland in Group Seven. Spain, who had been runners-up to France in the last European championship, were favourites to win the group. It had been determined, however, that whoever finished second in Group Seven would be offered another chance to qualify in a play-off against the winners of the Oceania group.

Scotland recognised the importance of this unexpected lifeline to Mexico. But neither was its significance lost on Wales who hadn't forgiven Scotland for qualifying at their expense in 1978, largely by way of the notorious penalty incident involving Joe Jordan.

Iceland represented the unknown. And every team in the World Cup was due at least one good game, according to Stein: you just hoped not to be around when fortune smiled on the other side. In fact, Iceland, who lost 3–0 at Hampden in the winter of 1984, scared Scotland witless in the return match in Reykjavik seven months later; contriving to lose by the narrowest possible margin, 1–0.

Consistently inconsistent, during the same period of a few months, Scotland had been able to defeat the might of Spain, appearing at Hampden in November 1984, with surprising ease. Scotland hadn't beaten Spain at Hampden since 1957. But in that match at Hampden on 14 November they played magnificently with Graeme Souness, in arrogant mood, commanding the mid-field against all-comers.

The teams at Hampden appeared as follows: *Scotland* – Leighton (Aberdeen), Nicol (Liverpool), Albiston (Manchester United), Souness (Sampdoria), McLeish (Aberdeen), Miller (Aberdeen), Dalglish (Liverpool), McStay (Celtic), Johnston (Celtic), Bett (Lokeren), Cooper (Rangers). *Spain* – Arconada, Urquiada, Camacho, Maceda, Giocoechea, Gordillo, Senor, Victor, Santillana, Urtubi, Rincon. *Referee* – A. Prokop, East Germany.

Before the match Stein told reporters: 'It would be nice to get a goal in the first 20 minutes. But it would be just as important if it came along in the final 20 minutes. One more goal than them will do me.'

His players couldn't quite deliver a goal in 20 minutes. But just as satisfying to everyone hoping Scotland would produce a good performance, and obtain a positive result against the group favourites, Souness and his men were two up, and looking good, after only 42 minutes.

The first goal followed a fierce shot by Nicol which Arconada couldn't hold. Johnston, moving quickly, dived low to head the ball into the net. Time: 33 minutes. Nine minutes later another well-timed header from the little Celtic player, connecting with a marvellously placed cross from Bett, put Spain further behind.

Thirteen minutes into the second half and a goal by Giocoechea saw them back in the game: Camacho took a free kick to the far post, Leighton appeared to hesitate, and Giocoechea rose high above the Scots defence to head the ball into the net.

All three goals had been the result of headers. But it was the fourth goal of the match which people remembered long after the event.

Graeme Souness commanded the midfield against all-comers when Scotland met Spain in a World Cup qualifying match at Hampden on 14 November 1984. Scotland won 3–1 and Miguel Munoz, the Spanish coach, admitted later: 'I have never seen such a strong Scottish team'

Kenny Dalglish, with 95 appearances for Scotland to his credit, had been nursing a knee injury and didn't train with the rest of the squad before the match. 'He was a borderline case,' Stein admitted. Taking his cap count to four short of 100, Dalglish had been right when he argued rest would cure his knee.

Spain were hacking at everything that moved. But they also looked capable of snatching a draw; until Dalglish took possession from a throw-in, deep in Spanish territory. Running across the face of the box he beat three defenders with joyous ease. Arconada, in the Spanish goal, sensed danger. But there was nothing he could do as Dalglish unleashed a tremendous left-foot shot, from at least 18 yards, high into the net.

There couldn't have been a better, or more significant, goal scored at Hampden. It didn't just settle the match for Scotland. Finally, after years of trying, it brought Dalglish level with Denis Law's long-standing record of 30 international goals for Scotland.

Following the match the Spanish coach, Miguel Munoz, was forced to admit: 'I have never seen such a strong Scottish team.'

Nevertheless, as the qualifying stage neared its end, it was Spain, the group leaders, who were almost guaranteed a place in Mexico and Scotland who were struggling to qualify. Scotland needed to draw with Wales in Cardiff to ensure another chance in a play-off against the winners of the Oceania group.

The result of the first qualifying match between the two countries, on 27 March 1985, had been a shock for Scotland. Wales rarely won at Hampden. But on this occasion, despite expectations, a typically opportunistic goal by Ian Rush sent them home happy. Nobody in the 62,000 crowd doubted it was a good result for Wales and a calamity for Scotland: points lost at home heightened the agony and made the job of qualifying for the World Cup finals doubly difficult.

The teams then were: *Scotland* – Leighton (Aberdeen), Nicol (Liverpool), Albiston (Manchester United), Souness (Sampdoria), McLeish (Aberdeen), Miller (Aberdeen), Dalglish (Liverpool), McStay (Celtic), Johnston (Celtic), Bett (Lokeren), Cooper (Rangers). *Wales* – Southall, Slatter, Jones, Ratcliffe, Jackett, Phillips, James, Nicholas, Thomas, Hughes, Rush. *Referee* – A. Ponnet, Belgium.

When the two countries met for the second time, in front of a 39,500 crowd in Cardiff on 10 September 1985, Scotland were lying second, behind Spain, in Group Seven, but ahead of Wales on goal difference.

Eight years earlier the Welsh FA elected to play their crucial home qualifying match against Scotland in Liverpool; and the volume of support clearly favoured Scotland. Everybody recognised it was a mistake which probably cost Wales the match – and a place in Argentina. This time the visitors would be exposed to the intimidating atmosphere of Ninian Park, Cardiff. The teams lined up as follows: *Wales* – Southall, Van Den Hauwe, Ratcliffe, Jackett, James, Phillips, Nicholas, Thomas, Rush, Hughes. *Scotland* – Leighton (Aberdeen), Gough (Dundee United), Malpas (Dundee United), Aitken (Celtic), McLeish (Aberdeen), Miller (Aberdeen), Nicol (Liverpool), Strachan (Manchester United), Sharp (Everton), Bett (Aberdeen), Speedie (Chelsea). *Referee* – J. N. Keizer, Holland.

For most of the match Wales looked the better side. And for most of the match they were ahead by a single goal; scored, after only 13 minutes, by Mark Hughes.

Less than ten minutes from the end, those who remembered how Scotland defeated Wales at Anfield in 1977, with the help of a dubious penalty, could be forgiven thinking history was a sour, and repeatable, feast; quenched from a poisoned chalice. Then it was Jordan's hand that landed Wales in trouble. This time it was Phillips' arm. Cooper's left foot also figured prominently.

Many people thought Scotland didn't deserve a penalty, claiming Phillips collided with the ball accidentally. Nobody with a desire to see Scotland in Mexico paid any attention to the subtlety of this argument, not least Davie Cooper who entered the match as a substitute for Gordon Strachan. A penalty in the closing minutes of a crucial World Cup qualifying match was an offer Scotland couldn't refuse. And Cooper didn't waste it. Directing the ball past Southall from the penalty spot, in the dense, tense atmosphere of Ninian Park, the popular Rangers' player demonstrated courage as well as skill.

He also ensured Scotland left Cardiff ahead of Wales in their group. It was that single, precious point which provided Scotland with an opportunity to scrape home against Australia, winners of the Oceania group, in a play-off.

Alex Ferguson was now in charge of Scotland's fortunes following the death of Jock Stein – but only for the duration of the 1986 World Cup, as he repeatedly made plain.

Denmark, West Germany and Uruguay were ranged against Scotland and a place in the second final round in Mexico. One goal, scored against West Germany, and a solitary point, obtained at the expense of Uruguay who played for most of the match with only ten men, wasn't much of a record. But by now it was about all most people expected.

After qualifying for four World Cup finals in a row the public at large appeared to believe Scotland would continue to qualify as of right. It was a dangerous assumption.

The seeding system ensured the presence of at least one major rival in every group. In four consecutive qualifying campaigns Czechoslovakia, twice, West Germany and Spain provided formidable opposition. Similarly, Scotland's route to the 1990 finals in Italy couldn't have been harder with France, Yugoslavia and Norway, together with Cyprus, against them.

Scotland, under Andy Roxburgh, started well. A month of hectic activity, during the autumn of 1988, earned three points from a possible four: Norway were defeated in Oslo, and Yugoslavia, favourites to win the group, were held to a draw at Hampden.

Four months later, Cyprus, who weren't expected to cause any of the other teams in the group the slightest difficulty, almost succeeded in destroying Scotland's chances with their play-defying methods in Limassol, although the loss of two goals to a no-hope team, in the course of the prescribed 90 minutes, didn't help. It was fortunate for Scotland that the referee responded boldy to the home side's flagrant time-wasting. It was at least 100 minutes following the kick-off before Richard Gough succeeded in making the score 3–2 in Scotland's favour.

That evening in Limassol everyone who travelled with the Scotland party was happy to agree that the referee should be congratulated on his sense of justice and sturdy commitment to some of the game's finer principles. It would be interesting to speculate, however, on the probable reaction at Hampden if a referee ever added ten minutes to a World Cup qualifying match and Scotland lost as a result.

Most people thought Scotland would dispose of Cyprus with ease. The way the team struggled, and the extraordinary amount of time they were allowed to achieve their aim, presaged trouble with France at Hampden the following month.

France, who finished in the last four on both occasions, had been one of the most attractive sides in the World Cup finals held in Spain in 1982, and in Mexico four years later. Given fairer treatment by the referee, when goalkeeper Schumacher of West Germany, felled Battiston in the 1982 semi-final, it seems certain they would have contested the final against Italy. Now, with Michel Platini, the former star of their great days on the world stage, in charge, they were the undisputed glamour team of Scotland's group.

Before the match at Hampden on 8 March 1989 there had been a total of eight meetings between the two countries from which Scotland could claim five victories and France three. The last time they met was in preparation for France's successful assault on the European championships in the summer of 1984. The result was 2–0, going on eight, as one visiting journalist was forced to admit, in favour of the nascent champions.

The indignity inflicted upon Scotland in Marseilles hadn't been forgotten, not least by Alex McLeish. He had been made captain for the night at Hampden, in honour of 60 appearances in the national side, and could be forgiven pondering 'a wee bit of revenge'.

Before the match regular team captain, Roy Aitken, appealed to the home supporters 'to get right behind the players. There is nothing better than having the encouragement of a big vocal support in a game like this.'

The teams were: *Scotland* – Leighton (Manchester United), Gough (Rangers), Malpas (Dundee United), Aitken (Celtic), McLeish (Aberdeen), Gillespie (Liverpool), Nicol (Liverpool), McStay (Celtic), McCoist (Rangers), Ferguson (Rangers), Johnston (Nantes). *France* – Bats, Amoros, Silvestre, Sonor, Battiston, Sauzee, Durand, Laurey, Papin, Blanc, Xuereb. *Referee* – J. Stiegler, Czechoslovakia.

The weather was dreadful. Hampden looked battered and forlorn. Its sell-by date had been posted long ago. Despite its hugely reduced capacity, however, as if heeding Roy Aitken's pre-match appeal, when Scotland appeared, its decaying slopes erupted in a mighty roar.

The wet and windy conditions discouraged the kind of stylish, polished play people were entitled to expect from a crucial World Cup qualifying match between two ambitious sides. But those who braved the elements were treated to one of the most exciting nights in the history of the famous old ground.

Andy Roxburgh likened the mood of the evening to the time John Greig scored against Italy in 1965 and Joe Jordan headed Scotland into the World Cup finals, against Czechoslovakia, nine years later. 'The night John Greig scored for Scotland against Italy was the first time I can remember being part of the Scottish passion at Hampden,' Roxburgh revealed. 'Then, when Joe Jordan scored against Czechoslovakia, you were overwhelmed by the atmosphere.'

According to Roxburgh, in his experience, the game against France was the one night which came remotely close to matching those previous electrifying occasions. 'The French were hot favourites but Scotland played out of their skins, like men demented,' Roxburgh recalled. 'It was just one of those incredible World Cup nights and to be involved in it was probably one of the biggest thrills I've ever enjoyed in football.'

These were heady days for the former Celtic and future Rangers star, Maurice Johnston, who scored both Scotland goals. Johnston's past and future career was spattered with controversy. And his contribution to the destruction of France at Hampden certainly wouldn't endear him to the stout burghers of Nantes where he was currently employed. But no-one could complain about the little man's daring and skill in front of goal. Johnston could now claim a tally of five goals from his last four appearances in a Scotland jersey; a more-than-respectable count by any standards.

Scotland's two-nil victory over France put them alongside Yugoslavia as one of the two teams who were favourites to qualify for Italy. Certainly, the man in charge of Scotland at Hampden, didn't doubt the importance of the team's performance against France. Long afterwards Andy Roxburgh reflected simply: 'That was the night we qualified for Italy.'

Once in Italy, of course, no-one was very much surprised when Scotland found the means to self-destruct badly in their opening match against Costa Rica. The national capacity for pain had been rigorously tested in six previous campaigns.

A convincing, and thrilling, victory over Sweden, one of the strongest teams around, did nothing to make amends, or change the public perception of how Scotland would perform in the World Cup finals.

It would have been easier on all concerned if the various squads who represented Scotland in the World Cup finals between 1978 and 1990, in particular, played closer to their own commendable abilities. This could have meant winning most of the games that were lost, or carelessly drawn, and losing on those occasions people expected defeat.

Winning against Holland in Argentina, and Sweden in Italy, could be judged perverse, at the very least, considering what went before; a draw with Iran and defeat by Costa Rica. But, usually, too much was expected from everyone involved, with only a thin divide, nationwide, between an unsustainable euphoria and near-manic depression.

Anyone who claimed, with a shrug, that this was all part of the unpredictable nature of the Scottish character might be right, of course. But it was still a dangerous tendency loose in the national psyche.

CHAPTER SEVENTEEN

On an evening of heavy rain, the Minister for Sport in the Scottish Office, Alex Fletcher MP, was among the guests who gathered early at Ibrox on Friday, 7 June 1980, to witness Jim Watt successfully defend his world lightweight crown against Howard Davis of the United States.

Earlier that same day, a meeting of Hampden Park Ltd had been informed of the government's intention to contribute £5.5 million towards the cost of a new national stadium for Scotland.

Hampden Park Ltd, which represented the Scottish Football Association, the Scottish Football League, Strathclyde Regional Council, Queen's Park FC and the Scottish Sports Council, had been formed to acquire and develop the stadium and its surrounding acres. 'We proposed spending £11 million on the new stadium, based on April 1978 prices,' Ken Hutchinson, former Chief Executive of the Scottish Sports Council, and a member of the development committee, explained. 'Before our meeting, at which the announcement was made, we received a letter from the Scottish Office confirming the size of their contribution and letting us know how the money would be paid,' Hutchinson added.

Following the meeting at Hampden on Friday, 7 June, a statement was expected in the House of Commons, during Scottish Questions, the following Tuesday. Until then the Government's decision to support a scheme for a new national stadium at Mount Florida would be kept from the general public.

Across town, a few hours later, in a hospitality suite at Ibrox, Alex Fletcher joined Rangers' chairman, Rae Simpson, for a pre-fight chat.

Nobody associated with Hampden Park Ltd expected the Government to renege on its offer. Contractors were told to begin removing the top of the east terracing. 'We were also instructed to look at demolishing the north stand which offered special problems,' project architect, Roy Wilson, disclosed.

Ernie Walker, then secretary of the SFA, made no attempt to hide his disappointment. 'The demolition people were on site, ready to start work, when the Government withdrew its support,' he said. 'I still feel bitter, absolutely bitter, and frustrated, when I think about it. One senior civil servant wrote to me privately and said he had never been associated with anything so shameful. What happened was disgusting,' Walker declared.

If the written commitment offered by the Scottish Office had been leaked in

Concern about Hampden's future, in the face of marching time and rising costs, appeared the least of its troubles on 21 October 1968 when fire threatened the main pavilion and centre stand. Four detachments of the Glasgow Fire Service were needed to subdue the blaze which also put the historic Queen's Park trophy room at risk

Scotland's national stadium, barely 70 years old, already looked dilapidated by the time Hampden Park Ltd, a consortium of interested parties, was formed to acquire and develop the stadium and its surrounding areas. A government offer of £5.5 million to assist with the work was withdrawn in 1980

Ernie Walker, secretary of the SFA, and Ken Hutchinson, chief executive of the Scottish Sports Council, announce the latest threat to Hampden's survival. Walker admits he felt bitter when the government reneged on its £5.5 million promise of support. It was Hutchinson who signed cheques worth nearly £2 million of public money in compensation to contractors

advance of a statement to the House of Commons, the attendant publicity could have forced the Government to honour their part of the deal, Ken Hutchinson believes. 'But we played the game, as requested, and the news was kept private over the weekend,' Hutchinson added.

Acting on behalf of the Scottish Sports Council, who represented the Scottish Office, Hutchinson signed cheques for nearly £2 million for abandoned costs with nothing to show for it.

In the months that followed Hampden looked doomed. Alex Cameron, writing in the *Daily Record* on 25 November 1980, warned his readers: 'Hampden could be dead and buried before Scotland's next game in the World Cup.' Cameron, who believed Scotland without a national stadium would be like the Derby minus Epsom or the MCC without Lord's, didn't blame Queen's Park. 'They have done a good job keeping Hampden Park from falling down all these years,' the man from the *Record* insisted. 'They are due our thanks.'

For more than a decade architect Roy Wilson struggled to keep the old place open for business. 'There was a feeling among a lot of people that if they could keep the ground open, and it was safe, and could hold the numbers, then they would get to a stage where they would have the ability to look at the future,' Wilson explained. 'It was agreed that we should try and do the ground in sections so that it would always be available with a capacity greater than other places,' Wilson added.

James Rutherford, the Queen's Park secretary, believes it was Wilson who led Hampden out of the dark days. 'His vision saved the ground,' he said.

Between 1981 and 1985 around £6 million was spent on ground improvements. The top tier of the east terracing was removed and the north stand demolished. Some 23 miles of under-soil heating, connected to a new boiler in the south stand, allowed Queen's Park to claim they could host games except in very extreme weather. A special terrace was constructed for disabled spectators. Additional crush barriers, turnstiles and toilets were installed. The west covered terracing was converted to accommodate 11,200 seats; then emblazoned with an enormous St Andrew's Cross to leave no-one in any doubt that this was Scotland's national stadium.

But all this time the arguments for and against Scotland actually needing a national stadium continued to rage.

During the most recent debate on the future of Hampden various groups appeared, waving assorted development plans for a new national stadium to be located outside Glasgow, complete with leisure facilities, shopping malls, offices and other amenities. However, as *The Herald* noted pointedly, private enterprise was 'brave with plans and ideas for rival schemes but never bold with cash'.

When the SFA negotiated the use of Ibrox as a temporary home for the national side against Portugal and Italy, in the qualifying round of the 1994 World Cup, there was every chance that Rangers, who were rightly proud of their magnificent facilities, would have been happy to make the arrangement more or less permanent.

Rangers' owner, David Murray, believed that any money which could be made available, from inside football, or the Government, for a new national stadium, should be shared among the clubs to assist with extensive ground improvement imposed by the report of the Taylor Committee on ground safety. A newly built, or refurbished, national stadium was hardly a priority, and would be a waste of money, with Ibrox waiting and ready to be used, Murray argued.

There was force and logic to his argument. But in Scotland, especially, football and logic don't always mix. In a country notoriously divided on religious and social grounds there was never much chance of Murray's argument succeeding. There was also a strong, general opinion throughout the country that, as a matter of pride, if nothing else, Scotland needed a national stadium.

Murrayfield, home of the Scottish Rugby Union, was a popular choice, largely among people with no direct financial interest in football. Ernie Walker, now chairman of UEFA's stadium committee, and still a powerful voice in world football, was adamant on the subject. 'There is no case to be made for the Scottish national football team generating money for another sport,' he declared bluntly. 'Football needs every cent that it can generate for itself, as does rugby. Rugby would never contemplate playing at Hampden with the money going into the coffers of football. Football would rather play at Ibrox, or at Pittodrie, or at a decent Parkhead, than go to Murrayfield,' Walker insisted.

However, as the various sides adopted fixed positions, it wasn't difficult to conclude that there would be no new national stadium for Scotland without Government support.

Early in 1992 the only political certainty Britain could contemplate was the approaching general election. As always, in recent years, the Tory Government was in trouble in Scotland.

Support for a new national stadium might be dismissed as a cynical pre-election sweetener to earn votes. But the National Stadium Committee, which comprised the Scottish Football Association, the Scottish Football League and Queen's Park FC, as owners of Hampden, would have been delighted, and unlikely to complain, if the Secretary of State approached them offering money.

Manchester had been promised £55 million to assist its Olympic bid. People in Scotland were entitled to believe the National Stadium Committee was equally deserving.

On 19 February 1992, the Secretary of State for Scotland, Ian Lang, wrote to the SFA offering £3.5 million over three years, provided the National Stadium Committee raised a similar amount. There were no loud cheers in Scotland at the news. The sum on offer, with strings attached, wasn't much compared to Manchester. It also compared badly with the £5.5 million which had been offered and withdrawn in 1980, as Ken Hutchinson, former chief executive of the Scottish Sports Council, pointed out. 'The £5.5 million which was briefly on offer in 1980 was based on 1978 prices and would be worth around £21 million now,' Hutchinson reckoned. 'This means the Government is offering to contribute a sixth of what was proposed all that time ago.'

Still, it was better than nothing. Together with £5 million from the Football Trust, which the Secretary of State considered Government money from a different source, it allowed the National Stadium Committee to begin work on the first phase of a £24 million plan to rebuild Hampden.

At a meeting in Glasgow on 13 April 1992, after years of bickering and scheming, the SFA council accepted their proposals: Hampden, long recognised as the heart of Scottish football, would continue as the national stadium.

Most people welcomed the news. 'It would be a bereavement to God knows how many thousands of people if it was never rebuilt,' the national coach, Andy Roxburgh, maintained. 'Hampden is steeped in the tradition of the business and you can't buy tradition.'

Work on the first phase of the development, which began in June 1992, was scheduled to cost £12 million. It included two new cantilever covered stands, located on the old east terracing and the north stand area, with seating available for nearly 20,000 spectators. Enormous lighting pylons, which dominated the ground for more than 30 years, were replaced with modern lamps, sited along the rim of each stand. Major improvements, with landscaping and resurfacing of the

SFA chief executive, Jim Farry, believes Hampden Park will be the national stadium well into the next century. But he is still seeking another £12 million to complete work on the present conversion

approach roads, were scheduled for outside the ground.

'This is not minor refurbishment,' architect Roy Wilson insisted. 'A complete rebuild is planned.'

As the first phase neared completion, SFA chief executive, Jim Farry, was already working on how best to raise another £12 million to cover the cost of phase two. 'What we have in mind is a cocktail of funding which will include the private sector,' Farry explained.

If the National Stadium Committee achieve their objective the money will be used, primarily, to provide a new roof for the west stand and a two-tier replacement for the existing south stand. The new south stand will accommodate 16,500 spectators and, Farry believes, compare with anything in Europe. Ironically, revenue-gathering schemes pioneered at Ibrox during the last few years will be used to support the national stadium.

Farry wants to see refreshment areas, hospitality suites, boxes and conference rooms within the new structure. He will examine the value of debenture schemes and season tickets for all Scotland's matches. Nor does he discount suggestions that the Scottish Football Association and the Scottish Football League could become tenants of Hampden. 'If there is sufficient space available we would be willing to sell our existing premises and move the administration to the national stadium,' said Farry.

But first Farry must find the money. And deal with anyone who continues to argue the folly of developing the Mount Florida ground as the national stadium long into the next century.

His old mentor, and former boss, Ernie Walker, could prove a forceful adversary. The former SFA secretary originally favoured upgrading Hampden but later changed his mind. 'You can't knock down Mount Florida to accommodate car parks,' he reasoned. According to Walker a stadium that can seat 50,000 people needs parking facilities for more than 15,000 cars and buses in the immediate vicinity. 'Can you think of a place in Glasgow that could provide that kind of space?' he demanded.

Hampden, in its refurbished state, will provide a good, modern stadium with cover over the seats and all the facilities people need, Walker stressed. 'My problem concerns its long-term future. You don't build a stadium for next year. You build it for the next century as the visionaries did at Hampden almost 100 years ago.'

Walker's dream stadium would be located between Glasgow and Edinburgh, ideally at Strathclyde Park. There would be a retractable roof and the playing surface would be covered with a solid, rigid floor, to be utilised for other purposes, between matches. 'You can build a 30,000–seater, roofed and floored, for £50

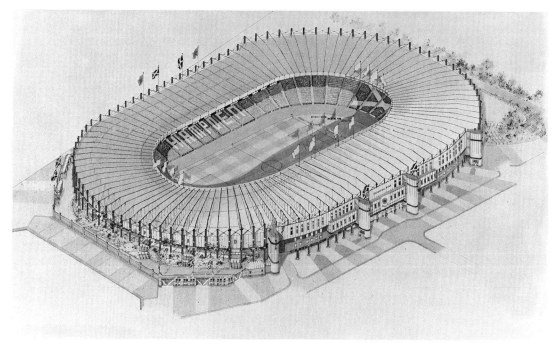

Hampden as future generations of Scottish football fans could know it. Work on the first phase, now complete, cost £12 million. Another £12 million is now needed to meet the demands of the next century

million at 1993 prices,' said Walker. 'I think you could build a 60,000–seater, which would meet everybody's needs, for £100 million.'

The man responsible for stadium standards throughout Europe foresees a time when all top-class football will be played on plastic that will look, feel and smell like grass. 'Millions of pounds are spent on the World Cup final. It attracts television viewers world-wide. But the whole event can be reduced to a shambles by nature. That isn't sustainable, really,' Walker maintained.

In visionary mood he is prepared to overlook the differences which divide Scotland and contemplate how, in addition to the national side, commercial considerations might encourage Rangers, Celtic, Hibs and Hearts, and as many other clubs as the week will accommodate, to book time in Scotland's super stadium. 'Who said football must be played at three o'clock on a Saturday afternoon?' Walker inquired.

One day there would be a national stadium on a green-field site. 'But it requires Government assistance. It cannot be achieved by football or commercial interests acting alone,' Walker conceded.

Who owns Hampden? With £3.5 million of taxpayers' money committed to the first phase development, and another £5 million on offer from the Football Trust, people are entitled to know.

'Queen's Park own Hampden,' Jim Farry, chief executive of the SFA and former secretary of the Scottish Football League, replied. 'The foresight that was shown by the men who first built Hampden was nothing short of remarkable,' Farry added. 'I think it's fair to say the same degree of foresight is required today.'

Farry represents an attitude, widespread in Scotland, which welcomes the SFA's continued close association with the country's oldest club. 'Queen's Park have a special relationship with the SFA. I have nothing but admiration for them,' said Farry.

Roy Wilson, the architect closely associated with several Hampden renewals, explained: 'The directors of Queen's Park are the people who are actually signing all the bits of paper so far as Hampden is concerned. We report to the National Stadium Committee but our client is Queen's Park.'

James Rutherford, secretary of Queen's Park, who receive 25 per cent of the net gate at international matches, and 20 per cent for other games, including cup finals, confirmed: 'It's our ground, we own the title deeds. But whether that will continue in the long term I can't say.'

Planning permission for the current main development was granted on condition the adjacent ground would be used for activities compatible with the national stadium.

Before negotiations with the Thatcher Government collapsed in June 1980, it was suggested a consortium, representing the Scottish Football Association, the Scottish Football League, Strathclyde Regional Council, the Scottish Sports Council and Queen's Park should asssume control of Hampden. Queen's Park would have been expected to transfer the title deeds to the ground at no cost – in return for managing the stadium and using the ground for home matches.

Jim Farry, the association's chief executive, discounts any suggestion that it would be a natural progression for the SFA to become owners of the national stadium; like the SRU with Murrayfield. 'We have no desire to own a football stadium,' Farry added. 'Our job is to foster and develop the game at all levels. Owning a stadium is not part of our remit.'

The chief executive of the SFA will be happy to see Hampden fully restored. 'That means at the end of phase two of the present development when we have completed work on the south stand. Then we can look to the future,' he said.

Farry's view of the future includes Scotland playing host to the finals of the European championships. He believes the huge success enjoyed by the 1989 World Youth Cup was proof of Scotland's ability to tackle an event of this complexity. It also offered a message of hope and pride to every fan who dreams of Scotland one day succeeding at the game's highest level.

'When we lost the final against Saudi Arabia on penalties there was disappointment and a few tears were shed by the youngsters involved,' Craig Brown, assistant national coach, and the man in charge of Scotland's youngsters, admitted.

Brown, like everyone else who saw them play, thought the Saudis looked older than the regulations allowed. 'It was really a question of boys playing men. But there was no hostility, even when we lost,' Brown said. 'I thought it was a great day out and a wonderful advertisement for football.'

The 1989 World Youth Cup was also a reminder of Hampden Park at is most compelling. It was no longer the finest football stadium in the land, far less the world. It had been close to demolition many times and survived. Its future could be considered uncertain at best. But once again the crowd was held enthralled, captured by the magic of its spell.

In the football folklore of Scotland – an uncertain tale of hope and despair, triumph and tragedy – Hampden will survive.

SELECT BIBLIOGRAPHY

Ian Archer and Trevor Royle (eds.), *We'll Support You Evermore* (London 1976)

Tom Campbell, *Glasgow Celtic 1945–1970* (Glasgow 1970)

Bob Crampsey, *The First 100 Years of the Scottish Football League* (Glasgow 1990)

Bob Crampsey, *Mr Stein* (Edinburgh 1986)

R.A. Crampsey, *History of Queen's Park 1867–1967* (Glasgow 1967)

Stephen Halliday, *Rangers; a Pictorial History* (London 1989)

Jim Hossack, *Head over Heels: a Celebration of British Football* (Edinburgh 1989)

Denis Law with Ron Gubba, *Denis Law: an Autobiography* (London 1979)

Clive Leatherdale, *Scotland's Quest for the World Cup* (Edinburgh 1986)

Roger Macdonald, *Soccer: a Pictorial History* (London 1977)

Bob McPhail with Allan Herron, *Legend: The Story of Bob McPhail* (Edinburgh 1988)

Bill Murray, *The Old Firm: Sectarianism, Sport and Society in Scotland* (Edinburgh 1984)

Pele with Robert L. Fish, *My Life and the Beautiful Game* (London 1977)

John Rafferty, *One Hundred Years of Scottish Football* (London 1973)

Richard Robinson, *History of Queen's Park 1867–1917* (Glasgow 1920)

Jack Rollin, *Soccer at War 1939–1945* (London 1985)

Graeme Souness with Ken Gallacher, *A Manager's Diary* (Edinburgh 1989)

Hugh Taylor (ed.), *Scottish Football Book* (London)

Brian Wilson, *Celtic: a Century with Honour* (Glasgow 1988)

George Young Talks Football (London 1958)